CAMBRIDGE LIBRARY COLLECTION

Books of enduring scholarly value

Printing and Publishing History

The interface between authors and their readers is a fascinating subject in its own right, revealing a great deal about social attitudes, technological progress, aesthetic values, fashionable interests, political positions, economic constraints, and individual personalities. This part of the Cambridge Library Collection reissues classic studies in the area of printing and publishing history that shed light on developments in typography and book design, printing and binding, the rise and fall of publishing houses and periodicals, and the roles of authors and illustrators. It documents the ebb and flow of the book trade supplying a wide range of customers with products from almanacs to novels, bibles to erotica, and poetry to statistics.

The Grammar of Lithography

W. D. Richmond's The Grammar of Lithography (1878) is a comprehensive and instructive work on the many varieties of lithography - with all their attendant materials and instruments - described and explained in practical terms for the active participant and the amateur enthusiast alike. Richmond's Grammar should also be understood as part of a wider movement of nineteenth-century industrial disclosure, where pockets of masterly knowledge previously available to apprentices and company employees alone were being made more widely available through impartial manuals and guides. This noble cause was intended to bring down the walls of ignorance and trade secrecy and to foster an open atmosphere of mutual understanding. In the realm of lithography, Richmond's Grammar was the first treatise to achieve this. While the work forgoes any historical or overly theoretical discussion, it does provide an excellent example of practically oriented expertise in the graphic arts.

T0370841

Cambridge University Press has long been a pioneer in the reissuing of out-of-print titles from its own backlist, producing digital reprints of books that are still sought after by scholars and students but could not be reprinted economically using traditional technology. The Cambridge Library Collection extends this activity to a wider range of books which are still of importance to researchers and professionals, either for the source material they contain, or as landmarks in the history of their academic discipline.

Drawing from the world-renowned collections in the Cambridge University Library, and guided by the advice of experts in each subject area, Cambridge University Press is using state-of-the-art scanning machines in its own Printing House to capture the content of each book selected for inclusion. The files are processed to give a consistently clear, crisp image, and the books finished to the high quality standard for which the Press is recognised around the world. The latest print-on-demand technology ensures that the books will remain available indefinitely, and that orders for single or multiple copies can quickly be supplied.

The Cambridge Library Collection will bring back to life books of enduring scholarly value (including out-of-copyright works originally issued by other publishers) across a wide range of disciplines in the humanities and social sciences and in science and technology.

The Grammar of Lithography

*A Practical Guide for the Artist and Printer
in Commercial and Artistic Lithography,
and Chromolithography, Zincography,
Photo-lithography, and Lithographic
Machine Printing*

W. D. RICHMOND

CAMBRIDGE UNIVERSITY PRESS

Cambridge, New York, Melbourne, Madrid, Cape Town, Singapore,
São Paolo, Delhi, Dubai, Tokyo

Published in the United States of America by Cambridge University Press, New York

www.cambridge.org
Information on this title: www.cambridge.org/9781108009072

© in this compilation Cambridge University Press 2009

This edition first published 1878
This digitally printed version 2009

ISBN 978-1-108-00907-2 Paperback

This book reproduces the text of the original edition. The content and language reflect
the beliefs, practices and terminology of their time, and have not been updated.

Cambridge University Press wishes to make clear that the book, unless originally published
by Cambridge, is not being republished by, in association or collaboration with, or
with the endorsement or approval of, the original publisher or its successors in title.

THE

GRAMMAR OF LITHOGRAPHY.

A PRACTICAL GUIDE

FOR THE ARTIST AND PRINTER.

WYMAN'S TECHNICAL SERIES.

Second Edition, crown 4to., price 1s.

WYMAN'S DICTIONARY OF STATIONERY AND COMPENDIUM OF USEFUL INFORMATION for the Office, Counting-House, and Library.

Price 6d., Post-free, 7d.

A KEY TO ONE OF THE MAIN DIFFICULTIES OF ENGLISH ORTHOGRAPHY : Being an Alphabetical Collection of nearly 3,000 Words resembling others in Sound, but differing in Sense, Spelling, or Accentuation. Compiled and arranged by HENRY BEADNELL.

Crown 8vo., cloth, price 2s. ; Post-free, 2s. 2d.

WORKSHOP MANAGEMENT. A Manual for Masters and Men, being Practical Remarks upon the Economic Conduct of Workshops, Trade Charities, &c. By FREDERICK SMITH.

Crown 8vo., cloth, price 1s. ; Post-free, 1s. 1d.

ENGLISH CHINA AND CHINA MARKS. Being a Guide to the Principal Marks found on English Pottery and Porcelain : with Engravings of upwards of 150 marks.

Crown 8vo., cloth, price 4s. ; Post-free, 4s. 4d.

PRACTICAL CABINET-MAKER. Being a Collection of Working Drawings of Furniture, with Explanatory Notes. By a WORKING MAN.

Medium 4to., cloth gilt, bevelled boards, price 10s. 6d.

CABINET - MAKERS' PATTERN BOOK. Being Examples of Modern Furniture of the Character mostly in demand, selected from the Portfolios of the leading Wholesale Makers. To which are added Original Designs by First-rate Artists, comprising various Designs for Hall Furniture, Library Furniture, Dining-room Furniture, Drawing-room Furniture, and Bedroom Furniture.

Crown 8vo., cloth, price 5s. ; Post-free, 5s. 4d.

GRAMMAR OF LITHOGRAPHY. A Practical Guide, for the Artist and Printer, in Commercial and Artistic Lithography, and Chromo-lithography, Zincography, Photo-lithography, and Lithographic Machine Printing. With an Appendix containing Original Recipes for preparing Chalks, Inks, Transfer-papers, &c. By W. D. RICHMOND.

LONDON: WYMAN & SONS, 81, GREAT QUEEN STREET, W.C.

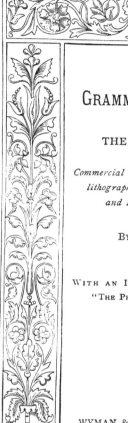

THE
GRAMMAR OF LITHOGRAPHY.

A PRACTICAL GUIDE FOR

THE ARTIST AND PRINTER

IN

*Commercial & Artistic Lithography, & Chromo-
lithography, Zincography, Photo-lithography,
and Lithographic Machine Printing.*

BY W. D. RICHMOND.

EDITED AND REVISED,
WITH AN INTRODUCTION, BY THE EDITOR OF
"THE PRINTING TIMES AND LITHOGRAPHER."

LONDON:
WYMAN & SONS, GREAT QUEEN STREET,
LINCOLN'S-INN FIELDS, W.C.
1878.

TABLE OF CONTENTS.

PART I.

DRAWING, TRANSFERRING, AND PRINTING.

PART II.

LITHOGRAPHIC MACHINE-PRINTING.

EDITOR'S INTRODUCTION.

HERE formerly existed a deep-seated and it must be admitted an unreasoning prejudice, against technical hand-books treating practically of any trade or profession. It was sedulously instilled into the minds of the young especially, that an acquaintance with the processes of the different industrial occupations could be acquired only by observing and imitating the methods of adepts. This idea was fostered by persons possessed largely with a selfish motive : they had gained their own knowledge of their art in the tedious and irksome manner which, in their case, was the only possible one, and were determined, as far as lay in their power, that such knowledge should be obtained by their successors in the same unintelligent way.

The rise of trade journalism, which is coincident with the establishment of *The Builder*—a periodical that has, in a variety of ways, been of signal service to the industrial community—and the gradually increasing influence and importance attained by the newspapers which each trade and interest soon brought into existence, showed the fallacy of the old prejudice ; and it proved what was even of more consequence, the great and substantial use which might be made of the Press in imparting technical instruction, partly supplementary to and partly independent of workshop and laboratory practice. A large class of persons became accustomed to find their practical knowledge, even in their own peculiar *métier*, increased and enlarged by the perusal of articles in serials of this character; and it was only a natural development of things when the articles grew into treatises, when isolated facts, hints, recipes, and instruction were welded together into connected grammars, guides, and hand-books of the different departments of craftsmanship.

In the conduct of a journal devoted to printing and the auxiliary arts—THE PRINTING TIMES AND LITHOGRAPHER—the Editor has been constantly called upon to answer questions of an elementary character, and consulted on points more abstruse, connected with Lithography and the processes allied with it. The correspondents' column was too circumscribed for sufficiently detailed replies; and the information desiderated by one reader was only partially required by others. He therefore resolved to cause to be written a series of chapters on Lithography which should embrace every practical exigency that might arise in the ordinary pursuit of the art; and in a form suitable not only for the initiatory instruction of the mere tyro, but for occasional reference by the more advanced practitioner.

He was confirmed in his resolve by another consideration. Repeated requests for the name of a complete treatise on the subject had to be answered with the statement that there was really not a work on Lithography of practical utility in the market. For nearly half a century no treatise of practical value on the art had appeared in the English language. The last considerable work of the kind was that issued by Mr. Hullmandel, and was intended chiefly for amateurs.

Indeed, it may be said that, from the date of the publication of the English translation of the Manual of Lithography issued by SENEFELDER (1819), no other work of importance commensurate with the subject has been given to the public. There was every reason, therefore, that the hiatus should be supplied, and that one of the most beautiful, useful, and progressive of the Reproductive and Graphic Arts should have its processes formulated and its methods scientifically described in a thoroughly practical and complete treatise, brought up to the present time.

Experience showed that a book of the kind was wanted, not merely by amateurs but by many persons who are already engaged in the practice of Lithography. In these latter days the exigencies of trade competition demand a division of labour that has a strong tendency to keep an apprentice ignorant of many things connected with the art of printing from and drawing upon stone. In the larger towns, the reputation made by certain firms for special work favours this division so much, that there are many respectable offices where, for instance, little beyond the ordinary routine of printing in black for commercial purposes is seen. While this systematic division, perhaps, increases the money-value of a workman to his employer, it decreases his general capability. This is soon discovered when he is employed as the working manager of a small general business, a position in which he is required to carry out, in a respectable manner, almost any kind of work that may be brought to the office.

This want of acquaintance with the minutiæ of the manifold varieties of printing and preparation of work is especially observable among artists and writers. In London, many lithographic artists know very little of printing, while printers are equally ignorant of drawing. This is un-

doubtedly the cause of much heart-burning and recrimi-
nation between the two parties.   The printer perhaps thinks
the draughtsman should draw so firmly that there should
be little fear of over-etching, while the artist thinks the
printer ought to be able to print anything, just as it is put
upon the stone.   There should be a desire to do the best
on both sides; but it is feared that not unfrequently the
one is more bent on proving the correctness of a pet
theory, than on doing the best he can for his employers.
A more extended knowledge would frequently prevent
these little differences, and it is hoped that the study of
the following pages will tend to a better understanding
between the different grades of practitioners of the art.

With these considerations in view, the Editor, after
rejecting more than one compilation, eventually selected a
practical lithographer of unusual experience and ability in
every department of the art, Mr. W. D. Richmond, to
prepare the present Treatise.   It is believed that his more
than twenty-three years' experience, acquired under circumstances accorded to few, his facility for explaining in clear
and simple language the various processes involved, and
above all his thorough acquaintance with the *rationale*—the
chemical and mechanical basis—of the art, have amply
justified the selection, and that this "Grammar of Lithography" is undoubtedly the most useful and practical, as it
is certainly the most full and complete, Hand-book of the
kind that has yet made its appearance.

It will be observed that no specimens of Lithography have
been given in this volume.   To have done so would have
been to increase the cost of the book without imparting to
it any corresponding increment of practical value.   Nearly
every shop-window, if not every street-hoarding, affords
examples of the different styles, and to reproduce what is
so accessible and so commonplace was needless.   Nor has

any portion of the available space been occupied in historical details. These would possess great interest, but as yet they need such an amount of collection, investigation, and classification as to require a separate and independent work for their adequate treatment. This we may some day attempt, in the mean time we can only admit the want, and suggest the interest which would attach to a work which should supply it.

The Editor has gratefully to acknowledge the valuable assistance with which he has been favoured by several gentlemen of high position in the profession of Lithography and the world of Art. Amongst others he must not omit to name Mr. Louis Haghe, the eminent artist, who was himself formerly a lithographic draughtsman and whose name alone is a guarantee of the importance of the co-operation which he has so kindly accorded; Mr. Michael Hanhart, who is identified with the progress of Artistic Lithography in this country; Mr. William Simpson, the famous artist and traveller, who, in his younger days achieved so high a reputation as a practical Lithographer; and Mr. Harry Sandars, of Oxford, an expert of exceptional talent and ripe practical knowledge. These gentlemen have each carefully read and corrected the proof-sheets of the different chapters prior to their appearance in the Printing Times and Lithographer, and their concurrence in the principles and processes here detailed affords to the Editor every confidence in the accuracy, utility, and comprehensiveness of this Treatise.

Office of The Printing Times and Lithographer,
81, *Great Queen Street, London.*
October, 1878.

PART I.

DRAWING, TRANSFERRING, AND PRINTING.

THE

GRAMMAR OF LITHOGRAPHY.

———o———

CHAPTER I.

Introductory.—Chemical principles on which Lithography is based—
Principal branches of the Art—Materials employed by the artist—
Stones : their varieties, characteristics, defects, and prices—Inks—
Chalks—Transfer-paper, writing, and drawing—Water—Tracing-
paper.

THE object of the following treatise is to present a full and explicit account of the ART OF LITHOGRAPHY in its various branches, adapted to the requirements alike of the amateur and professional. In its manner, an endeavour has been made to adopt a style simple enough for the learner and the self-educator ; while the matter will, it is hoped, be comprehensive enough to be regarded as a useful compendium and *vade-mecum* for those who already possess a knowledge of the general principles and ordinary practice of the art.

The *plan* of the treatise is to give, in the first place, a description of the materials, tools, implements, and machinery ; then to show their application. The subject is divided into two chief portions,—those appertaining to the provinces respectively of the Artist and the Printer.

B

The principal subjects are referred to in independent paragraphs, numbered consecutively. This plan insures facility of reference, avoids repetition, and obviates unnecessary recapitulation.

1. The art of LITHOGRAPHY is based upon a chemical principle,—that of the attraction and repulsion of various natural substances, and more especially upon the antagonistic qualities of grease and water, or of those substances which are soluble in water and those soluble in oil.

Every one must have observed that grease will not directly combine with water. On this property depends the whole principle of Lithography, however simple or complex the result may be, from the ordinary circular in black to the highly-finished imitation in colours of water, or oil painting.*

2. Practical Lithography may be divided into two distinct branches, viz., *Drawing* and *Printing*.† The former includes drawing and writing both upon stone and transfer-paper ; the latter, those multifarious operations necessary after the drawing or writing has left the hands of the artist or writer.

3. Before pursuing this interesting and, to many, fascinating study, it will be necessary to become acquainted with the *materials* ‡ necessary for its practice. Some fifty or more years ago, when the art was in its infancy, its pursuit was attended with many difficulties which do not now

---

* Stated more precisely, the art of Lithography rests upon the following properties of the substance forming the printing surface :—

1. That a drawing made upon it with fat ink adheres to it so strongly as to require mechanical force to remove it.

2. That the parts of it free from the drawing receive and retain water.

3. That a roller or other instrument covered with fat ink, being applied to the printing surface when wetted, the ink will attach itself only to the fatty drawn parts, and will be repelled from the wetted parts.

† Those who practise the two branches are respectively known as lithographic *artists*, *draughtsmen*, or *writers*, and lithographic *printers*.

‡ The materials necessary for drawing and colouring upon paper, &c., will also be required for the complete equipment of the lithographic artist ; but it is considered unnecessary to detail them in this treatise, the student of lithography being supposed to be already acquainted with them. His attention will therefore be mainly solicited to the specialites connected with the subject in hand.

confront the Lithographer. At that time it was necessary that he should make, or cause to be made under his immediate superintendence, presses, rollers, varnishes, writing and printing inks, crayons, and any other instrument or material that was peculiar to, or necessary in, Lithography. Of course the chances of failure were *then* very great; but at the present time they are reduced to a minimum, for not only in the metropolis, but also in the provinces, may be found persons whose business it is to supply the trade with every preparation and appliance required.

Every person in commencing is recommended to purchase his requirements from some well-known dealer, as he then may feel confident, if any mishap occurs, that the fault is with himself, and not the material he is using; and this will greatly conduce to his progress. It is only when he has learned to know and appreciate what good materials are, that he may safely venture to make them for himself. Everything that it will answer his purpose to prepare, this treatise will make him acquainted with; it is, however, economical to purchase ready-made many things which he is actually able to prepare for himself. It is nevertheless advisable that every one who aspires to a thorough acquaintance with the art of Lithography should spend some little time in experimenting on the manufacture of the materials, as valuable information is gained thereby,— information that cannot be so well or so thoroughly acquired in any other way. Experiment teaches him to judge not only of the quality of the article, but to estimate the difficulties that attend its production. The beginner should only do so when he has pretty well mastered the use of those materials that are obtained from persons who make their actual manufacture a study and a business.

4. STONES for the purpose of Lithography are imported chiefly from Germany. They may be obtained from dealers who carry on business in London or elsewhere. Lithographic stones are very compact homogeneous limestones, varying in colour from a light cream, dull yellow, drab, or grey, to darker shades of the same colours. The light tints are softer than the dark, and the grey are harder than the cream-coloured stones. Some are uneven in colour, having light and dark patches, which render them

unfit for drawings of which the artist requires to see the effect he is producing during the progress of his work ; but for ordinary transfer-work this appearance is usually unimportant, as also in show-card and other simple ink-work. *Chalky* stones have *light spots* scattered about in patches, or these may occur all over the stone : these places are soft, and render the stone unfit for any but the commonest work, and should *never* be used for chalk-work, because the acid used in etching attacks those parts with greater energy, and produces similar spots in the impression. For the same reason they must not be used for *etched tints*.

Among the ordinary defects of stones may be mentioned *holes*, and *specks* termed pins. The latter are hard points, usually of a dark colour, but are not of very frequent occurrence, nor of much disadvantage in use. Neither chalky stones nor those having holes will do for engraving upon.

Veins are frequently found, and appear to arise from cracks at some period of the stone's history. Through them has percolated water charged with the carbonate of lime of which the stone is formed. In process of time this crystallizes and cements the portions of the stone together so firmly that it is a rare thing to find a stone break in the direction of these marks. Being of the same chemical nature, they behave in ink-work as the rest of the stone ; but as they differ in mechanical structure, when a stone is grained for chalk-work they receive the grain differently to the other parts, so that when the drawing is made the vein shows darker than the rest of the drawing. Some veins are scarcely visible, while others are not only broader, but sometimes patches occur in the course of their length which distinctly show their crystalline character.

While any stones of the description before-mentioned will do for common purposes, great care should be exercised in selecting those required for particular work. This advice pre-eminently applies to chalk-work, in selecting stones for which, preference should be given to those which are of an even grey or drab colour ; and though these are not of so agreeable a tint to the artist as the lighter ones, yet experience has shown them to be the best for the purpose of chalk-drawing.

Stones are sold by weight. Small ones may be had as

·ıow as ıd. per lb., while very large ones command as much as 4d. Thin stones and grey stones are a little higher in price. *Double-faced* ones, on account of the difficulty of obtaining stones equally good all through, command as much as sixty per cent. more than *single-faced* ones.

Stones have been found in France, England, and other parts of the world, which will yield impressions in the lithographic press, but none possess the qualities of the best German stones in a sufficient degree to become successful rivals.

No other surface, yet discovered, fulfils the necessary conditions of lithographic drawing and printing so completely as the Solenhofen limestone, yet other substances are in use, possessing advantages peculiar to themselves ; the most important of these being zinc plates, and the chromatized gelatine films used in the Albertype and other kindred photo-mechanical printing processes.

Any compact substance that carries a good face and has an affinity for both grease and water, may, no doubt, be used for printing by the lithographic method with varying degrees of success ; hence, surfaces of metal, artificial stone, glass, wood, &c., have been at various times used and advocated. For the present, however, the student's attention will be confined to the methods applicable to the use of lithographic stones.

5. LITHOGRAPHIC INK.—The manufacture of this important preparation will be described in due course, but at present it will be only necessary to mention that good ink may be bought from any dealer in lithographic materials. The inks of Lemercier and Vanhymbeeck have deservedly gained a high reputation ; but there is, in the eyes of many artists, one drawback to their use on stone, and that is a deficiency of black. Good lithographic ink should contain as much black pigment * as is consistent with the necessary

---

* This black pigment is added to the ink merely for the purpose of enabling the artist or writer to see what he is doing and to estimate what the effect of his work will be when printed. If more black be put into the ink than is required to attain this object thoroughly, it will probably be injurious, because the artist could then see to use it, though it might be too weak to fulfil the conditions necessary to success in transferring and printing.

strength for rolling up, and should flow freely from the pen or brush without a decided tendency to spread, though in this respect it differs considerably from either common writing or China ink, as from the same pen a much thicker line is made with the lithographic ink.   The mode of using will be mentioned in its proper place.

The price of this ink is from 1s. per cake.

6. LITHOGRAPHIC CHALKS, OR CRAYONS.—Those most generally used are manufactured by Lemercier, of Paris, and are so well known that every printer experienced in chalk-drawings knows how to treat a subject in which they have been used.   They are made of several degrees of hardness.

The *copal* chalk is hardest, and is used for outlining. Next in order come Nos. 1, 2, and 3.   There is also a *stumping* chalk, though not so much used.

These crayons are very carefully manufactured, and may be relied on for great, if not absolute uniformity ; so much so, that the lithographer should, under all ordinary circumstances, use no other.   This rule may be departed from when the quantity used is very large, or when some competent person is at hand to make them. This duty usually devolves upon the foreman printer in such cases, as he is responsible for the drawings after they leave the hands of the artist.   If such a printer should supply the artist with crayons of his own production, they may be used with perfect confidence.

There are at present no crayons in use for Lithography which equal in facility of manipulation the black-lead pencil or the conté crayon, when used on paper ; but as these substances are in no degree qualified for printing purposes, the artist must necessarily make use of those special productions prepared for his use, which have been found to not only answer his purpose, but that also of the printer.

7. TRANSFER-PAPER FOR WRITING AND DRAWING.— The facilities afforded to Lithography by transfer-paper are so many that its importance cannot be too highly estimated. Its use obviates the necessity of working backwards, as must be done on the stone.   When a piece of writing, for example, is transferred face downwards to the stone, and

the paper upon which it was written is removed, the back of it is then seen ; and when this in turn is inked by the printer, and a piece of paper laid upon it and an impression taken, this impression shows the same appearance as the original piece of writing upon the transfer-paper.

Transfer-papers are prepared by coating the surface of paper with gelatine, starch, or gum, either singly or in combination, or united with other substances. The object of this coating is to interpose a soluble film between the writing or drawing, in lithographic ink or chalk, and the paper. Paper being more or less porous, would, if used alone, absorb some of the ink, instead of permitting the whole of it to be transferred to the stone. Hence the necessity of covering it with some substance which, during the process of transferring, can be moistened through the back of the paper, which is then peeled off, and the work, with the whole or part of the mucilaginous film, left upon the stone.

There are two distinct kinds of transfer-paper for drawing in the ink style and writing, one prepared on ordinary paper and the other on transparent or tracing-paper. These have smooth surfaces ; but the transfer-paper for chalk drawings has a finely granulated surface adapted for receiving the lithographic crayon. There are also transfer-papers for taking impressions from copper-plate, type, and designs upon stone, to be transferred to stone for the convenience of printing more impressions at once than that obtainable from the original alone.

The use and manufacture of these papers will be hereafter fully described, though they may be bought ready prepared at about 8s. per quire, demy size. Chalk transfer-paper 24s. per quire, imperial quarto.

8. WATER is used for dissolving the ink for writing or drawing on stone or paper ; and inasmuch as soap is used to render the other materials of the ink soluble, it is important that hard water should not be used, but distilled or rain-water filtered through blotting-paper. A four-ounce bottleful, with a nick cut in the side of the cork, so that it may be shaken out a drop at a time, will last for a long while if kept for the purpose.

9. TRACING-PAPER for making clean and neat copies

of the work to be done, and *red* tracing-paper for transferring the same to the prepaied paper or stone, will be required by the artist. (See *Appendix.*)

10. The foregoing constitute the principal *materials*** required by the writer or artist. Instruments will be treated of in another place, as well as the machinery and tools required by the printer.

CHAPTER II.

Mechanical and Chemical Principles of some of the Lithographic Materials used in Printing.—Varnish—Printing-ink, black and coloured—Gum-water—Plate Transfer-paper—Plate Transfer-ink—Retransfer-paper — Retransfer-ink — Type Retransfer-ink — Nitric Acid—Sponge—Damping-cloth—Sand—Pumice-stone—Snake-stone—Turps.

HAVING referred in the preceding chapter to the principal Lithographic agents — stones, ink, and water, as materials required in lithographic drawing and writing, we now proceed to notice the chief materials used in printing.

11. By VARNISH, in Lithography, is understood the vehicle in which pigments are ground to form the printer's ink. It is made by subjecting the best linseed-oil to the continued influence of heat, until it becomes more or less thick and viscid. The heat must be raised until the oil will take fire, and must be kept at that heat until the varnish is brought to the proper consistency. The operation is very dangerous, inasmuch as the flame from the burning oil will sometimes reach a great height, even though the quantity of oil be only a quart or two, and, for that reason, every precaution should be taken in its manufacture.

One reason for making varnish for one's self would be to obtain an article known to be pure, for comparison with that which may be bought, as it is possible to thicken the

---

* " Materials " are here intended to mean those matters that require frequent renewing, or are used up in the operations in which they are employed.

varnish with resin (as is done with varnish for letter-press ink), instead of producing the viscidity by burning only.

As varnish is an article manufactured on a large scale, there is no difficulty in purchasing it of a quality to answer the lithographer's purpose. It is made of several degrees of strength, known in the trade by the terms *thin, tinting, medium,* and *thick.* The more transparent and free from colour it is, the better it answers the purpose of Chromo-lithography, as frequently the ink, in this style of printing, is only varnish, stained, as it were, with a little colour or pigment. If this is light or delicate, it is essential to have the varnish as colourless as possible.

Varnish is sold by the gallon, but smaller quantities can be bought. The price varies from 10s. to 18s. per gallon.

12. PRINTING-INK.*—This important material is sold to the trade ready ground, to suit various classes of work, and the price varies from 2s. to 40s. per lb., a good medium ink, for ordinary black printing, costing about 5s. per lb. It is put up in tins, and most inks keep well.

In the state in which it is bought, Lithographic ink is too thick for use, and requires to be thinned down with varnish to answer the printer's purpose. Considerable experience, united with a keen appreciation of the nature of the ink and varnish, is necessary to enable the printer to master this part of his trade ; and though much assistance may be given him by pointing out principles for his guidance, yet it is only experience that can qualify him to carry on his printing with success.

Ink made with *thin varnish* leaves the roller freely for the stone, and will soon spoil a drawing if used by an inexperienced hand—*first,* by adding to the greasy properties of the work already upon the stone ; and *secondly,* by spreading under the pressure. This is caused by, *first,* having too much ink on the roller ; *secondly,* rolling too slowly ; *thirdly,* rolling after the stone has begun to dry ; *fourthly,* the weather or the stone being too warm. This result will be aggravated by the paper being too hard and

---

* The nature of this ink is more fully treated of in paragraphs 116 and 117.

non-absorbent, and the ink not having sufficient tenacity to clean up the work as the printing proceeds.

Now, ink made with *strong varnish* behaves very differently. It soils the stone with difficulty; and if the stone should be made dirty by being rolled after it is dry, on re-wetting the stone and passing the roller over it, the stone is cleaned by the roller again taking up the superfluous ink. It requires slow and heavy rolling to transfer this ink from the roller to the stone, because the varnish is so tenacious, that its particles do not part easily. By using it with a *quick* motion of the roller, the drawing may be almost torn from the stone, so that any delicate parts are sure to suffer if so treated for any considerable number of impressions. The mode adopted in applying this strong ink, causes it to stand, to some extent, in relief upon the stone, and thus may be expected to "smash" in taking the impression; while it is so strong, that it will probably tear soft paper when the latter is being lifted.

The less the body of ink upon the impression, consistent with the proper degree of colour, the better it will be; so, the less varnish there is in the ink, compatible with ease of working, the more suitable will it be for the printer. Temperature is found to modify the varnish very much, and *medium* varnish in summer approaches the nature and properties of *thin*, while in winter it becomes more like *thick* or *strong* varnish; so that the printer must regard temperature as an important element in his calculations. It is clear that a middle course must be taken between the two inks previously described, and it is here that the experience of the printer is required to produce a large number of satisfactory impressions from one drawing.

13. Though the printer is not called upon to make his own black ink, yet he has frequently to produce his coloured inks. To do this he takes a small quantity of medium or medium and thin varnish, and rubs as much colour as he can into it with his palette-knife; and then with the muller he grinds it upon the slab. After it has been thus spread over the slab, he gathers it up with the knife, and adds more colour. By repeating this operation frequently, the ink gradually becomes stiffer, till no more can be added with the knife, and the colour has to be added by dropping a

little here and there upon the slab, and forcing it in with the muller. The ink has now become so stiff that the muller is forced over it with difficulty, and has to be ground with the angle or edge of it instead of its flat face. It must be frequently gathered up with the knife and spread out again with the muller before it is sufficiently ground. Colours that are soft to the touch are more easily ground than those which feel hard or gritty. Hard colours, such as Prussian blue, should be soaked in turpentine *before* grinding ; the varnish displaces the turpentine as the latter evaporates. This saves much of the grinding.

Though ink may be used as soon as ground, it is better when kept a few days, and the same remarks apply to its use as those before made on black ink.

The lighter the tint required, the more varnish must be used ; but if a light body-colour is wanted, flake or zinc-white must be ground up with it to produce the necessary effect ; but this will be more fully treated of hereafter.

When a large quantity of coloured ink is required, ink-mills, which may be driven by steam power, are in use for grinding it.

14. GUM-WATER. A solution of gum-arabic in water is essential to the lithographic printer, and must be always at hand. It is made by putting a quantity of gum—say, four ounces or more—into an earthenware pot that will hold about twice as much, and dropping upon it a few drops of carbolic acid.* It must then be covered with water, frequently stirred during the next day or two until dissolved, and when strained through a cloth or sieve it will be fit for use.

---

* We are indebted to the kindness of Mr. M. Hanhart, the eminent lithographer, for another and important application of carbolic acid. It is well known in the trade that after a stone has been set aside for a considerable period, it is liable to some kind of decomposition that causes light spots, varying in size from a pin's head to a shilling, to appear among the tinting of the drawing. These spots are so troublesome to rectify that not unfrequently the drawing has to be re-done. In investigating the cause of this phenomenon, Mr. Hanhart came to the conclusion that it was due to a fungoid growth affecting the drawing itself. After trying many antiseptics, he has chosen carbolic acid as the most powerful, which he applies with the gum when the stone is finally gummed in. Since adopting it he has been rarely troubled with those "spotty" stones.

Care must be taken not to use it when sour, but, if it should become so, a little chalk or whiting put into it will correct the acidity, though, if the carbolic acid be used in the making, it will keep a long while, even in summer, without becoming acid. The attention of the trade should be specially directed to the properties of carbolic acid, because it is a cheap and simple preventive of sour gum, but one that is not yet generally in use.

To get the best result from gum water it should be applied when the stone is *dry ;* it then penetrates better, and holds more securely. It is usually spread, not thickly but evenly, with a sponge, and allowed to dry, and then it unites with and fills so thoroughly the pores of the stone, that no subsequent amount of washing with mere water will effectually remove it. After a drawing or transfer is made, the gum unites with that part of the stone that is free from the greasy ink or chalk, and assists very materially in checking the tendency of that, or of the subsequently applied printing-ink, to spread further than intended.

The draughtsman also uses gum in *preserving* part of his work, as will be explained in its proper place.

Besides using gum in the first preparation of the stone for printing, the printer should always use it whenever he has occasion to leave his stone, even if only for a few minutes.

Gum-arabic is frequently adulterated with other and cheaper gums, and notably with gum-senegal, which comes nearest to it in properties and appearance. Gum good enough for Lithography cannot be bought much under 1s. per lb., at which price it can be bought from oilmen and druggists in London, while in other towns 1s. 6d. and more will have to be paid for the same article. Common gum is sometimes sold at about 6d., but its dull and dirty appearance, and insolubility, will condemn it at once.*

15. PLATE TRANSFER-PAPER is used for taking impressions from copper and steel plates, from type and stone, and, afterwards, for transferring them to stone. There are two distinct kinds on sale—viz., India retransfer-paper,

---

* Of course prices vary with the market, but those given refer to the present year.

which sells at 16s. per quire; and Scotch, which is about 8s. per quire. The latter is to be preferred, because the surface is slightly absorbent and takes a better impression, while the great body of composition upon it allows it to be successfully transferred, and its swelling up under the operation of damping helps to prevent the lines from spreading under the pressure.

16. PLATE TRANSFER-INK is sold at from 12s. to 16s. per lb., or 1s. per oz. It is sufficient to have in use one ounce at a time, as that quantity will yield a large number of transfers.

17. RETRANSFER-INK, "STONE TO STONE," is about the same price, and four ounces will suffice for a small establishment. It is put up in tins, and keeps any length of time.

18. TYPE RETRANSFER-INK is also sold; but, in our opinion, the last-mentioned, with the addition of a small quantity of soap, answers the purpose better, and is less troublesome in use. The ink in ordinary use for letter-press printing may also be used, and, from containing a portion of soap, very good transfers are frequently made from it.

19. NITRIC ACID must be kept in glass-stoppered bottles. It is used for preparing and cleaning the stone by an operation termed etching. It should be obtained only at one place, so as to insure, if possible, the same strength being always employed. The price is from 8d. per lb.

20. SPONGE is used for applying water to the stone, damping paper, &c. The price varies from 10s. per lb. to twice that sum. That at 10s. will answer the general purposes of the lithographer, the smaller pieces serving for gum and acid sponges. Before using a new sponge, it must be well beaten to get the sand out of it; there will then remain small pieces of shell that must be picked out. They may be felt on squeezing it when it is damp. If some pieces then remain out of reach, they may usually be got rid of by putting the sponge into weak acid and water, and letting it stay until all effervescence ceases upon the addition of some more acid. After washing well with plain water, it will be fit for use.

21. DAMPING-CLOTH must be provided, and may be obtained from the dealers in lithographic materials at about 1s. per lb. It is made from old sheeting, sugar-bags, &c., and must be of linen or flax, and soft when wetted: hence new material does not do so well. As much must be taken for use at one time as will, when it is doubled and the corners folded to the middle, make a pad a little larger than the hand. It will be about damp enough if it is saturated with water and then wrung as dry as may be.

22. SAND is used for rubbing the stones down to a level surface, and for taking off old work. SILVER SAND is generally used, and may be bought of nurserymen, oilmen, and others, at about 3s. per bushel. It must be dried thoroughly, to enable it to be sifted through the proper sieves. Sand for *graining* stones to receive chalk drawings is a fine brown sand sifted through sieves of the proper degree of fineness for the work to be done. If the silver sand be first sifted through fine sieves, and preserved for use, it will suit many purposes better than the brown sand, while the coarser portion will answer equally well for grinding purposes.

23. PUMICE-STONE, which follows the sand in use, may be bought at 6d. per lb., from oilmen, ironmongers, &c. The largest pieces should be selected, and a flat side filed on them in a direction at right angles to the fibrous appearance of the structure.

24. WATER-OF-AYR STONE, or SNAKE-STONE, in blocks of about two inches square by six inches long, is used to finish the polishing. Smaller pieces, termed PENCILS, are useful for polishing parts of the stone in making corrections and alterations, as also for use at the press for cleaning purposes. They may be had as small as one-fourth of an inch square. The price for snake-stone is 6d. to 8d. per lb. Small slips from 2s. per dozen.

25. A mixture of two parts spirits of turpentine, usually called TURPS, and one part olive oil, should be kept for washing out drawings when necessary, and spirits of turpentine should always be at hand.

PAPER as a material in lithography and its preparation for printing will be treated of later on.

CHAPTER III.

Instruments, Tools, and Appliances used in Drawing and Writing.— Brushes— Pens—Mezzotint-scrapers—Crayon-holders—Hand-board —Turntable.

OUR last two chapters have prepared the way for an account of the appliances used in lithographic drawing and writing, which we now proceed to give.

26. For drawing upon stone and transfer-paper, the artist will need all the usual appliances of the draughtsman's office, but he will require to have the ruling and circle pens in more than usually good condition. In addition, he will require brushes and pens of a finer character than those required in any other kind of drawing.

27. LITHOGRAPHIC BRUSHES are good red sable crow-quill pencils, with a portion of the hair cut away all round, so as to allow only the central part to be used. If any single hair protrudes beyond its neighbours, the brush will not be good, but this may in part be remedied by wetting it and passing it rapidly through a gas flame to burn it off, the wetting protecting the rest and exposing the single hair only to the flame. It is not every pencil that will make a good brush, so that when one is obtained it should be treasured. It is well to possess some half-dozen or more, as a brush that will not do for one purpose may do very well for another. Brushes are made that are intended to be used without cutting, but they are generally made of too fine hair, and are not sufficiently springy and elastic. Some artists make up their own brushes by cutting off portions of a larger red sable pencil and tying them to suitable pieces of cedar-wood and then mounting them by any convenient means.*

---

* Mr. Sandars, of Oxford, has communicated a somewhat ingenious mode of cutting a brush. Dip it in gum-water, draw it to a fine point, and let it dry hard, remove the outer hair with a sharp penknife to the degree thought necessary and wash out the gum. This often produces a first-class brush, but the method has the disadvantage of not permitting it to be tried at intervals during the operation. No more hair should be removed than is necessary to produce a brush suited to the particular work in hand.

A ready mode of mounting brushes is to attach them to pieces of wood in such a way that a quill may be used as a cover to protect them when not in use, and to form the handle when required. This is similar to some pocket penholders, which, by the way, may be adapted to the same purpose.

The beginner is recommended to cut at least half a dozen, as by so doing his chances of obtaining a good one will be six times as great ; and unless he has had the opportunity of trying a known good one, he would hardly be able to judge whether he had or had not obtained one by the first trial.

In addition to the brushes used in drawing and writing with the lithographic ink, others of a coarser kind (duck and crowquill red sables) will be required for various purposes, such as " stopping or gumming-out " (see article 81 *et seq.*), making coloured sketches, &c.

A flat camel-hair brush about two inches wide will also be wanted to remove any loose particles of dust or dirt from the surface of the stone or transfer-paper while at work.

28. LITHOGRAPHIC PENS.—All ordinary pens are useless for any of the finer purposes of lithography, such as circular and ornamental writing and drawing. Perhaps the nearest approach made by steel pen manufacturers is " Perry's Lithographic Pen"; but even these are short of the perfection required by transfer-writers, who have to fall back upon those of their own production. These are usually made from the best quills scraped down before cutting, until the barrel of the quill will yield to the pressure of the nail. For this purpose, broken glass may be used. A short slit is then made in the quill, and the nibs formed by means of a sharp penknife. This requires much skill and practice, and as it cannot be attained without much perseverance, the tyro can perhaps make a better attempt at the preparation of steel pens.

If the work is not *very* fine, Perry's pens will be found to answer the purpose, and they may be further improved by delicately sharpening them on Arkansas oilstone. Some persons take any very fine pens and sharpen them as before mentioned, and then reduce them in thickness by treating them to a strong solution of nitric acid in water, and by such means pens equal to the best may be produced, while they are superior to quills in point of durability.

The use of steel pens was known in the early days of the lithographic art, and the mode of making them is thus described by M. Bregeaut in a work published in 1827.*

"Take a watch spring, and get rid of any grease that might have adhered to it, by rubbing it with some fine sand or a soft piece of pumice-stone ; place it in a dish, and pour on it equal parts of nitric acid and water ; allow the acid to act on the steel, until it has lost three-quarters of its thickness, and is reduced to about the substance of a sheet of paper.

" During the action of the acid, the spring must be taken out occasionally and wiped with a rag, to render the action more equal.

" When of the proper thickness, the spring must be well washed and wiped, and cut into lengths of about one inch and a half. Each piece must now be rounded in the shape of a gouge, by placing the steel on a piece of cardboard laid upon a lithographic stone, and striking the steel with the small end of a hammer, lengthways ; by this operation the steel will take a curl.

" A small and sharp pair of scissors must now be taken, and the slit made with them at one extremity of the piece of steel ; each side of the pen must next be shaped with the scissors : the difficulty of the operation consists in forming each nib perfectly equal and with a very fine point : great practice is required in making a good steel pen."

Steel of the proper thickness for such pens may now be obtained at various places in London. It is a good plan to put the steel between a wooden holder and a quill, so that when a new pen is required the steel may be drawn down, the old nibs cut off, and new ones made.

In forming these pens a pair of small forceps will be found useful in setting the nibs in their proper position.

---

* And by Senefelder in 1819, in his "Complete Course of Lithography." The language differs, but the description is even fuller, though conveying no more information.

29. MEZZOTINT* SCRAPERS (Fig. 1), sold at about sixpence each, are useful for correcting work upon stone either for the use of the artist or printer; but in default of possessing one, a penknife or the ordinary erasing-knife (Fig. 2), may be employed.

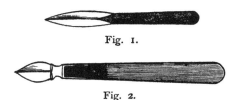

Fig. 1.

Fig. 2.

30. CRAYON-HOLDERS, as usually bought from the artists' colourman, are instruments rather unpleasant to use, more especially as compared with the smoothness and lightness of the lead-pencil. It is advisable to saw or file them into two parts, and fit cedar or other handles† to them; the ring will then be out of the way, and the holder will answer very well for any work excepting delicate tinting, for which purpose a lighter one will be necessary. A holder easily made and fairly light may be formed out of a large-barrelled magnum bonum steel pen with the nib part broken away. By neatly cutting and scraping the crayon, it may be so adjusted to the barrel as to form a neat light tool, and when the chalk is worn nearly to the steel, it may be projected from the other side.‡ Holders may also be made of writing-paper pasted and rolled round a smooth pencil or similar mould. When dry, they are stiff and very light,

---

* *Mezzotint* is applied to a process of engraving, so called because it was at first supposed to require a large amount of middle tint or half-tone in the distribution of masses of light and shade. The ground is *scraped* away to the various degrees of lightness required.

† Such crayon-holders are now to be had of artists' colourmen. The metallic part being of steel is lighter and thinner for the same strength than the old brass and German silver holders were.

‡ In making these holders, it is well to give them long tapering handles, so that when held near the middle they are so balanced that they give scarcely any pressure due to to their own weight, leaving the hand alone to apply what is required.

and a good stock may be made in a short time. It is well to have several, for reasons which will be referred to hereafter.

31. A HAND-BOARD will be found exceedingly useful and almost essential to the lithographic draughtsman. It is a piece of wood about six inches wide, and about six inches longer than the stone; but if longer, will not probably be much in the way. It should be about three-eighths of an inch thick along the middle line, and made thinner towards the edges, which should be straight. Some thick strips of millboard should be gummed or pasted in places round the edge of the stone, to keep the board away from that part which is to receive the drawing. By using this handboard, the drawing, either in chalk or ink, may be effectually protected from injury. The edges will occasionally be useful in ruling lines.

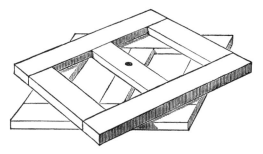

Fig. 3.

32. A TURNTABLE is a luxury to the draughtsman on stone, as the largest stones, when placed upon it, may be easily moved into any position. To make one, strips of oak, or similar wood, 3 in. wide and 1 in. thick, are framed together by mortise and tenon to form a square of 12 to 18 in. There should be five pieces in each frame, so as to have one across the middle. Two of these frames are required. Into one frame let in four small friction-wheels, such as are used in sliding frames to upright glass cases, equally distant from a centre pin a quarter of

C 2

an inch thick, projecting about half an inch. In the other frame make a centre hole for the pin to work in, and screw on an iron ring, or piece of sheet iron, to prevent the friction-wheels from imbedding into the wood. When these two frames are placed together, the turntable is complete, and presents the appearance shown in Fig. 3.

A very simple though not efficient substitute is obtained by folding up a piece of stout brown paper into eight or more thicknesses, and placing it under the centre of the stone, which may then be moved with a little exertion. The great defect of this is that the paper bruises the table if the stone is any considerable weight ; but this may be prevented by putting the paper on a piece of stout sheet iron.

The special appliances for the Draughtsman having been reviewed, it will now be necessary to speak of those required by the Printer.

CHAPTER IV.

Instruments, Tools, and Apparatus used in Printing.—The Press, varieties of Construction—the Framing—the Cross-head—the Pressure Screw—the Press Key—the Scraper Box—the Bed or Carriage —the Tympan Frame—the Cylinder—the Handle—the Brasses— the Eccentrics or Cams—the Lever—Tympans, how to stretch them —Scrapers—Elastic Beddings—the Roller, how prepared for use— Roller Handles—the glazed Roller.

AS we have already described the general properties of the materials used in Lithography, from the stones up to the appliances by which the drawings are put upon them, we are now prepared to give an account of the construction and principles of the apparatus by which the prepared and drawn stones are made to give an almost unlimited number of impressions.

Foremost among the apparatus used for this purpose stands the PRESS, which we will fully describe.

33. THE LITHOGRAPHIC PRESS (Fig. 4) is a comparatively

simple piece of mechanism, and consists of the following parts :—

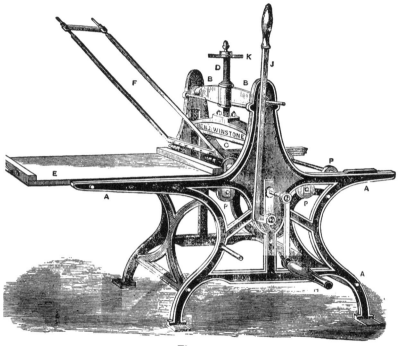

Fig. 4.

1. The framing, A A.
2. The cross-head, B B.
3. The scraper-box, C.
4. The pressure-screw, D, uniting Nos. 2 and 3.
5. The bed, E, to which is hinged
6. The tympan-frame, F.
7. The cylinder, to which is attached
8. The handle, H (in larger presses there are two).
9. The handle and lever, secured to
10. The Eccentrics * and their shaft.

---

* An eccentric is a mechanical contrivance consisting of a circular

In the presses mostly in use at the present day the bed slides upon two projections upon the sides of the frames, while in some improved forms it runs upon friction-rollers (see P P P, Fig. 4). This latter form is much to be preferred, as effecting a saving in labour, in lubricating-oil, and wear of the beds. In some kinds of presses the cylinder can be taken out, and, with the brasses in which it works, can be cleaned without taking the press to pieces. There are other kinds which combine both these improvements. Presses are sold without tympan, elastic bedding for the stone, or scrapers ; but these things should be ordered with the press, in order to have it complete. It is better to purchase a large press than a small one, as by having an extra tympan of a smaller size small work may be executed with facility. A press, for example, 39 by 26 inches, fitted with friction rollers and smaller extra tympan, can be easily worked for an octavo circular, certainly with greater ease than in a smaller press *without friction-rollers*.

34. The FRAMING in all modern presses is invariably of cast iron. The two sides should be united by cross frames of cast iron, and held by nuts and bolts. The sides in some older kinds are held together by bolts only, with flanges to keep them at the proper distance from each other. This pattern is very weak, and should be avoided, as, purchased at any price, they are dear in the end.

35. The CROSS-HEAD is tapped to carry the screw by which the pressure is regulated, and is preferably made of wrought iron ; but really strong and useful presses are made with cast-iron cross-heads, a greater quantity of metal being used to make up for the inferior strength of the cast iron. This extra quantity is best located chiefly on the upper side of the cross-head, so as to make its cross section of the T form, as the mechanical condition of the cross-head is that of a beam fixed at the ends, and loaded in the middle, but the pressure being from below, the greater quantity of material must be applied to the opposite side.

---

disc attached to a shaft, but having its centre at a small distance from that of the axis of the shaft. Though called eccentrics by printers, these parts of the press are really what engineers call " cams," the sides of the eccentrics being cut away to give a greater rise and fall to the cylinder, and through it to the press bed.

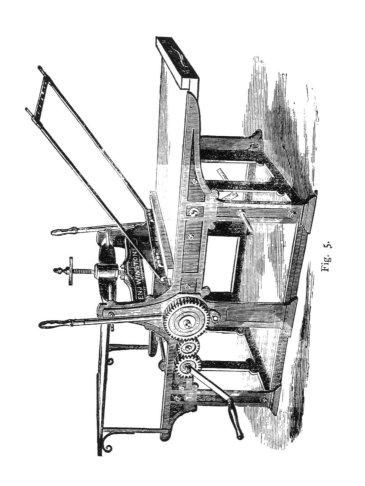

Fig. 5.

36. The PRESSURE SCREW has at its lower extremity a flange which works in a small socket screwed to the upper side of the scraper box, which is thus hung to the screw. Its upper end is hexagonal, and usually carries the

37. PRESS KEY, K, whose ends are formed into spanners, to be used for raising or lowering the tympan to the thickness of the stone, or unscrewing the various parts of the press.

38. The SCRAPER BOX should be smooth and even inside, or it and the scrapers may either be broken or give unequal pressure. It should have one or two screws in its front to hold the scraper sufficiently to prevent its dropping out.

39. The BED, or Carriage, is made of wood of an equal thickness throughout, and bound on the under side with strips of broad hoop-iron. There is a cross-piece at each end, one to carry the tympan-frame, and the other to form a stop for the stone.

40. The TYMPAN FRAME is united to the carriage by hinges, so made that the frame can be adjusted to the thickness of the stone, and, by withdrawing the centre pins of the hinges, the frame can be altogether removed. There are loose plates at each end, held to the frame by screws, between which the leather or metal tympan is firmly secured. The top of the frame slides on the sides, and by means of nuts the tympan can be stretched to any desirable extent.

41. The CYLINDER must be of wrought iron, turned very true and parallel, and adjusted exactly in the vertical line of the eccentrics, scraper box, and cross-head. Neither it nor the bands on the under side of the carriage must be permitted to get greasy; for, if they become so, there will be a difficulty in moving the carriage when the pressure is on. All oil must be wiped off these parts, then washed with turps or benzoline, and rubbed with whiting. The cylinder and the bed will then "*bite*," and the printing may proceed with any reasonable pressure.

42. The HANDLE is attached to an elongation of the cylinder shaft by a taper pin passing through both. To presses above 24 × 16 there should be two handles, and to those of 36 × 24 a tooth-wheel and pinion so

arranged that the printer has not to pass to the other side of the handle to work the press. This is accomplished either by the pinion working in an internally-toothed wheel, in which case two handles cannot be applied to the pinion shaft, or, as in Fig. 5, by an intermediate wheel between the larger wheel and its pinion. In either form the parts should be so arranged that the press may be worked with the handles applied directly to the cylinder.

43. The BRASSES in which the cylinder runs have on each of their under sides a plate of hardened steel, against which work

44. The ECCENTRICS, or Cams. These are placed under the cylinder brasses, and are pieces of steel welded to a shaft that crosses the press. Their office is, by a quarter revolution, to raise the cylinder, bed, and stone to the scraper, and to give the necessary pressure. This is done by means of

45. The LEVER, secured to the eccentric shaft. It stands, when out of use, in an upright position; but by being depressed horizontally against a pin in the side of the press (which prevents its being set too low), the stone and tympan are brought to the scraper, and, by turning the handle, the friction between the cylinder and the bed-bands or straps forces the stone under the scraper, though the pressure may amount to some tons.

46. TYMPANS* are made either of leather or metal, each of which has its advantages. Good leather tympans cost about 4s. per square foot, and will last for years. If the press is bought new and a leather tympan supplied, it will

---

* There is a fundamental difference between the tympan of the letter-press and that of the lithographic press. The former is a frame attached at one end to the carriage on which the paper is laid in position before being printed. It serves as a guide for laying the sheets on the type. In lithographic printing the lay of the paper is not thus secured; the sheet is placed directly on the printing surface. In typography, however, the tympan-frame is also used as a means of interposing some elastic substance between the platen and the printing substance. The same object is served by the tympan in lithography. In the one case paper and blanket contained in the tympan-frame come between the type form and the platen; in the latter "backing sheets," or blanket and leather, or thin metal, come between the scraper or the impressing surface and the stone, or the printing surface.

require preparation. Thus : put in the press as large a stone as it will take, cover it with clean paper, and lower the tympan upon, it. Rub the side that comes against the scraper with tallow, suet, or lard, to which a large quantity of blacklead has been added ; the scraper, previously levelled upon the stone, must be brought down upon the tympan by lowering the lever, and the carriage drawn through with a light pressure. The result will probably be that the tympan stretches. Now after drawing the tympan to its full length, before the pressure is released, take up the "slack" of the leather by running up the nut against the top sliding piece. By repeating this operation under gradually increased pressure, and the application of grease and blacklead, the slack will be brought to a mininum, and the tympan may be considered fit for use.

47. For METALLIC TYMPANS zinc is sometimes used, but brass is much to be preferred. Zinc tympans are 9d. and brass 1s. 6d. per square foot. They are similarly prepared, but the scraper must be covered with leather as described in next article.

48. SCRAPERS are made of boxwood from 3 to 4 inches wide, and $\frac{7}{8}$ in. thick, and of a length suitable to the work in hand. If the stone is not thick, the scraper should be nearly as long as the stone is wide, or a breakage might be the result. The edge that is applied to the tympan must be of a V section, about $\frac{3}{8}$ths wide at the bottom.

In all cases of transferring, the scraper should be *set* to the stone, by placing a sheet or two of coarse cabinet paper upon it and rubbing the scraper over it, taking care to slightly round its face. When the scraper gives signs of touching all along, its edge may be considered true.

Scrapers for metal tympans are covered with leather, which may be bought at from 2s. per lb., in strips of about $1\frac{1}{2}$ inch wide. Take a piece about 3 inches longer than the scraper and wet it ; then with about $\frac{3}{4}$-inch tacks secure it to one end, and with a pair of pincers strain it over the face of the scraper as tightly as possible, and nail down the other end : when dry it will be fit for use. In default of a pair of pincers, make a hole in the end of the leather, and put a strong string through it. This may be tied to a portion of the press, and the scraper brought to bear upon the same portion, so as to form a lever and thus stretch the leather.

The objection to nailing the leather to the scraper is, that it cannot be conveniently removed to set the latter; but this may be remedied by the following method :—

At about the middle of the ends of the scraper drill a three-sixteenth inch hole about one inch deep, pointing obliquely to about the centre of the face of the scraper; fit a pin projecting about one-quarter inch, make a hole in the leather, and put it over the pin at one end, strain it over the face, and mark it for the other hole, which, when made, may be slipped over the second pin. The leather may then be removed at any time.

49. ELASTIC BEDDING should be secured to the face of the bed. This consists of thick kamptulicon, costing about 9d. per square foot. A board or two about three-quarters and one inch thick should also be provided to make up for a deficient thickness in the stone, as each stone must be brought up to the lowest position of the tympan.

50. The BACKING-SHEET is an appointment of the press used to protect the stone from any grease that may find its way through the *tympan*, and in other ways to assist the progress of the printing. It is usually made of a piece of well-rolled cardboard, of about six-sheet thickness, fastened by string to the tympan frame. It is sometimes fastened only to the upper end of it, and hangs loosely over the tympan, the thumb being applied to the sheet in bringing the tympan down to the stone so as to keep it in place. The object in having it so loose is, that when secured by its four corners it is generally torn by the stretching of the tympan in taking the impression. This may be entirely avoided by putting an eyelet-hole at each bottom corner, passing through it a small india-rubber band, and then by string fastening it to the corners of the tympan-frame. By adopting this contrivance the sheet is kept properly in position, while the elasticity of the bands prevents the breaking out of the holes.

This backing-sheet is sufficient for ordinary commercial work, but for better purposes it is supplemented by a few sheets of soft printing-paper, which the printer lays on the back of the paper to be printed. When it is passed through the press, the sheets are lifted off again and laid aside for the next impression. This delays the work, and might be entirely avoided by fastening to the back sheet a piece ot fine printer's blanket, which would be more permanently elastic than the loose sheets of paper.

For *transferring*, the fine blanket backing is exceedingly useful, as it not only moderates the pressure and assists in preventing the "smashing" of the lines, but helps to modify any slight inequalities in the stone, backing-sheet, or tympan ; and these same qualities are almost equally useful in taking the impressions. It may be used as a loose sheet if it is not thought worth while to fasten it up, and may be made portable by brushing over a cardboard some book-binder's glue, laying the blanket upon it, and running it through the press.

For printing from engraved stones the blanket may be regarded as a necessity.

51. The ROLLER. This consists of three parts. 1st, the *block*, which is of wood, about four inches thick and eleven or more inches long, with a taper projecting handle at each end; 2nd, the *flannel*, with which the block is tightly covered; and 3rd, the *skin*, which is outside all. This last—very important feature—is made of the best part of a fine calf-skin, very tightly drawn over the flannel, and secured at the ends by a string passed through holes, and the leather closely gathered up. Though rollers that have been in use for some time are undoubtedly better and easier to use than new ones, yet the novice must be forewarned against purchasing "*rollers ready for use*," or "in working order," from the dealers, as they are frequently merely rolled up in black ink, which, drying in the leather, nearly spoils it ever afterwards.

Rollers are prepared for use by rubbing into them before a fire some kind of grease that will not dry, such as *lard* or *tallow* ; * after this they are to be rolled in *strong* varnish frequently for a day or two, with an occasional scraping

---

* Some printers prepare their rollers with olive-oil and other sub-stances, but the principle is essentially the same, viz. :—A previous saturation of the leather with some substance of a less drying nature than the varnish employed in the ink.

off of the varnish with a knife. The knife should be dull in the edge, so as to avoid cutting the roller. A roller once used for black ink should be kept for that purpose only; but when used for colour, it may be made to answer the purpose for printing any colour with due precautions. As *dryers* are usually put into coloured inks to make them dry promptly, it is necessary to clean the rollers immediately after they are done with. This is effected by scraping as much ink as can be got off, then washing with turpentine, and scraping again; finally, washing with turps and wiping with clean rag.* If an entire change of colour is to take place for one of a pure character, the roller must be cleaned more carefully than would be necessary if the next colour were only a secondary or tertiary colour, in which the former colour on the roller entered into the composition of the one to be next used; or, than if the next change was to be one of a lighter or darker tint of the same colour. When a colour-roller is done with for a time, it should be well cleaned, and tallow or lard rubbed into it. It should then be wrapped up and put away. Before using again, the grease must be carefully scraped away, and the roller washed with turps, to entirely free it from grease. Nothing is more injurious to a roller than allowing the colour on it to get dry; this and bad scraping spoil more rollers than years of use.

Fig. 6.

With rollers are invariably used ROLLER HANDLES, made of leather. The leather should be thick, such as is used for mill-banding, &c. Sufficient should be cut to cover the handle without overlapping. The leather is then to be wetted, tied round with a piece of string to keep it in shape, and allowed to dry, after which it will be found to retain its shape. These handles allow of free motion of the rollers

---

* In refractory cases salt is sometimes used in conjunction with turpentine; but on what chemical principle we fail to discover. Probably, the salt being insoluble in "turps," acts mechanically only.

when held lightly, but by gripping them more or less the roller is controlled as desired. For light rolling they are held loosely, and for heavy rolling they are gripped tightly. Fig. 6 shows rollers and handles.

52. The GLAZED ROLLER is very useful in many cases upon polished stones, by reason of the ease with which it may be cleaned. It may be prepared by taking any smooth roller whose leather is thin and nicely strained over a rather soft flannel, and rolling it in an ink composed of red lead and varnish. When dry, rub it down with fine cabinet paper, roll it again in the colour; then rub down a second time, when, if not smooth, the operation is to be repeated until it becomes so. A roller so prepared may be very quickly cleaned with turpentine and some rag. These rollers should be washed at the close of every day's work and at the end of each job, ready to be wrapped in clean paper and put away.

CHAPTER V.

Accessories to the Lithographic Printing Press.—Acid Stumps—Mortar and Pestle—Palette Knife—Ink Slab—Backing-sheet—Marking Leads—Squeegee—Appliances for stone grinding and polishing—The Trough—Levigator—Sieves—Straight-edge—Callipers—Stone-horse—Mallet and Chisel—Rasp, File, and Crowbar.

OUR last chapter described the *press* and the *roller*. Accessory to these all-important appliances are many things used in the art which now require notice, such as the tools for spreading equably or distributing the ink, which appertain to the roller, and the backing-sheets, which appertain to the press.

53. ACID STUMPS are small pointed pieces of box or other hard wood, to be kept at hand and used with strong acid or (better still) gum and acid, for removing any specks of dirt from the stone. Taking these in the right hand, a water or gum sponge is held in the left to wash away instantly the acid when it has removed the dirt.

54. A MORTAR AND PESTLE of a small size will be useful to reduce rosin into a fine powder for purposes where the work requires an extra strong etching. It is used either by tying it up in fine muslin, or it may be dusted on with cotton wool, the finer parts being found to adhere to the ink in preference to the larger parts.

Fig. 7.

55. A PALETTE KNIFE (Fig. 7), for taking up the ink, spreading it on the roller, and various other uses, should be had for each press. A knife from seven to nine inches in the blade, costing from 1s. to 1s. 6d., is a convenient size. Care should be taken in warming the knife for any purpose, as it may easily be spoiled by being overheated.

56. An INK SLAB is essential for each press. Nothing is better than a thin litho stone about 17 by 13 inches, with strips of wood tacked round it to the bench to keep it in its place. It should be set level.*

57. MARKING LEADS are used for making marks upon the stone for laying the sheet to, it being the practice in lithography to adjust the paper direct upon the stone, instead of to the tympan, as is done in letterpress printing. A piece of "four or six to pica lead" obtained from the compositor will answer the purpose exactly—it will make a mark that can be plainly seen, and will neither wash away with the sponge and damping cloth, nor take the ink from the roller.

A mark made with common ink will answer the same purpose and possess similar properties, but the lead is decidedly to be preferred, because, besides being portable, it can be, and usually is, used upon the stone while it is wet.

58. The SQUEEGEE is a very useful tool to both printer and stone-polisher, though as yet almost unknown in the

---

* If space can be spared, a stone about 2 feet square should be set up for grinding colours, as the ordinary ink slab is too small to grind sufficient colour for jobs of many impressions.

trade. It consists of a piece of india-rubber a quarter of an inch thick, about two inches wide, and any convenient length, set in a frame with about one inch of its width projecting, being mounted just in the same manner as the modern ink-erasers and paper-cleaners. When a stone is polished and washed, one or two strokes of this instrument will denude it of all surface water more effectually than any other method, and it is far superior in every way to either the use of blotting-paper, rag, or setting the stone on end to drain ; beside this, other uses will be found for it later on.

59. In our first chapter (§ 4) were described the characteristics—mineralogical and chemical—of the stone used for lithography. Before the stone can be used, however, it requires to be ground and polished. The materials and apparatus used in these several operations are the following :—

The STONE TROUGH is used as a convenient rest for the stones during the operations of grinding, polishing, and graining, and as a receptacle for the waste sand, water, &c. It must not on any account be used as a washing-place for dirty cloths, &c., nor for any use whatever whereby the thorough cleanliness of the stones may be in any way endangered. It should be emptied at least once a week. Many jobs are spoiled through a want of care in the stone-grinder, in using the stale water in the trough instead of fresh clean water.

The trough may be made of pine, 1½ to 2 inches thick, about 11 inches deep. Its superficial area may be according to convenience ; say about 4 feet by 3 feet. It may be lined with zinc or lead, preferably the latter, but if well jointed it will do without either, as it is intended to contain always water, which will keep the wood swollen. It should be placed on a strong stand about 18 inches high, and if the trough be ledged at the bottom, the ledges may be so contrived as to keep the trough in its place on the stand. It is better to have them made to separate, as the trough is then easily lifted off the stand if required, while it can be made equally firm as when constructed as one piece. Four or five cross pieces about 4 inches by 2, notched 2 inches deep at the ends, on the under side, to keep them in place, and a groove across on the upper side, about

2½ inches from their ends, to prevent the water running over the trough, will serve to hold the stones during the operations of grinding, polishing, &c. Where convenient, the water should be laid on from the main or a tank, terminated nearly opposite the centre of the trough by two or three feet of india-rubber pipe, to which should be attached a 3-inch rose nozzle. Where this cannot be done, a shelf must be provided for a bucket of water, and a jug or other handy vessel kept for pouring the water over the stone.

A tap should be placed in a convenient position about two inches above the bottom of the trough, by which the water can be drawn off and the sediment be taken out afterwards with a small hand-shovel, or similar tool.

Fig. 8.

60. A LEVIGATOR or "JIGGER" (Fig. 8) is an instrument of cast iron about 10 inches in diameter, with holes passing from the top through it. It is surrounded by a rim, and has a handle placed eccentrically at about one-fourth the tool's diameter from its edge. It is used for grinding purposes by strewing sand and water over the stone and on the top of the levigator, which is then set in motion by grasping the handle and performing rapid circles all over the stone to be ground.

61. SIEVES are used for sifting the sand previous to grinding and graining. They are of fine woven wire gauze, preferably of copper, but usually of brass, mounted in

D

wooden hoops, as seen in Fig. 9. They must be carefully
kept in a dry place, as they are very easily injured. Damp
air corrodes the brass and makes it rotten. If a few
broken places occur, they may be repaired by gumming over
the holes with small pieces of paper, or otherwise preventing
the sand passing through such faulty places. Sieves
are numbered according to the meshes per lineal inch.
No. 60 will answer well for ordinary grinding purposes,
preceded, if necessary, by No. 40, when much grinding has
to be done. No. 120, the smallest size made, will be necessary for ordinary fine grains, and No. 100 for coarser grains.
These will answer all the requirements of the lithographer
in producing grains for any subject. The prices run from
3s. 6d. to 7s. 6d. each.

62. A STRAIGHT-EDGE will be necessary for trying the
surface of the stones. A very useful article may be made
by selecting a piece of iron three or four feet long, two
inches wide, and one-quarter inch thick, and sending it to an
engineer to be planed along one edge, so that it will stand
upon it. A stone may be considered true enough if a small
piece of writing-paper is *held* by the straight-edge at each
of several places along its edges and middle when the
straight-edge stands upon it.

Of course various substitutes for such a straight-edge will
suggest themselves.

The back of the stone should be tested also, and made
generally level, if found not so. Breakages are the result of
inattention to this, as stones break in most instances by
reason of the backs not fitting the bed of the press. If the
upper and lower surfaces of a stone are two parallel planes,
no amount of pressure applied in printing will break it.
The press may be broken, but not the stone. Any lumps
may be taken off the back with the chisel and mallet, and,
if necessary, finished by the levigator. Yet, when every
care is taken with the back, if the face is not parallel to it,
the printer may by clumsy packing reduce it to the condition of an uneven back, and break it in consequence.

63. A PAIR of CALLIPERS * should be at hand for testing

---

* Callipers are a species of compasses with legs bent in such a form
a to render them available in measuring the thickness of solids.

the thickness of the stones, so that they may be got parallel in their under and upper surfaces. The callipers should have cross-pieces at the ends, so that the point shall not drop into any hollow place in the back of the stone.

The callipers should be used every time a stone has to be ground, and the stone ground more at the thick part; thus, without doing it all at once, they may be gradually got quite even, and then kept so.

Fig. 9.

Fig. 10.

Attention to this point will pay, as it will prevent many breakages and save the draughtman's time in re-drawing. It also renders unnecessary the loss of the printer's time in "packing."

A STONE-HORSE for drying the stones upon may be constructed in various ways. It is commonly framed of wood, inclined backwards, to prevent the stone falling forwards, with a step for the stone to stand upon. It is used before an open common or gas fire.

A MALLET and CHISEL for trimming broken stones, a large *rasp*, and large smooth *file* for preparing their edges, with a small *crowbar* or lever for raising the corners of heavy stones, will complete the equipment of the stone-grinder. The *trolley* (Fig. 10) will be found useful for moving heavy stones.

CHAPTER VI.

Grinding and Polishing Stones.—Marking the Depth to be ground—
Instances in which Grinding may be dispensed with—Grinding
without a Levigator—The Gradation of the Sand—Polishing—
Testing by the Magnifying-glass—Rounding the Edges of the
Stone—Stone-grinding Machines.

IN the preceding five chapters we have, we trust, conveyed to the Student of Lithography a clear idea of
the nature and uses of the different materials used in each
of the two great divisions of the art—drawing and printing.
He is, therefore, prepared now to utilize his knowledge of
the materials and to enter upon the practical operations
required in this kind of printing.

The stones have been described in the *first* chapter; the
appliances for preparing them in Chapter V.; the *modus
operandi* in the process of preparation now requires to be
detailed.

64. GRINDING.—As it will fall to the duty of the foreman
printer to determine what stones are to be ground, it will
be well for him to *scratch* a cross deeply into the stone,
making the scratch deeper in those stones that have been
standing the longest with work upon them. This gives the
stone-grinder to understand that the cross must be ground
out. It is a simple matter that will save the printer's
temper and the master's pocket by insuring the thorough
grinding of the stones.

It is astonishing to what a depth the stone is affected by
the greasy particles of the ink without being perceptibly
greasy. The residuum of the ink acts also by preventing
an equal absorption of water and gum with the rest of the
surface, so that this part, drying soonest and being less protected by gum, favours the spreading of any work that
might have been drawn or transferred over it. It is very
annoying to the artist to see a nice even chalk tint spoiled
by the influence of the old job causing every speck of
chalk to become thicker at that place; very vexatious to
the master who has perhaps to pay for a new drawing, and
very discreditable to the stone-grinder, whose carelessness
has been the cause of it.

As a stone-grinder's wages are much lower than those of a draughtsman and printer, it will be true economy in any office to have the stone thoroughly prepared, and in order to prevent any shirking of duty, the little expedient before mentioned may be resorted to as a means of insuring that a certain depth is taken off each stone.

There is a class of work in which it is unnecessary to grind the stone every time—viz., law-stationers' work, or other work where only a few impressions (from three to a score) are taken rapidly off and the stone done with. In such cases a good rubbing with pumice or snake-stone, or both, is all that is necessary, followed by a good washing and a stroke of the "squeegee." The stone is then to be rapidly dried, and it is ready again for the press; but even here, when the stone is thoroughly dried and the polishing has not been sufficiently done, the last job will often make its appearance. It might not, however, have done so if the stone had not lost all trace of the water used in polishing.

In some offices, where law work is done extensively, as soon as the printer has pulled the number of impressions wanted he takes a basin of clean water, a clean sponge and rag (not one used in printing), a polishing-stone, and prepares his stone *in the press* for the next transfer, using a piece of clean paper to finish the wiping dry of the stone. Under these circumstances it is not often that the old work reappears.

This mode of polishing can be carried on to a limited extent only, the stones requiring occasional grinding to correct the unevenness that must be caused by the use of small abrading surfaces.

65. The grinding may very satisfactorily be done without the levigator (par. 60) by grinding smaller stones on larger ones, moving them about with a circular motion, and keeping them fed with sand and water, having first one side towards the grinder, and then another, going over the edges and corners of the under stone to prevent its getting hollow, and being careful not to allow the stones to rest for a minute in one place. In the latter case the cohesion may become so strong, owing to the exclusion of the intervening air and the vertical pressure of the atmosphere, that there will be a difficulty in separating them. Rub the last lot of

sand down finer than the previous ones and that will save
time in the next operation. Two stones containing one
square foot each should be ground on a stone containing
two square feet, and so on in proportion ; but if the under
stone has been lying with the ink upon it longer than those
to be ground above it, a proportionate number may be
done upon it as a compensation. After completing one
upper stone, try the under one with the straight-edge, and
use the next stone in such a manner as to render the under
one level. This will be found an excellent and practical
method ; but where the stone is too large to be easily moved
by hand the levigator may be resorted to, and used in the
manner described in par. 60.

66. POLISHING succeeds the grinding, and is commenced by taking a large piece of pumice-stone, filing a
flat place at right angles to its fibre, and rubbing the stone
with it and water from end to end, or, if the stone be too
large, across it. Take the pumice-stone in both hands and
press firmly on it from the shoulders, exerting the principal
pressure as it is pushed *from* the person, which should
accompany the motion of the hands. Light, quick rubbing
has very little effect. The use of the pumice-stone must be
continued until the sand-holes have disappeared. The
scratches caused by the pumice are then taken out by the
snake-stone (par. 24), which is used in a similar manner ;
but instead of keeping a flat face, a kind of rocking motion
is applied in using it, thereby forming a curved rubbing surface that cuts more quickly. More water is necessary in
using the snake-stone than the pumice requires, because the
adhesion is so great that the fluid is pushed before it, while
the pumice-stone is porous, and carries the water with it.

A finer polish may be given by using a woollen pad and
finely powdered pumice-stone ; but the other method, when
well done, gives a sufficiently good surface for all kinds of
work. For fine ink-work, engraving, chalk transfers, and
transfers from finely-engraved plates containing tinting,
there should be no scratches seen under a magnifying-glass
of such a power as is ordinarily used for viewing photographs, &c. ; but for the general run of commercial lithography the scratches commonly met with are of no importance. The same remarks apply to sand-holes, which, for

the delicate styles of work before mentioned, should be carefully looked for. Subsequent to the grinding, a rasp, followed by a fine file, is necessary to give the stone a curved edge for about half an inch all round, finishing with pumice and snake-stone, which should be kept for the purpose, because the edges will spoil the flat surfaces of those used for the flat-polishing. In stones for the machine, this part requires great attention, and more of the edge should be taken away, especially on that side that comes nearest the gripper.

After polishing, it is very essential that the stone be thoroughly washed, to effect which it may be treated as for grained stones (par. 89).*

Of late years, in large works, stone-grinding machines driven by steam-power have been adopted. These do their work in a very satisfactory manner, but they must not be expected to keep the stone perfectly level without care and intelligence on the part of the stone-grinder. The stones will require testing with the straight-edge the same as if they were ground by hand. Stone-grinding machines usually work on the levigator principle, the chief difference between them and hand-work being, that in the machines the stones are kept moving as well as the levigator ; while in hand-grinding they are stationary, and the levigator only is moved.† No doubt these self-acting mechanical movements are well designed for keeping the stones as level as machinery is likely to accomplish ; but, as before said, they must not be relied upon entirely. These remarks apply very forcibly to stones for machine-printing. The cylinder of the printing-machine cannot be adjusted to the stone as the scraper of the hand-press may be, so that it is essential for equality of pressure that the stone be true on its face, even if its upper and under surfaces are not strictly parallel.

---

* In cases where a stone is wanted immediately after polishing, it may be warmed and dried very rapidly by pouring hot water over its surface, taking care not to apply too much at a time at one place. The water soon parts with its heat ; and when the stone is sufficiently warm the water may be struck off with the squeegee. The stone will then dry rapidly, because little moisture remains upon it to be evaporated.

† In a machine recently introduced the levigator principle is omitted, the stone being ground face downwards upon a revolving iron table.

CHAPTER VII.

Lithography on Paper, or Transfer Lithography.—Preparation of the Ink—Mode of Making in Large Quantities—Law Writing—Architectural Bills of Quantities—Directions for Writing Law, Text, Old English, Copperplate, and Ornamental Styles—Drawing with Instruments and the Brush—Tracing Transfer-Paper—Chalk Transfer-Paper—Facsimiles—Autography.

FORMER chapters will have placed the student in possession of the *theory* regulating the employment of Lithographic Stones as well as the *art* of preparing them for printing. He has also been shown the uses and nature of transfer-paper, and the materials for writing and drawing upon it. He is now ready to commence the actual practice of Lithography.

As the latter is a very comprehensive and complicated subject, it may be well to take it up at that part which offers fewest obstacles to the beginner. For this reason we begin with LITHOGRAPHY ON TRANSFER-PAPER

67. To PREPARE THE INK.—Take a small white delft or china saucer, or a small tin patty-pan about three inches in diameter, and having warmed it at the fire or over the gas until it is as hot as it can well be borne in the hand, rub the stick of ink round and across it so as to cover it thinly. Then out of the bottle (*see* par. 8) shake a few drops of water, and with the second finger of the right hand rub it until the ink is dissolved. Then add more water cautiously, until it is brought to a proper consistency for use, which can only be learnt from an adept, or by experience. If it is very pale and flows too freely, it is too thin and may not transfer properly; if too thick it will not work pleasantly, and will spread in transferring. As a rule thinner ink may be used with the writing-pen than with the brush (*see* pars. 27, 28),*

---

* Our eminent *confrère*, Mr. William Simpson, advises, when the brush only is used, to put a small bit of ink in the upper part of a saucer placed upon a slope, and a little water in the lower part. The brush may then be dipped in the water, rubbed upon the ink, and tempered upon the dry portion of the saucer until it becomes fit for use.

while the ruling-pen requires an ink to be nicely prepared, so as to be not so thin as to spread in use, nor so thick as to smear when dry.

68. INK FOR LAW WRITING, when much is used, may be conveniently mixed in larger quantities, and ought to keep well for a month after preparation. It is usually used with ordinary fine-point steel pens depositing a good quantity of ink, which latter consequently may be made much thinner than is usual with other styles of work. Take a piece of stick ink and cut it into fine shavings ; put it into a small clean saucepan, cover it with distilled or filtered rain-water, make it simmer over a fire until dissolved, and then add more water until brought to such a condition that it will flow quite freely from the pen when used with rapidity. Cork it up in a bottle, and use it as wanted from small ink-pots, to economize.

69. The TRANSFER-PAPER is supplied ready ruled for use to the LAW-WRITER, who has simply to attend to the following rules :—

I. Write upon a pad of blotting-paper, but never use it to blot off the writing.

II. Be careful to use a piece of clean paper under the hand when writing, and scrupulously avoid handling the paper or even touching. it with the fingers, except at the edges where no writing is to occur. *Finger-marks from a moist or greasy hand roll up black.*

III. Corrections may be made, if small, by removing the ink with india-rubber or ink-eraser, or, if large, by washing it out with clean spirits of turpentine or benzoline. In either case it must be taken out without leaving any of the previous ink, or the whole intended correction may roll up black. Sometimes it may be better to paste (using as little as possible) a clean piece of transfer-paper over the part to be corrected, but *gum must not be used*.

IV. If the paper works greasily, rub it with powdered whiting or chalk, or wash it clean with spirits of turpentine or benzoline, or rub it well with clean india-rubber.

As the water is close to the ink, the artist can always by this plan have the exact amount of fluidity he may require, because he mixes the water and ink just as an artist mixes his colours on a palette.

70. SHEETS OF QUANTITIES, for architects and engineers, in addition to the cross lines for writing upon, have *down lines* identical with the down lines of the sheet upon which they are to be printed. They should be ruled by the machine-ruler at the same time as the transfer-paper is ruled, and kept in stock. When the transfer is laid down, the place of its margin is marked with the lead upon the stone, and a correct "lay" thus made for the sheet to be printed.

In writing "old English" or "German text," take either a quill or steel pen, and form a nib of nearly the width of the letter required ; with this make all the thick strokes, with very little ink in the pen, taking it up as often as required, being careful not to deposit upon the paper sufficient ink to spread, nor so little as not to transfer properly. When the thick strokes are dry, the thin ones may be put in with a fine pen. It is usual in practice to carry all the writing forward and slightly pencil the words for "texting," which is then done afterwards.*

71. THE COPPERPLATE STYLE AND FINE ORNAMENTAL WRITING is executed in a more careful and methodical manner on a finer and *thinner* paper. The learner will require very fine pens, the points, if steel, being so sharp that they will hitch in the paper in making the upstroke if it is laid on a flat surface in the ordinary way. This is to be avoided, in using both the steel and quill pens, by placing the left hand underneath the top edge of the paper so as to raise it from the table, the strokes may then be made on the yielding surface of the thin transfer-paper much more delicately and safely than when the paper is resting on the pad. Although this method will be found difficult at first, it is necessary to be accomplished to become a transfer-writer. The letters must be made as carefully and slowly as may be found necessary to produce the forms required. Lines in pencil may be ruled all over the paper at about an angle of 40° with the perpendicular,

---

* It may be useful to point out that in making pens for these broad strokes, the smaller the cylinder of which the pen forms a part, the less liable is the ink to be deposited on the paper in inconveniently large quantities.

to keep to the correct slope ; and double lines to write between to get the letters all one size ; and if a middle line be
added, a good guide will be obtained for the tops and tails
of the letters. Writing thus kept uniform in size and slope
will look very fair, even if the letters themselves are not
formed so well as desirable. The writing should fill the line
if possible, without dividing the words ; but in this respect
judgment must be used, as when the words ending the lines
are long ones they must be divided if necessary, because the
attempt to avoid it may cause ugly gaps. The learner is
recommended to lightly pencil out his words before writing
them in transfer-ink, so that he may know how much will
come into a line.

Any ornamental writing, &c., may either be first sketched
in pencil on the transfer-paper, or on other paper, and
traced down upon the transfer-paper with a red sheet. For
this purpose red chalk paper is to be preferred, because no
mistake can then be made as to which is an ink line ; but
such an error might easily occur if black-lead paper were
used instead.

72. WHEN A DRAWING HAS TO BE MADE WITH INSTRU-
MENTS OR THE LITHOGRAPHIC BRUSH a stouter paper is
better to work upon, and is best for use when strained in
the following manner :—

Sponge the back with water in proportion to the thickness
of the paper, sparingly if thin ; let it lie a few minutes for
the water to be absorbed, gum or paste it round the edges,
and attach it to a smooth drawing-board ; take a piece of
plain stout paper, wet it well until pliable, and lay it upon
the transfer-paper, folding back the edges so as to leave the
pasted edge free. The side in contact with the transfer-
paper should not be wet. A piece of calico wetted, well
wrung and shaken, may be used instead of the paper, if a
piece of thin paper be interposed between the cloth and
transfer-paper. The result sought is to get the edges dry
first. The paper or cloth is then removed, and the transfer-
paper will dry with a nice tight surface. If this method be
not adopted, the transfer-paper, especially when thin, will
sometimes follow the ruling-pen when in process of being
lifted from the paper, and alter the character of the line.
The unstrained paper, under the influence of the moist

breath of the artist, will sometimes rise from the surface upon which it has been placed, suddenly react upon the brush, and make a black speck where it should not be.

The following points must be carefully attended to :—

I. All lines are to print quite black, and consequently

II. No attempt must be made to get effect by using pale ink.

III. Thick ink will spread in transferring, and must therefore not be used in producing deep shades by lines lying close to each other.

IV. Thin lines with very pale ink will probably fail altogether.

V. The ink being dissolved in water, the latter has a tendency to soften the composition on the transfer-paper; it therefore becomes necessary not to go over, with the pen, the same place twice while the ink is wet, or the result may be that the composition will become mixed with the ink and destroy its qualities.

73. TRANSFER TRACING-PAPER may be used most conveniently in the same way. When all the outlining has been done upon it, a cut may be made down one edge and a piece of white paper slipped between it and the original, so that the shading may be done without the interference of the shading of the pattern. With these precautions, and a little patience, very fair work may be produced upon tracing-paper ; and, when it is taken into consideration that by this method the operations of tracing in pencil and retracing in red are avoided, the method has much to recommend it. It is much to be regretted that the gum-resins used in rendering the paper transparent prevent the absorption of water so necessary in transferring, so that the same quality of work upon the two different papers usually produces two different results when transferred.

We have given much study to the use of tracing transfer-paper, and hope further on to show how the largest transfer may be put upon the stone with certainty and success.

A secondary result, but a very useful one, of the practice of damping and straining transfer-paper is that the copies are nearer the size of the original. This is brought about by the contraction of the paper after it is cut from the board, and its re-expansion when damped for transferring, whereas if the transfer-paper was first drawn upon without being strained, the damping necessary to transfer it would so expand it that the prints would be considerably larger than the original. The system of transferring to damp stones hereinafter treated of would certainly produce a similar result, but it is not every printer who can be brought to make use of it, nor is it after all *quite* so reliable as the damp transfer process.

74. THE CHALK-TRANSFER PAPER is a revival of an old process known almost as long as Lithography itself, and though it possesses peculiar advantages, its use was known only to the few, until it was made the subject of a patent by Mr. Nelson.* Though Mr. Nelson seems to have claimed too much in his specification, it is only fair to say that his method of graining the paper by means of stippled plates produced a paper that could be more easily drawn upon than the older way of using a sand-grained stone or plate. The etched stippled plate produces a series of points which rise to the same height from the body of the paper, and are so close to each other that the point of the crayon cannot penetrate between them, while the sand-grain consists of pyramids or cones of varying size and height. The practical difference is that in drawing on the paper grained by the stippled plate there are no intermediate lower dots to receive the chalk when more pressure† is applied to deposit a greater quantity, and the work is consequently more open and better fit for transferring and printing from than the sand-grain, in which such favourable conditions cannot exist. Nevertheless, the stippled plate, by its mechanical mode of production, produces a kind of pattern that is objectionable to the practised eye, which, added to its high price, has given an impetus to the use of paper prepared by the older method.

Grained paper is eminently suited to the purpose of the amateur by reason of its extreme portability as compared

---

* The patentee's claims were canvassed in the pages of the LITHO-GRAPHER at the time, and much light thrown upon the subject.

† For the same reason a harder chalk, such as copal, can be used for this kind of paper, while for the ordinary grain Lemercier's No. 2 will be found better.

with stone, and not requiring the drawing reversed as regards right and left. This latter quality will recommend it to the artist for the production of drawing copies, because he can then set before the student a pattern that does not appear in the disposition of its shading and foliage touches to have been produced with the left hand, which is often the case with those drawn direct upon stone.

In using this paper it is recommended not to use much pressure in tracing the subject down, for fear of flattening the grain; and to take every means of keeping the work open. In light tinting the paper may be held up from the board as described in par. 71; the darkest touches may be done with ink, and lights taken out with a sharp knife.

The artist must proceed in his work with caution and decision, because this kind of work will not admit of any such correction as requires the removal of the grain and substitution of other work in its place. Of course a tint may be darkened to any extent, but the only means of lightening one will be to hatch it with lines with a sharp point or knife, the methods hereafter described of lightening chalk work on stone not being applicable to similar work on paper. Small black specks may be taken out with the knife. Sometimes it may occur that corrections may be more easily made after the subject is transferred to the stone, but these minute points of detail will occur to the student and be settled by him, as he proceeds with his practice.

75. FACSIMILES of writing are produced by placing a piece of tracing transfer-paper over the manuscript to be copied, and carefully going over the whole with a pen or brush. If required for mere commercial work, less care may be bestowed upon it—unless the customer is unusually fastidious—than for purposes required for courts of law and copies of curious or old manuscripts. Ordinary pens, fine pens, fine pens ground off a little at the point, and brushes, may be used in imitation of various styles of writing. All writings may be imitated with the brush, but by the pen it may frequently be done as well, and in much less time, while at other times the brush will be found the best in every way. When the pen is used and the writing is heavy, the ink must be much thinner, or it may smash in transferring.

Some customers prefer to have paper and ink supplied to them to write for themselves, but unless they have some experience, or are possessed of considerable manipulative skill, the result is not so satisfactory as when their writing is imitated by the practised lithographer, because, upon the transfer-paper, and from the pen, the ink flows in a manner very different to what common ink does upon ordinary paper. This may in a measure be overcome by a process sometimes called—

76. AUTOGRAPHY; a term applicable to all kinds of writing upon transfer-paper, but usually restricted to writing upon plain hard-sized writing-paper, with a strong lithographic ink. This process, though yielding fair results, is yet inferior to writing upon transfer-paper, because only part, instead of the whole of the ink, is left upon the stone in transferring.

It is a useful mode in the hands of the man of business, to whom it is unpleasant to be called upon to write with a different pen, ink, and paper, and yet produce similar writing to his ordinary hand, for the very fact of using a finer pen to counteract the spreading tendency of litho' ink and paper, would most likely cause the result to be unlike his usual handwriting ; but if he is given his favourite pen and paper, the ink will not make so much difference.

77. Occasions may arise when in some rough litho' tracing, such as is frequently required in arbitration cases, a little shading effect of the chalk kind may be necessary, and the time requisite for line shading cannot be afforded. Under such circumstances, if a piece of fine sharp cabinet-paper be placed under the tracing, it may be worked upon by the crayon, or if a sharp-grained plate be at hand that may produce a better effect.

CHAPTER VIII.

Ink Writing and Drawing on Stone.—The preliminary tracing—Circular writing—Relative advantages of working on stone and paper — Ornamental Lettering—White letters on black ground—Stopping out for transferred machine ruling—The sprinkled method—Stippling—Distinction between and relative advantages of the two methods—Corrections on polished stones during the work, and after rolling up—Theory of drawing on stone—Precautions to be observed.

DRAWING and writing on *paper* having been described in our last chapter, we now proceed to treat of

78. WRITING AND DRAWING ON STONE.—The principal difficulty experienced in drawing and writing on stone arises from the necessity of reversing the work, and this, conjoined to the drawbacks of always having to trace work to the stone, and the great bulk and weight of the latter, places working on stone at a disadvantage in comparison with transfer-paper; on the other hand, the accidents to which transfers are liable cause stone to be more generally used in most establishments.

Transfer-paper is more suited to the use of the writing pen than stone; but for the brush, crayon, and mathematical work, the surface of the stone is to be preferred, and it will hereafter be shown that it allows of a greater variety of work than the transfer method.

79. INK DRAWING ON STONE,—THE TRACING.—In proceeding to work upon stone, the student must bring himself to acknowledge and appreciate the value and importance of a good and correct Tracing, and feel assured that nothing can be gained by neglecting so essential an aid to success. It is made either in pencil or ink, placed in the *reversed* position upon the stone, and the red chalk tracing-paper with its prepared side downwards, is interposed between it and the stone. The corners are now gummed, pasted, or held down by paper-weights (avoiding the use of wafers), and the work traced over with a HHH pencil, or other hard tracing point, until a facsimile, in red, of the tracing, is

transferred to the stone.   In this manner all kinds of work are put upon the stone in faint red outline for whatever purpose it may be required, and whether the stone be polished for drawing, or grained.   Other methods of tracing, applicable to photographs, pictures, and subjects requiring greater transparency than ordinary tracing paper possesses will be found in paragraph 130.

The tracing having been made, the student may proceed to apply the ink by which the stone is made capable of multiplying the artist's ideas.   This ink may be applied either by the brush, steel pen, or the mathematical pen.

The brush has been described in paragraph 27.   With this instrument almost any kind of work may be accomplished that partakes of a freehand character.   To use it properly requires considerable practice ; but a few hints may assist the tyro who is making his first attempts.   The brush must be dipped into the ink, the superfluity removed by drawing it over the edge of the saucer, and a point finally given to it by patting it, as it were, upon a piece of smooth paper, the thumb-nail, or other similar clean surface.   It may now be applied to the stone to produce what the draughtsman requires.   It must, to produce fine lines, be held so that only the extreme point touches the stone.   At first the student may content himself by placing the stone in such a position that he can make the lines by drawing the brush towards him.   He will soon find, however, how far this system may be departed from, and that some brushes will permit of much greater freedom of manipulation than will others.   Thicker lines may be drawn by greater pressure upon the brush, more being required as the ink in it approaches exhaustion.   On account of the delicate structure of the brush, the ink in it will require frequent renewal, and much patience will be wanted on the part of the young artist, who will in all probability be tempted to work faster than consistent with the object aimed at, this manipulation of the brush to bring it into working condition occupying a considerable amount of time.

In tinting, the student should not endeavour to make a long line at once, but to effect his object by a series of short ones.   In doing this, however, he must avoid making ugly gaps between each set, though good effects are sometimes produced by leaving such places, and afterwards stippling them. The study of good bold etchings by some first-class engraver on copper will do much towards forming a good style; but the peculiarities attending this style of drawing should never be lost sight of. The etcher on copper and steel has this advantage: he can re-bite his work, and make it darker if his first proof is not satisfactory; but the lithographer must get the effect he desires before he passes the stone to the printer for proof. Nevertheless he has the advantage of easily getting heavy masses of *black*, which he can lighten either with steel or diamond points, and thus produce effects similar to woodcuts.

Tinting by means of irregular waved lines is easier to perform than by straight lines, and the effect is good if suitable to the subject. Mathematical precision of course must be avoided, but it must be done with some amount of regularity to look well. The convex side of any curve in a line must not be opposite the convex side of its companion line, but opposite its concave side, so that though the lines may be really irregular, yet the general effect may be that of parallelism.

The steel pen spoken of in paragraph 28 may also be used, and will be found especially useful in foregrounds, near foliage, &c.

The mathematical steel pen will at first require much practice and attention to master it so that very fine lines may be made with it; but this tool, as also that for making circles, is of the very greatest importance in all branches of lithographic drawing; therefore it is quite essential to master any difficulties that it may present. In any work of an architectural or mechanical character it may be accepted as a *general* rule that these pens must be used in preference to the brush wherever possible. Attention to this will enable the draughtsman to execute his work with a firmness and precision that will recommend itself to any architect or engineer who may chance to employ him, because it is an axiom with them that nothing should be done in the freehand manner that can be performed by ruling and compass pens.

It is usual among lithographic draughtsmen to put in any

dotted lines with a continuous stroke of the pen, and afterwards to scrape them in such a manner as to make dotted lines of them. While fully admitting the neatness of this method, we must be permitted to point out some attendant defects. 1. The scraping is liable to be omitted. 2. If insufficiently scraped, the lines roll up again; and, if deeply scraped, the proofs show an unpleasant embossing at that part. And 3. They often look too thin and ineffective when one half the line is thus taken away. In consideration of these points, we rarely, in our own practice, make use of the method, as we find no difficulty in dotting them as we proceed, with good ink of proper consistency. If the ink be too thin, all ruled lines have a tendency to run thick at the end of the stroke when using the ruling pen, and this is aggravated when making the short strokes of dotted lines. The student may therefore make this a test when preparing his ink.

The learner may find it useful to have the margin of the stone to practise upon, but it is not to be recommended to the practical lithographer. If the edges are gummed over with thin gum before commencing it will save the printer a good deal of trouble.

To assist the student in reversing his drawing, he will require a looking-glass of any convenient size. It should have a piece of wood or other contrivance attached to its frame, by which it may be made to stand pretty securely on its edge.*

80. WRITING ON STONE FOR CIRCULARS must of course be reversed, and the first essays of the learner may be assisted by tracing; but, as tracing for this purpose is inadmissible for real work, the sooner it is laid aside for the next stage, the better.

Take a piece of round pencil-cedar, or other wood, cut it very taper, so as to be about $\frac{1}{8}$-inch thick at its end. On these tapering faces make a thin groove in the direction of its length, and with a piece of thread or silk

---

* A finely polished steel or silvered copper plate, or a piece of glass silvered by the chemical method will be found superior to ordinary looking-glass, as there is then only one reflection, while when the ordinary mercurial silvering is used there are two—one from the metallic surface and another from the outer glass surface.

bind in each groove a common pin in such a manner that the points are level. If the pins, before binding, are flattened a little with a hammer, they will be more manageable. A tool is now produced by which two parallel lines may be drawn at one stroke as a guide for the size of the writing. A more expensive tool, with a wider scope, is a needle-pointed spring bow-pen, substituting brass pins for the needle points.*

A brass point, mounted as described in paragraph 139, for engraving tools, will also be required for sketching on stone, as lead pencil is unsuitable, by reason of its marking too black.

Proceed by sketching out rapidly in pencil, on paper, the words of the circular, so as to see how much space it will occupy.

Now lay out and mark a space on the stone, and, having fixed upon the size of the letter, rule the stone with the before-mentioned tool into a series of double lines, to correspond to the sketch. Across these rule any convenient number of single lines at an angle with them, of from 45° to 50°, as a guide for the slope of the letter. Now, having first obtained a good specimen of copper-plate or lithographic writing, by the help of the mirror consult its reversed position, and carefully copy each letter by means of a fine lithographic brush. It will be as well to sketch them out, but more especially the capitals, by the help of the pin-points, and, as confidence is gained, sketch the capitals only. It will be found that both the up and down strokes of the writing must be made with *down strokes* of the brush : make the down stroke, and then add the up stroke. Much practice will be necessary, and, as the plan-draughtsman on stone *must* be able to letter backwards, it will be only a further extension of his skill to be enabled to write a circular.

When the lithographic student has mastered the difficulty of writing backwards, and is able to produce a decent

---

* For this purpose engravers use small steel gauges, which are sold in sets, and numbered. These may be used by the lithographic writers on zinc direct, or on stone by interposing a piece of red tracing-paper.

circular, he may proceed to do without such of the before-described helps as his skill will permit of.

With respect to the question as to which method (stone or transfer) is best in practice, it will usually happen that the subject is practically beyond the control of the employer. He may have a clever general hand, and must be guided by his attainments, while if he engage a circular-writer the probability will be that he will be a transfer-writer. The general question may be disposed of by saying that the transfer method is quickest, but more liable to accident; while the writing upon stone is usually more firm, will yield perhaps more impressions, and is liable to no accident that is not equally likely to happen to a transfer *after* it is upon the stone.

ORNAMENTAL lettering may be practised in a similar way, but all large letterings, &c., should be treated as drawings, a complete sketch being made and traced to stone (§ 79). They are to be outlined, in their straight parts, with the ruling pen, and the large letters on show-cards, &c. may advantageously have the compass-pen employed upon their curved portions.

81. WHITE LETTERS UPON A BLACK GROUND are produced by using a mixture of gum-arabic solution and vermilion acidulated with a little nitric acid. It must be made as wanted, because when once dry it cannot be properly re-dissolved by reason of a chemical change in the gum produced by the action of the nitric acid. The more acid is added to the solution the more decided is the subsequent insolubility. Experience must be the guide for the proportion of gum, pigment, and acid.

Gum too thick.	Will not work pleasantly, especially in ruling pen.
Gum too thin and too much pigment.	Will not stop out effectually.
Too much acid.	A decided effervescence will take place, and the lines spread beyond their limits.

Perfection will be attained in the mixture when it works pleasantly, and shines upon the stone after drying. The

letters are to be made with this preparation,* and when dry
are to be covered over with litho writing-ink dissolved in
spirits of turpentine, or other convenient fatty matter. When
the job is complete and put into the hands of the printer,
the water will dissolve the gum and leave the letters clear
upon a black ground, the result being not only more rapid
but more satisfactory than when the ground is painted in
and the letters are left white upon the stone.

82. STOPPING OUT FOR TRANSFERRED MACHINE RULING
is effected in a similar manner, but no acid must be
used, because it would partially obliterate the drawing over
which it was necessary to put it. It is useful in plan and
other work where lines, &c., are required which would
involve great skill and occupy much time to put in by
hand, but are easily and expeditiously transferred from
machine ruled and dotted plates. Vermilion and gum, free
from acidity, is painted over all parts of the drawing that
are not to be covered with the machine work in question,
and when dry, and a mark put upon the stone to indicate
the direction of such lines, dottings, &c., it is handed over
to the printer, who transfers a suitable impression, which
unites with the stone in those parts only that are uncovered.
When the stone is washed with gum-water, if the operations
have been properly performed, the effect will be that the
gummed portions remain quite clean, and the transferred
lines, &c., will almost equal copper-plate, and be very far
superior to what hand-work could possibly accomplish.

83. THE SPRINKLED METHOD is effected by taking a
quantity of litho writing ink in a tooth, nail, or other similar
brush, and drawing it across the blade of a table-knife or
other like instrument, over that part of the stone to be
sprinkled. The sprinkling is confined to proper limits by
having all other parts "gummed out," as in par. 82. When
the first light tint is sufficiently strong, the parts required

---

* If the letters are of a kind to admit of the proceeding, it will be
found very advantageous to first rule a strong line at the top and
bottom of the line of lettering, in litho ink. The gum mixture not
dissolving, the ink will not penetrate through it to the stone, and the
result will be a straightness and definition which could not be hoped
for without such assistance.

to be kept at that strength are "gummed out," and, after drying, the process may be repeated until the desired effect is obtained. The operation requires care, and trial should be made (at each renewal of ink in the brush) upon a piece of paper, to be sure that the dots are of the desired size and distance apart. The less ink in the brush the finer the dots, and the nearer it is held to the stone the closer they will be together. The ink for this process should have the minimum quantity of soap to render it soluble, and therefore less tendency to dissolve and penetrate the gum protection.

The cases in which this style may be used must be left to be decided by the taste and discretion of the artist.

One grave defect of the process is, that though a transparent gum solution may be used, yet the effect cannot be observed during the operation, because all is covered alike with the dottings, the gum protecting the several stages. It is only when the gum is washed away that the effect is seen; if then it is not what is desired, it may be remedied by going over again where necessary—first preparing the stone as in article 86.

84. STIPPLING,* though a process more peculiarly adapted to chromo-lithography, may be occasionally employed in the more modest ink-style now under consideration. It yields a very soft and pleasing effect when introduced to tone the harshness of unhatched line-shading by stippling minute dots between the lines. The dots should be in proportion to the lines among which they are placed, never thicker if possible. When the dots are desired to be very fine, they may be done with the brush; but the pen, of various degrees of fineness in the nibs, will be found a most efficient tool for the medium and larger one.

The great distinction between sprinkling and the more laborious stippling consists in the precision with which the dots may be applied just exactly where required in the latter mode; whereas in the former they fall at haphazard.

When a graduated effect is to be produced by stippling alone, the dots must be fine and open, followed by

---

* "Stippling" is a species of engraving which is effected by a series of dots instead of lines. The word has a similar meaning in water-colour painting.

others larger and more close, until they approach a solid black.

Roundness of dot and succession of them in lines are to be avoided, as producing hardness of effect. If a good stippled engraving be examined by a magnifying glass, it will be seen that the dots are triple ones, which conduces much to the *softness* of effect observable in this style.

85. CORRECTIONS ON POLISHED STONES IN PROCESS OF WORK are almost invariably made with a sharp mezzotint scraper. Sharpness of the knife is essential to taking the work perfectly out without going deep into the stone, which must not be done, because the pressure would be taken off at that part in the printing. The part scraped out is certainly not so pleasant to work upon as before, but yet when neatly done the work may be put in again in such a manner as to draw no attention to it as a correction. The over-running of lines at corners and junctions are removed by this means, and lines are usually dotted by the scraper after being drawn continuously.

Where the alteration required occupies much space, and the nature of the work will permit, the best way will be to take the snake-stone and polish the stone where necessary, when of course it may be treated in the same manner as if no work had been upon it. Small snake-stone pencils, one-fourth of an inch square, will be found useful in getting at small portions, and by means of a file they may be made of any convenient size and shape at point. Such pieces may also be used for finally polishing the stone after scraping.

86. CORRECTIONS AND ADDITIONS AFTER ROLLING UP.— When an addition is to be made in a place where there is room to use the scraper, remove the surface with that instrument and put in the addition with litho ink.

When previous work has to be removed polish it out with the snake-stone if there be room; if not, use a sharp scraper, and be sure the old work is well cleared away. In using the knife or scraper it will be found that it has a tendency to jump over the greasy lines, more especially if the edge be dull, leaving them somewhat in relief; but it is essential to remove all trace of the ink, or it will roll up among the new work.

The aim of the artist must be to scrape effectually, yet

without reducing the surface to such a degree that neither the roller nor pressure will reach the part. Consequent on this it will be seen that it is imperative that the correction must be effective, or the work will have to be gone over again, thus producing a still greater depth below the surface. If the roller will not reach the part, the printer must use his finger with ink upon it, or make a small dabber to apply the ink to the depressed part, while the pressure may be made to reach it by pasting paper upon the tympan at that place.

When additions have to be inserted among the work and none is required to be removed, a mode altogether different had better be employed. Without entering into the subject of printing, to which it properly belongs, it will be advisable to lay down the theory on which the method depends.

a. In all lithographic printing the stone is varnished, as it were, with a solution of gum arabic which dries not only *on* but *in* its surface, and is there held so tenaciously that no amount of washing with plain water will remove it.

b. This coating of gum, filling up the pores of the surface, prevents the absorption of ordinary litho ink unless it contains an amount of soap more than usual. This is sometimes added to make work " stand," but it spoils the good working qualities of the ink.

c. It is evident this coating must be removed, and anything that will dissolve carbonate of lime (of which the stone principally consists) and will not dissolve the ink, may be used for preparing the stone previous to retouching, because if the surface of the stone be dissolved the thin gum coating dissolves with it.

Most acids, and some salts, will effect this purpose, but choice is given to the weaker acids of vegetable origin, which form soluble salts with lime. ACETIC ACID is an old favourite, but CITRIC ACID is preferable, and may be used as follows :—

Roll up the job as for an impression, wash it well to free it of all gum that can be removed by that means, using hot water by preference ; dry ; and apply with a camel-hair brush of a convenient size the solution of citric acid of such a strength as to taste a little weaker than lemon juice ;

watch it, and if bubbles of gas arise at once it is too strong, and must be washed immediately with clean water.   If of the proper strength it may remain about a minute, when it must be washed with clean water.   The ink must now be removed by pulling two or three impressions* from the one inking, so that the artist in working upon it shall have no superfluous ink to attach to his "hand paper" to be carried about and soil the stone.   Any touching-up or additions may now be done with ordinary lithographic ink, which will now be found to work nearly as pleasantly as upon a newly polished stone.

It has been here recommended to roll in with ink previous to the acid preparation, because it assists in protecting the work from its action, while the usual plan is to take off the superfluous ink first and acidulate afterwards; but it is evident that weaker acid is then necessary.

All sponges, &c., used in this process must be scrupulously clean, or success must not be expected.

Solutions of alum and common salt, or sal ammoniac, or both combined, form very good washes for clearing the stone from gum, and they probably act not only by dissolving but by bringing away the gum as the salts crystallize.†

87. PRECAUTIONS TO BE OBSERVED IN DRAWING ON STONE.—All the cautions given regarding the handling of transfer-paper apply equally to the stone; but the stone being a better conductor of heat than paper, and of greater bulk, condenses the breath of the artist upon it in cold weather, causing him to waste time in drying the stone.   It is recommended to place the back of the stone to the fire the first thing in the morning, and allow it to get moderately warm through, when it will be found to keep free from this

---

* The paper should be well rolled printing or plate paper, so as to avoid "slurring."

† A very practical method for the printer who requires a job touched up, is the following :—After cleaning the work, roll it up pretty full, and etch with perfectly clean nitric acid and water and clean sponge, which will remove the gum at the same time; well wash, and take off a couple of impressions without re-inking.   When dry, send it to the artist to have the corrections made.   Gum the stone, and allow it to dry, when the job may be proceeded with.

peculiar annoyance for the rest of the day; whereas if the face had been warmed to the same degree only, it would have rapidly cooled again. If it is inconvenient to *warm* the stone in the manner described, a piece of cardboard, about 4 in. by 3 in., of an oval shape, and a bit of twine passed through two holes in it about $1\frac{1}{2}$ in. apart, and by this held between the teeth in such a manner as to cover the mouth and nostrils, will effectually prevent the condensation of the breath upon the stone.

a. In drawing upon stone, remember that friction is proportionate to pressure : therefore, let ruling pens glide over the surface, free from the weight of the hand and arm.

b. The parallel ruler must not rest on the stone, but on pieces of cardboard or folded paper. If the work is small, take a piece of cardboard and cut a circular, square, or oblong hole in it, and use it as a shield and rest for the ruler, &c.

c. Keep the side of the pen that slides against the ruler scrupulously free from ink, and for fine lines the outside also, so that the space between the nibs only may, if possible, determine the breadth of the line.

d. To set the ruling and compass pens, rub them on Arkansas oilstone; examine them carefully with an eyeglass after wiping off the oil, holding the pen in such a manner that the light from the nib ends is reflected to the eye; when each nib is reduced to an equal thinness and equal length, they may be polished on a piece of leather having a little crocus on it. The nibs being already comparatively thin, care must be taken that they are not rubbed too violently, or an unequal length and breadth will be the result. If this happens, bring them to an equal length by a motion on the oilstone, as if ruling lines, previously to bringing them to an equality of thinness. The Arkansas oilstone should not be mounted, because on such a one it will not be possible to get at both nibs of a spring bow pen. A useful stone for the work may measure about $4 \times 1\frac{1}{2} \times \frac{3}{8}$ inches.

CHAPTER IX.

Chalk Drawing on Stone.—Theory of the process—Peculiarities of the grain of the stone—How to grain a stone—Defects and remedies— Tracing the outline to stone—Pointing the chalks—Copal chalks —Occasions when ink may be used—Drawing—Cautions—Tinting—Importance of this department of Lithography.

NO part of our subject at all equals in artistic importance that upon which we are about to enter, viz. that of drawing in crayon or chalk upon the stone. By it an accomplished artist is enabled to reproduce the works of our best painters in a manner but little inferior to that of the best engravings; and we feel convinced that if the same study and talent were bestowed upon lithography as is necessary for engraving, our favourite art would be found quite equal to the successful reproduction of all classes of pictures.

88. The drawing on stone treated of in the last chapter refers more especially to that kind of lithography usually denominated "ink" or "line work," and executed on polished stones; while that upon which it is proposed now to enter is called chalk or crayon drawing, and derives its name from similar work upon paper, which it may be said to excel.

Instead of being polished, the surface of the stone is, for this kind of work, broken up into minute points, technically called "a grain," which, when drawn upon, receives the lithographic chalk in proportion to the pressure employed. This grain is most essential, not only in giving clearness of texture and transparency in the impressions, but, by reason of its hardness and sharpness, acting as a rasp to take off a sufficient quantity of crayon to give blackness and body to each dot. If the crayon be drawn over a polished stone and over a grained one, it will be found that the stroke in the former case is poor and grey, while in the latter it is bold and black. The former is nearly destroyed by an etching that the latter will stand well; for this reason, it is desirable to have a sharp grain.

The grain should be in proportion to the work in hand ; but manipulation has much to do with the appearance of coarseness or fineness of grain. Delicacy in outline and detail demands a fine grain, while boldness in these particulars admits of a coarse one ; but it will be found in practice that it is more easy to produce an appearance of coarseness on a fine grain than of delicacy and detail on a coarse one.

89. To GRAIN THE STONE.—Take a stone free from all veins, marks, and chalk-spots, and, if for best work, of a clear grey or dark drab colour. Grind it and pumice it free from any deep scratches. Now take a piece of stone similar to the one to be grained, about three or four inches square, with the corners and edges well rounded off with a file. From a sieve (No. 100 or 120, according to the grain,—*see* par. 59) sift sufficient graining-sand* to lightly cover the surface ; sprinkle a few drops of water over it, and place upon it the graining "muller." Move this about with a motion describing small circles along one edge ; then return at about three inches from the edge ; back again at about six inches from the edge, and so on, until the stone has been gone all over. As the work is proceeded with, more water will be required ; and as the sand wears out, more of that will be needed. If the stone be finished off with sand that has been but very little worn, it will probably produce a grain too coarse and sharp, while a contrary result will follow the using of the sand for too long a time, the grain then being "flat." To produce a good grain, the happy medium must be attained, and practice will be necessary to arrive at it. Every care must be taken that no coarser sand finds its way to the stone, or scratches, which will show as white lines on the drawing, must be the result. When it is thought that it is properly done, wash it well in clean water, rubbing it with the hand or a clean sponge, to free it from all traces of sand, &c.; strike off the superfluous water with the squeegee, and let it dry. Do not set it to drain while wet upon a dusty floor, or the dust will creep up the wet surface by capillary attraction, to prevent which set it upon a piece of paper that is free from dust.

---

* To be procured from the dealers in litho materials at about 2*s.* per gallon, sifted.

When dry, place it obliquely at a window, and with a magnifying glass seek for any scratches. A scratch or two may be of no importance in some jobs ; in such case consult the artist, who will know. If they prove vexatious, the stone must be gone over again. The stone should now be of a vellum-like texture *all over*, and the artist may try the grain with a crayon at various parts of the stone, making little patches of light tinting. These will not often interfere with the work, because they will either be absorbed in deeper tints, or may be scraped out in the finishing. If the artist is satisfied with the grain, the grainer's work is done; if not, it must be sought to know what the defect is.

If too coarse—	Take either a finer sieve, or work the sand down more before washing off.
If too fine—	Work the same sand but little before renewing it, or take a size larger.
If too flat, with lines running through it—	The sand has not taken out the marks of the pumice-stone. Continue the graining.
If very fine and flat, without lines—	The graining has been continued too long with the same sand. Grain again.
If wanted coarser in places, such as the foreground—	Roughly sketch an outline, and grain with a small muller where required with coarser sand or fine sand often renewed.

90. TRACING THE OUTLINE TO STONE will be the next operation. Proceed as in par. 79, but observe that the red tracing-paper must have but little colour upon it, because the grained surface takes off a greater quantity than the polished stone. Try it first, and if too red wipe it off the paper with a dry cloth, until the necessary colour is gained. It should be borne in mind that liquid ink will penetrate a strong line of the tracing, while the *dry chalk* might be kept from the stone by the interposition of the red chalk

line ; and hence the advisability of having the tracing very faint. If it can be distinctly seen, it is dark enough. For the same reason, if it should be necessary to sketch upon the stone, it should be lightly done with a hard pencil or brass point, a dark mark with a soft lead being very likely, when drawn over with the crayon, to show as a white line in the print.

A tracing may also be made in soft red or black conté crayon. When this is put upon the stone and a piece of hard writing-paper laid upon it, it may be transferred to the stone by rubbing with some smooth hard substance, taking care that it does not shift. The transfer of the tracing to the stone may also be accomplished by passing it through the press under a heavy pressure. This would give a more correct outline, and would be more quickly done than a second time going over every line with the point ; but so good a tracing of intricate work cannot be made in the first instance as can be obtained by a hard blacklead pencil.

Having got the subject traced to the stone, remove the tracing-papers and substitute for them a piece of plain paper fastened round the edge of the stone. Tear a piece out of the upper left-hand corner and proceed to work there, removing the paper as necessary until the whole is completed. The *hand board* (par. 31) must be used to keep all pressure from the newly-deposited chalk, because if the chalk be partly removed from the surface it will have less power to withstand the action of the etching, and the result may be spots and patches of lighter colour. The board keeps the hand further from the stone, and assists in preventing that condensation of moisture which takes place when a warm moist hand rests upon a cold stone with only the intervention of hand paper, and is of further use as providing a convenient arm-rest for working near the edge of the stone.

The use of loose paper to rest the hand upon is also objectionable, from the liability there is of thereby carrying particles of chalk from one part of the stone to another. They adhere to the underside of the paper, and are not seen excepting by the effects produced in various specks of dirt occurring over the stone, and which will probably cause a good deal of trouble to pick out in finishing the drawing. Prevention is here *easier* than cure.

The artist will find that the grained stone wears away the crayons so much faster than paper does, that much of his time will be employed in pointing them, so that, if it be valuable, it may be well to appoint an assistant to sit by and perform that operation for him.

Lithographic chalks are pointed with the knife, like conté crayons, by laying the point on the left forefinger as a guide, and cutting *from* the point. It is unnecessary to use the knife every time the crayon requires pointing. As long as it remains nicely taper, it may be brought to a good working point by rubbing it gently—turning it between the thumb and finger at the same time—on a piece of coarse printing-paper or other similar surface. This will give a better point, and more expeditiously, than the knife, and will usually be found to be less liable to break.

The friction the crayons undergo on the stone, and the warmth of the hand have a tendency to soften them, so that it will be found advantageous to have half a dozen pointed at a time; and it will be further convenient to make a distinction in the colour or form of the crayon-holder, so that the different degrees of hardness may be readily distinguished.

In drawing lines with the straight-edge as a guide, greater uniformity of breadth will be obtained by cutting the crayon to a thin wedge instead of to a conical point, and by *pushing* the chalk as well as *drawing* it, great firmness and strength will be given them.

The outlining should be all complete before commencing to shade, or lay in the "*tinting*." If it is an architectural or other subject requiring fine detail, it may be put in with *copal chalk* with a firm touch, as it will then better resist the etching. This chalk is made as hard as possible consistent with the quality of rolling up, but is not so strong as No. 1, and should not be used at all for tinting, nor for outlining, when No. 1 will answer the purpose. No. 2 is softer and stronger, and may be used for bolder drawings and deeper shading; while No. 3 is to be reserved for very deep parts, or such subjects as large bold portraits.

Where precision of outline is of more importance than artistic effect,—where it is more minute than the chalk point can well accomplish,—and where the nature of the subject permits or demands it,—ink may be used, either with brush or ruling-pen. It must be strong enough to permit of etching, and black enough to enable the artist to estimate his effect. If it is too thin, it will not work properly; the water separating and spreading beyond its proper limit, leaving the coagulated ink in the middle of the line, but becoming of a proper size on drying. Such lines must not be depended upon, as they do not sufficiently resist the etching.

For the first tint take a light crayon-holder and No. 1 crayon; hold the porte-crayon, in a slanting direction, as far from the chalk as can conveniently be done, and lay in the tint with light and regular strokes, taking care not to commence or leave off heavily, as that would make it spotty. In this way cross and recross it until the desired effect is obtained. The chalk should be constantly turned in the hand by *depressing* the thumb to cause the porte-crayon to rotate, thus bringing a new clear part of the point into work. If the crayon were made to rotate the reverse way by *elevating* the thumb, that part of the point having a *burr* upon it would be most likely applied to the stone, and cause a black speck. If the crayon be used without turning for a few strokes, a flat place will be worn, and when it is then turned, so sharp a corner will be introduced to the tint as will cause a clear, almost continuous fine black line instead of a succession of dots.

Pay particular attention to the first tint, as it influences very strongly the subsequent deposition of the chalk. If the tinting be too open for the subject, it may be made more close by using a finer point, held in a more upright position; thus bringing into use a secondary series of the grain-points that would otherwise have remained untouched; but it must be remembered that this will render the printing more difficult. This first tint may sometimes be very well accomplished by *stumping*. A piece of clean wash-leather is put over the first or second finger, and then rubbed upon a piece of stumping lithographic chalk; when charged, any loose particles must be detached by rubbing lightly on a piece of paper. It is now passed with a light circular motion over the stone, which then receives a more delicate tint, and with less labour, than is obtained with the point of the crayon. For ordinary work it should not be carried beyond this point, because if a middle tint were to be obtained with it, the subsequent chalking would be deceptive, looking darker on the stone than it would roll up, the particles of stumping-chalk being blacker chemically than they are visually. Having laid in a smooth even tint, *greater pressure and a more blunt point* may be used for the darker shades ; thus making the previously covered grain-points to accumulate more chalk, and, in still darker shades, some of them to join together.

Having completed the drawing with the crayon, little bits of pure black may be put in with ink to give effect where necessary ; lights may be removed with the scraper; transparency given to the shadows by the judicious use of the needle-point ; figures separated from the background by the same instrument ; and many little things done that taste and experience may dictate, previously to the drawing being handed over to the printer to prove. In giving effect by means of ink, it should be applied with a brush, as it is possible that a pen may scratch the stone, so as to leave white marks in the impression.

In working out the drawing, little bits of loose chalk will fall from the crayon, hands, and other sources, which may be removed by the frequent use of a flat camel-hair brush, kept for the purpose. Avoid blowing them off, because little globules of saliva and condensed moisture are usually hanging about the lips and moustache, which, being projected on to the stone by the puff of air, cause all subsequent chalking to be removed in the rolling up, and produce white or grey spots, known to the trade as "spittle-spots."

Other black specks of chalk will be found, that will not be carried away by the brush ; but by pressing the point of the crayon vertically upon the place, and suddenly lifting it off again, the chalk will be removed from the stone. In this manner, considerable portions of the stone may be denuded of chalk, and corrections made.

Tinting may be made even by pricking out little specks with the needle-point by the aid of the magnifying-glass, brushing away the portions removed, so as better to observe the effect. Care must be taken in this operation, because the part cannot again be easily worked over. Where tints are too dark, they may be hatched over with the needle-point in two or three directions, so as to avoid any formality of effect; but it is best to avoid this, if possible, unless the artist wishes thereby to introduce an effect not to be had by the simple chalking. In the use of the needle-point, it is to be remembered that the scratches cause the stone to look whiter, and consequently they will not show so plainly on the impression, as they do upon the stone.

Previously to commencing any kind of lithography, the head, face, and beard should be washed, or otherwise freed from dandruff, which will otherwise fall on the stone in small flakes, and if not at once removed by the brush, will, by lying on it a short time, penetrate it, and roll up as black specks, very difficult of removal. Not being of a dark colour, their effect cannot be estimated in the course of work, and must be left until the job is rolled up, and then carefully picked out with a needle-point.

If an error be committed of any large extent, the part must be grained out with dry sand and a muller proportioned to the surface to be removed. The sand must then be carefully and thoroughly brushed away, and finally wiped off with a perfectly clean dry soft cloth, until nothing remains to prevent the proper adhesion of the chalk subsequently to be applied. It will be useless to attempt corrections with the scraper, as in par. 85, because the grain indispensable to this style would be thereby removed.

Suppose the drawing finished, and a proof submitted to the inexperienced artist, his feelings on receiving it will be those, probably, of disappointment. He will perhaps find that his light tints have become more light; his dark shades too heavy and opaque; and the general keeping of the subject altered for the worse; the result being aggravated by the substitution of white paper for the pleasant neutral grey of the stone on which it was drawn. The remedy is obvious. The light tints, to stand an etching sufficient to keep the deep shades clear, must be drawn more strongly; the middle tints as desired; and the deep shades a trifle lighter than they are intended. Then, by printing the subject on a tint somewhat of the colour of the stone, with the addition of white high lights, now at command, it is possible to produce an effect more in unison with the wishes and expectations of the artist. If some of the works of English and French lithographic artists are at hand, much may be learned by a careful study of their means of producing effect. Sometimes, as in the works of Calame, they are printed upon tints even deeper than that of the stone on which they were drawn, while white is very sparingly employed. The works of Julien are perfect imitations of black and white crayon upon tinted paper, while those of Louis Haghe, J. D. Harding, and others, are perfect models of lithography as applied to landscape in simple black and tint.

A most important point in chalk lithography is to keep the point of the crayon proportionate to the tint sought. Fine points make fine tints, and coarse points coarse tints. If it be desired to produce a rough effect, as on old walls, roads, shingly beach, and such like, the point must be broad, and held at an acute angle to the stone; or a piece of broken chalk may be cut to a flat surface on its side, and rubbed in the direction required over the stone, on which it will produce a marvellously rough effect. By a judicious use of the scraper to take out some bits, and thereby reduce their uniformity, and the addition of slight touches to complete the resemblance to pebbles, &c., a good rough foreground may be produced with little expenditure of time. This mode has its weak points, and certainly requires the touch of the artist to prevent its becoming too mechanical.

The advice given in par. 87 is very applicable to the chalk style, and may be read in conjunction with this paragraph. Care and cleanliness are essential here, as in other styles of lithography, and the artist should be cautious in permitting persons unacquainted with the art to examine his work during its execution, as he thereby runs the risk of scurf from the hair, spittle-spots, and other similar accidents occurring to the stone. The artist, of course, should cultivate a cheerful temper; but he must bear in mind that laughter is a fertile source of spittle-spots; so that if he wishes to indulge in that, or a sneeze, he must jealously turn away from the stone.

The importance of chalk-drawing on stone should give

it the highest place in the estimation of the artist, and much careful practice should be devoted to it. Many artists have given up the practice of lithography to devote themselves to painting; while others, somewhat deficient in artistic feeling, yet excellent draughtsmen, engage some artist-friend to advise them as to effect, and to put the finishing touches to their work,—a course that may be adopted with great advantage, not only to the work, but to the young draughtsman himself.

CHAPTER X.

Etching Chalk Drawings on Stone.—Chemical principles of the operation—Action of acids—Four methods of etching—Retouching and correcting after printing.

LAST chapter completed the subject of chalk drawing, as far as putting the subject on the stone is concerned; but there is an intermediate process to be gone through before it is ready to be printed from, which is very important, as affecting, in a very marked degree, the good quality of the impressions. Our present chapter is therefore devoted to this operation, which is called—

91. ETCHING THE DRAWING.—This operation is usually performed by the foreman-printer; but as it does not essentially belong to printing, and might with advantage be done by the artist, it will be described in this place.

The term "etching," in lithography, is no doubt borrowed from the practice of etching on copper, but it is somewhat improperly applied. The etching process on copper consists in producing an effect by drawing with a point through a wax surface spread upon a metal plate, and afterwards fixing or deepening such work by "biting in" with dilute nitric acid. In Lithography the term "etching" is applied only to the acidulation of the stone by dilute nitric or other acid, the effect of which is rather to make the work lighter than stronger, and is thus diametrically opposed to similar operations on metal.

When nitric and most other acids are brought into

contact with the carbonate of lime, of which the lithographic stone principally consists, decomposition ensues ; the nitric acid seizes upon the lime, and sets the carbonic acid free, which then passes off rapidly in minute bubbles, producing the phenomenon known as effervescence. The necessity for etching chalk drawings may be understood by studying the following conditions :—

1st. Lithographic crayon is soluble in water by reason of the soap it contains, and would spread under the operation of damping the stone in printing, unless means were used to restrain it.

2nd. Soap is, from a chemical point of view, a combination of fatty acids with caustic alkalies, which latter render those fatty acids soluble in water.

3rd. When any mineral acid is brought into contact with the soap, it unites with its alkali, to the exclusion of the fatty acids, which then become again insoluble in water.

The lithographic chalk, being acidulated in the etching process, has its saponaceous character destroyed, and is rendered insoluble* in water, and thereby prevented from spreading under the influence of the damping process. This

---

* We have heard good practical printers doubt the action of the etching on the alkali of the soap ; but any person may try the experiment for himself in the following simple manner. Rub some of Lemercier's chalk in two places on a clean stone (a polished one will answer the purpose). Acidulate one with dilute acid sufficient to cause effervescence, but leave the other free. If a clean sponge and soft water be now taken, it will be found that the unetched chalk will be partially washed away, and become grey, while the other remains black and unmoved. Mr. M. Hanhart, in an article on "Chemical Printing" in Watts's "Chemical Dictionary," thus speaks of the probable nature of the etching and gumming processes :—

"The action in this part of the process is somewhat obscure, but it is probable that the nitric acid dissolves the superficial particles of the stone, and the resulting solution forms with the gum an insoluble gummate or metagummate of calcium. One thing is certain, that the gum becomes firmly fixed on the stone, and cannot be removed even by repeated washing with water. The nitric acid also acts upon the chalk by laying hold of the alkali and setting the fatty acids free.

"The stone, thus prepared, is next washed with water, to dissolve off the excess of gum and the nitrates of sodium and calcium, and afterwards with oil of turpentine, which removes the excess of grease from the drawing, and renders it nearly invisible. The fatty calcium salts formed by the action of the soap on the carbonate of calcium are,

etching, at the same time, removes the surface of the stone to some extent, and carries away the dirt.

In practical lithography there are two different ways of applying the acid : firstly, flooding the stone with acid diluted with plain water ; and secondly, brushing it with acid diluted with gum-water.

92. *First method.*—Provide a shallow wooden or other suitable box, of at least the full width of the stone, and sufficiently water-tight to answer the purpose. Into this box put sufficient etching solution to completely flood the stone, which must be fixed over a trough, sink, or other convenient place, at an angle of about 45°. Now take the etching-box, place its edge so as nearly to touch the upper edge of the stone, and pour its contents over it, so as to make, as near as may be, an uniform wave from top to bottom. The stone should now be reversed, and the operation repeated, because

---

however, insoluble in the turpentine, and remain untouched; and on subsequently wetting the surface of the stone with water, and passing over it a roller covered with printing-ink, composed of linseed-oil and lampblack, the ink adheres to those parts of the surface where these fatty salts are situated, while the remaining portion, which has been acted on by the gum, does not take up the printing-ink, because the fatty acids of the linseed-oil are incapable of decomposing the compound of lime and gum with which those portions are covered, and mechanical adhesion is prevented by the film of water on the surface.

"This view of the lithographic process represents it as altogether depending on a series of chemical actions. It is, however, more commonly supposed that the fatty matter of the lithographic chalk simply adheres to, or is partly absorbed by, the porous surface of the limestone; that the parts thus penetrated readily take up the printing-ink; and that the adhesion of the ink to the other portions of the surface is prevented by the interposition of a film of water. But if this explanation were correct, a piece of alabaster, or sandstone, or porous earthenware, or any other stone capable of receiving a granular surface, ought to be available for lithography as well as limestone; whereas it is well known that carbonate of calcium is the only kind of stone that will answer the purpose; moreover, the mechanical theory of lithography takes no account of the peculiar action of the gum, which appears to be an essential feature of the process."

Our own views are somewhat different from those of Mr. Hanhart, and are founded upon experience and experiments. Our object not being the discussion of obscure phenomena, but rather the production of a practical treatise, we will allow our readers an opportunity of forming their own opinions, when they have mastered the manipulative details in which we shall have the pleasure of instructing the m.

the acid in descending will, of course, remain longer on the lower portion than on the upper; but if the stronger part of the drawing be at the bottom, keeping it in the one position may be better than reversing it.

Acid cannot at all times and places be bought of equal strength; therefore it will be necessary to indicate how its strength may be estimated. For the purpose in view, it may roughly be stated as the strength of lemon-juice. Try it upon the margin of the stone, and if an effervescence takes place, accompanied with noise, it is too strong; but if the effervescence commences only after the lapse of a few seconds, it will be about the correct strength.

93. *Second method.*—Gum the clean edge of the stone with weak gum-water, and allow it to dry. Set the stone level, but in such a manner as to be able to give it a rocking motion. Convert the surface into a kind of tray by means of some engravers' bordering-wax, and pour the dilute acid into it, and as the bubbles of gas arise, rock the stone to detach them from its surface. It would be possible by this method to proportion the acid to the surface of the stone, and, by allowing it to become exhausted, to insure a proper amount of etching.

In these two methods, as soon as the etching is completed and the water drained off, the stone is to be gummed by a soft sponge or brush, and allowed to dry, when it may be put into the hands of the printer for proving.

94. *Third method.*—This is, perhaps, the one most generally employed, and has been found to give good results in most cases; by it additional etching can be applied to any darker parts that require it; but in this respect it is not so perfect as the method to be described in Art. 95. According as the drawing is composed of strong or delicate chalking, and the stone is of a hard or soft nature, the preparation is to consist of from 40 to 60 parts of gum-solution, of the consistency of linseed-oil, to one part of acid (nitric or muriatic). This is to be poured into a dish of convenient size, and well mixed. Now take a flat, soft brush, of not less than four inches in width, saturate it with the solution, and apply it to the stone in bold strokes from right to left, and left to right, until the stone is covered. Repeat the opera-

tion, and if there are dark parts requiring it, have ready a smaller brush to further etch them with the same solution. Now rinse off the etching-fluid, and gum in as before described, and dry. It is better thus to wash off the etching preparation, because all further action is stopped, which may not be the case if the gum and acid were allowed to stop on till dry.

The thickness of the gum-mucilage moderates the action of the acid very materially, plain acid and water of the same proportion acting much more energetically; it is therefore important to use much judgment ih any mode of etching, as, of course, if the operation be long-continued, a similar result will be arrived at as when the preparation is used of greater strength.

95. *Fourth method.*—This is founded on the desirability that exists for etching the darker parts of a drawing more than the lighter, and if carried out by a man of experience, on a suitable subject, cannot fail to give satisfaction, though a little more troublesome. Prepare an etching preparation as for method one, suitable to the lightest tints, and with that etch the whole of the drawing. After drying, instead of gumming the whole, apply the gum to the lightest tints, and etch again in the same manner. Wash well with plain water, and dry. Now stop out with gum the light and middle tints, and etch for the third time. The etching, in each case being momentary, will not dissolve the gum, which, for the short period the acid is on the stone, protects it. After the third etching, the stone may be fully gummed and put aside to dry. It must be noted that subjects having a continuous gradation from light to dark cannot be etched on this principle.

96. "However simple this operation may appear, it is extremely important as regards the success of the impressions. Two risks are run in its execution, and it is by practice alone that they can be avoided. If the stone be not etched strong enough, it is apt to run smutty; and if etched too strong, the delicate lines disappear. The difficulty is increased by this circumstance, that the etching-water which is proper for one stone is not so for another.

"In general it is better to etch weakly than strongly (as this defect has its remedy), particularly for highly-finished drawings; when, however, they are executed with spirit, or contain very dark parts, they may be treated with less precaution. This proves that it would be better to pour but little acid on the delicate parts, and more on the dark ones; for it is easy to understand that the acid must attack with much more strength the delicate places than those which contain a great deal of chalk; besides, the faint tints, not being inclined to run smutty, do not require such strong etching as those parts which are covered by chalk." *

While treating of the nature of acids and their uses in lithography, it may be desirable (although slightly out of the order laid down at the beginning of this treatise) to notice another application of them—viz., to retouching and correcting after printing.

97. RETOUCHING AND CORRECTING AFTER PRINTING on grained stones may be effected according to the instructions given in paragraph 86 for polished stones. If done with every care, and the additions made with No. 2 chalk, they may be expected to stand very well, though they will not equal in strength and firmness the original drawing.

The printer will have to use fine-pointed scrapers or needle-points to pick out black specks, and to use them in such a manner as to preserve the character of the grain and the work upon it.

98. As these chapters are written for the practical man, it will be well at this point to take up the subject of transferring and taking impressions from the work produced according to the foregoing instructions. It is true there are other modes to be treated of, and instructions to be given for producing them, but they will be left to another portion of the work. What has already been done includes the *usual* processes of working on stone in one colour, and real progress has been made by the student if he has mastered his subject thus far. By now going to the subject of Transferring and Printing, a better foundation will be laid for understanding the more complicated matters to follow.

---

* M. Raucourt.

CHAPTER XI.

Taking Impressions for Transferring. — Copperplate transfers —
Warming the plate—The jigger — Blanketing—The damp-book
—Method of taking the impression from plates—Failures and their
causes—Retransfers from stone—Transfers from type and woodcuts
—Condition of the stone in transferring.

STONES, after the *Etching*, described in the last chapter, are ready for the press. As we have, however,
given instructions for drawing in two styles on *paper ;* with
pen and brush (line work) and with chalk (grained paper),
we must show how they are to be put upon the stone previous to printing from them, or in the language of the
trade, transferring them. The transferring method applies
not only to work executed in the first instance by hand
labour, but also to the reproduction by Lithography of engraved plates, blocks, and type. We shall, therefore, take
this subject next in order, and devote a chapter to it.

99. ONE of the most important qualifications for the
foreman of a small lithographic printing-office, is the ability
to pull transfers from copperplate.

In these days of extreme division of labour it is not
every youth who has the opportunity given him for practice, and it is the more important, therefore, that this
treatise should attempt to supply the deficiency.

100. THE COPPER-PLATE PRESS may be used for pulling
the transfers, but the litho press will be found quite sufficient. It is as well to devote a small press entirely to this
purpose, and have conveniences at hand for use at any
time. A small lithographic press will cost less money than
a copper-plate press, and may be used for litho work as
well in a small establishment. If cost is of greater consideration than convenience, a larger press capable of any
ordinary work may be used without injury to it, if a
smaller extra tympan and frame be employed to save the
full-size one. Such tympan may be either of metal or
leather, see article 44.

101. AN APPARATUS FOR WARMING THE PLATE will be necessary. It may be simply held over an ordinary gas flame, but this is a mode to be avoided by any one who wishes to do his work neatly and cleanly, because it smokes the back of the plate and causes it to accumulate little hard spots of ink-like nature that soon develop into convex spots upon the surface of the plate. Even this might be avoided by greater attention to cleanliness ; and the employer if he finds his own and customers' plates getting into this state should warn his transferrer, and insist upon his exercising greater care. It may usually be regarded as an indication of careless or bad manipulation, certain to show itself in other matters connected with the trade.

The dealers in materials will supply a proper " *heater* " for the plates, to be fitted up by a gas-fitter, with a " ring burner " containing about a dozen fine holes. When the gas is lighted, the flame must be kept down so as to rise scarcely beyond the blue stage which indicates an absence of soot. It may also be heated by one of those cheap smokeless gas stoves that may now be bought from 2s. upwards.

For occasional use the cheapest and cleanest mode of heating the plate will be to employ an " air " or " Bunsen Burner," which may be bought of dealers in chemical apparatus from 1s. 6d. By this, the plate may be heated free from smoke, and little room occupied.

102. A JIGGER is a kind of light wood box open at the ends, to be placed near the heaters. It is used for laying the plate upon while it is being wiped, the open part underneath serving as a receptacle for " whiting," which is thus preserved from dust and grit. This apparatus, though useful, is by no means indispensable.

103. PRINTERS' BLANKETING is used for laying upon the plate, over the transfer paper, while the impression is being taken, serving by its elasticity to drive the paper into the lines of the engraving. Good flannel, such as is used for underclothing, if employed double or treble, will answer the purpose admirably. The paper and ink required are mentioned in articles 15 and 16.

104. THE DAMP BOOK is usually employed, when much

transferring is done, for preparing the paper previously to taking the impression, and also preparatory to laying it down upon the stone. It consists merely of 20 or 30 loose sheets of thick printing-paper, of a convenient size, wetted by dipping every alternate sheet, and then putting them in a heap under a weight until equally damp all through. It must not be used until the water is equally diffused through the whole. To prevent the mildew, to which it is subject, a little carbolic acid may be added to the damping water.

This book should be kept between thin plates of zinc, or some waterproof material, to reduce evaporation as much as possible; and, at the close of each day, more water should be sprinkled among its leaves, and a weight placed upon it, so that it may be in good condition for the next day.

Though recognizing the great convenience of this arrangement, and fully acknowledging the perfection with which a transfer may be *damped for the stone*, we do not consider it equally applicable in damping the transfer-paper previous to pulling the impression, for the reasons following :—

1st. The composition on the paper is made adhesive, so as to attach it firmly to the stone during the operation of transferring; and the damping-book acts admirably in bringing the paper into such condition by acting upon the composition and softening it.

2nd. In taking the impression from the plate, it is desirable that the composition should adhere sufficiently to prevent its shifting, but not so strongly as to leave it partly on the plate when the transfer is being lifted.

3rd. If the transfer-paper is damped upon the back with a sponge containing but little water, the paper may be rendered sufficiently supple and yielding as to easily penetrate the lines of the engraving at the same time that it adheres well enough to the surface of the plate without sticking too strongly.

For these reasons it is advisable either to damp the paper on the back with a sponge containing a little water, or to place a piece of clean, dry paper in the book on the face of the transfer-paper, to prevent its becoming too adherent when applied to the plate.

105. METHOD OF TAKING THE IMPRESSION FROM
PLATES.—Tie up a piece of transfer-ink (Art. 16) in sufficient old linen or silk to cover it.   This acts as a strainer
during the inking of the plate.   Warm the plate by one of
the modes mentioned in paragraph 102, until it can barely
be held in the hand, holding it by a piece of folded paper
or cloth to protect the fingers.   Rub the covered-up stick
of ink upon the plate, until sufficient is melted to cover it,
continuing to rub the ink into the lines of the plate, and
warm it as found necessary.

When it is well filled in, take a piece of soft rag, fold it
over the fingers, and wipe the superfluous ink off the still
hot plate, endeavouring in so doing not to wipe the ink out
of the lines, which is best done by wiping *across* them.

Shift the rag to a cleaner place, and wipe again until all
the ink is removed from the surface and the plate looks
clean.   Now carefully examine it, and see if any ink
remains in small specks, which will very likely happen.   If
so, remove them with the finger-nail or a splint of wood.
When quite free from surface ink, rub the hand on a piece
of whiting or soft chalk, and then wipe it over the other
hand or similar surface, so as to get a little only on it, and
with it polish the plate, thus removing the last trace of
grease from the surface.   Be careful to have but little
whiting on the hand, or it may stick to the ink in the lines,
in quantity sufficient to prevent its adhesion to the paper.

Place a small thick stone in the press, and upon it the
plate face upwards.   Upon the plate put a piece of transfer-
paper prepared side downwards, and previously damped as
in par. 104, and over that the flannel or blanket (par. 103);
turn down the tympan (44), and, by depressing the lever
(43), bring the scraper (46) down upon the tympan just
over one end of the plate,* and, with a good pressure, run
the plate through by the handle (41).

Now raise the lever, pull out the carriage, lift the tympan,
reverse the plate in the press, and repeat the operation.
This should now be sufficient, but occasionally it may have

---

* It is an excellent plan to have two pieces of millboard of the
thickness of the plate—one on each side of it—as the scraper may be
then set on the millboard, and a proper pull got all over the plate.

to be repeated twice or thrice. Take the plate from the press, and remove the flannel, when the cutting in the plate should show plainly at the back, if sufficient pressure has been applied. The transfer must *not now* be peeled from the plate for two reasons :—(a) the ink being cold and hard, will not readily quit the lines ; (b) the composition is damp, rotten, and deficient in tenacity. To bring all into proper condition, the plate must be gently warmed to soften the ink and dry the paper, which will then contract, and leave the plate with very little assistance.

The impression should now present the appearance of glazed enamel paper, with every line full of ink—distinct and sharp.

The failures and their causes are as follows :—

The paper does not adhere to the plate.	Damp it more before using.
The impression is doubled in places.	The composition has been too damp, so as to cause it to slide under the pressure.
The lines are broken.	The pressure may have been deficient ; the composition not tough enough ; or the plate may have been insufficiently inked.
The ink is thin and grey in places.	It has been too much removed from the lines in wiping the plate.

Another source of failure is, burning the ink in the lines by overheating the plate. By occasionally washing it out with turpentine, its condition in this respect may be ascertained. It is sometimes necessary, for the complete removal of old or burnt ink, to heat the plate, apply turps, and set it on fire, taking care to put out the flame instead of permitting it to burn out. This method usually is successful, but in refractory cases stronger solvents, like oil of tar, may be resorted to with good results.

If the impression is very full of ink, or the ink be too soft, so that there is reason to anticipate its spreading in transferring, it may be laid upon a piece of *clean printing* paper, and pulled through the press, when some of the ink will adhere to the clean paper. To separate, it will be safest to warm them slightly.

106. TO TAKE RETRANSFERS FROM STONE.—A small litho roller should be kept for this purpose, because it will then be always ready, while an ordinary printing-roller would require scraping both before and after using the re-transfer ink upon it. This is rendered necessary by reason of the soapy nature of the ink making it unfit for ordinary printing. An ink which may be used without injuring a drawing in taking a few transfers, might spoil it when employed in printing a quantity. The non-drying nature of this ink will be found to keep the roller soft and pliant for use, with an occasional scraping previous to applying new ink, and this furnishes an additional reason for appropriating a roller to this use alone.

Take some of the transfer-paper (15), sparingly damp the back with a sponge. Wipe off the superfluous water with a cloth, and in a few seconds the paper will lie flat, when it is ready to take an impression from the stone without sticking sufficiently to break the composition in lifting. It is now only required to roll in the work with the ink mentioned in par. 17, waft the stone quite dry, and to pull the impression on the previously-damped paper. It will be found to adhere strongly to the stone, and must be raised carefully at the edges, and peeled off.

It is as well to use the ink as strong as possible ; but if it is so strong as to tint the stone, some ordinary lithographic printing-ink must be mixed with it until it works cleanly.

If these instructions be followed with care and intelligence, impressions from the retransfers will compare so favourably with those from the original as to be scarcely distinguishable.

107. TRANSFERS FROM TYPE AND WOODCUTS are very useful, and, in some offices, have a wide application. The inspection of some commercial samples will show the student how they may be applied. It will here be sufficient to point out that it is no unfrequent thing to find letter-press invoice-headings, &c., transferred to stone, and printed at machine. The advantages are, that transferring is quicker than stereotyping ; that four to eight may be

printed upon a sheet; and that no impression is made to show upon the back.

The paper is to be less damp than in the last two methods; the ink (18) to be used with a letterpress roller, and a fine card to be laid upon the back to get a nice, sharp, clear impression. If the ink is not at hand, and the transfer is wanted quickly, it may be printed in ordinary stiff letterpress ink, which, containing soap, is of the nature of a transfer ink.

108. The fact that all the modes described in articles 105, 106, 107, may be employed in one piece of work, united with any of the modes of drawing or writing herein previously explained, shows that a power is possessed by lithography that can be found in no other mode of printing, for, in fact, it can successfully imitate the other two, while it possesses advantages peculiarly its own.

The mode of taking transfers having been, it is hoped, fully explained, it now remains to complete the subject by showing the methods employed in putting them on the stone, to which end it is very necessary to pay particular attention to the

109. CONDITION OF THE STONE.—The stone for the reception of transfers should be polished free from perceptible scratches, perfectly clean, and free from gum, grease, or dust. This latter cannot be easily seen by inspection, but may readily be detected by wiping the stone with a piece of dark-coloured cloth, velvet, &c., when the dust is visible on the stuff used.

The stone must have been dried, but its temperature may vary according to circumstances. For ordinary work, it is perhaps safest to have the stone slightly warm, but it is undeniable that transfers can successfully be made on cold stones, and even on damp ones, when, from the nature of the work, it is desirable to use them. The warming of the stone is said to open its pores and make it more susceptible of receiving the ink at the same time that it softens it. As, however, stone expands less than most other solid substances by heat, it is clear that the opening of its pores by such influence cannot be accounted a reason for so using it in transferring; yet it is known that transfers go down more strongly on a warm than on a cold stone, and the cause may be found in the fact that the warm stone softens the ink by contact, in which state it more easily penetrates the pores of the stone.

The qualities of the transfer-paper will sometimes determine whether the stone is to be used warm, for there are papers that will not adhere to cold stones. Such are those made of parchment size, or other varieties of hard gelatine, which do not become adhesive unless warmed to some extent, though they will absorb water at a low temperature. It frequently happens to these papers that when they are much damped, and the stone is very warm, the composition runs almost like water, while if the composition is properly damp, and the stone moderately warm, the transfer adheres with such tenacity as to necessitate the use of hot water to bring the paper away.

Transferring to damp stones finds but little favour among lithographers, because their past experience fully imbues them with the idea that grease and water are practically antagonistic; but any one who has rolled up a weak transfer before gumming the stone, must have noticed how easily the ink catches, even while the stone is wet.

———

CHAPTER XII.

Transferring.— Three methods of transferring—Transferring to dry stone—Transferring to a wet stone—Transferring by damping the transfer and wetting the stone.

THE methods of taking impressions suitable for transferring having been described in the last chapter, we proceed now to show the manner of putting them down upon the stone, so that they may be printed from. There are three distinct variations of transferring, each having its own special advantages.

1st. Transferring damped transfers to dry stone, either warm or cold.

2nd. Dry transfers to wet stone, and

3rd. Damped transfers to wet stone.

110. TRANSFERRING TO DRY STONE is the mode usually, and in some offices invariably, adopted. The stone may be warm or cold, but in all cases must be thoroughly dry. If the drawing, writing, copper transfer, or other work, is of an unusually fine character; or if the ink used is of a very hard nature, the stone may be warmed with advantage; but it should not be made hot, or the transfer-ink may spread, as it can hardly be expected but that some part of the work will contain heavy lines, which would, of course, be more liable to spread than finer ones.

The damping of the transfer-paper requires care and experience, and may be done as described in par. 104. It has before been stated that the object is to render the composition sufficiently adhesive to stick to the stone under pressure, and this may be ascertained by taking a corner of the paper containing no work, and squeezing it between the finger and thumb, to which, if it attaches itself by the composition, the transfer is ready for the stone. Care must be taken that the thumb and finger are not damp or the transferrer may be thereby deceived. A very convenient substitute for a damping-book is a piece of thick linen cloth dipped in water, wrung as dry as possible with the hands, and then opened out and taken by the corners, and well shaken with a jerking motion to straighten it. This is then folded, and used to put the paper between. If the coating on the transfer-paper is very soft, a piece of thin plain paper should be put upon the face of the transfer to prevent it absorbing the damp too readily.

It is almost imperative that patched-up transfers must be damped after the damp-book fashion, but single transfers may be readily damped by preparing a piece of plain paper with a sponge. Damp it each side, and wipe the superfluous water off; lay the transfer upon this, and damp its back in like manner. The composition lying upon the damp paper will become adhesive more quickly without becoming rotten, and is, in fact, prepared just the same as if placed in the damp-book.

Care must be taken that no loose particles of dust, dirt, or other extraneous matter become attached to the transfer, and to this end it is recommended to use a magnifying-glass to examine it. If any should be discovered, they may be removed with the point of a sharp penknife delicately used. It will be found much easier and more economical in practice to make the transfer clean, before applying it to the stone, than to make good any deficiencies afterwards.

While the transfer is lying in the damp, or previously, the stone must be put in the press, and it and the scraper made level. To level the stone, place over it a piece of clean paper, bring down the tympan, and adjust the scraper to give a light pressure at one end; now try it in the middle and other end, and if the pressure feels the same at each place, the stone will do. If a deficiency is found at either end, it may be made good by packing the stone with a thick paper called *casing*, or the wrappers of reams of paper. The paper is to be *torn* into strips having a *feather* edge—one being narrow, another twice the width, a third three times the width, and so on. These are then to be put together to form steps as it were, the feather-edges preventing a too abrupt transition from one to the other. This is now to be put under the stone at the thin end, and the pressure tried again.

The scraper may now be taken out of its box, and examined to see if it be bruised or not. It should then be placed across the stone in the same direction as it is in its box. If it will tightly hold a small piece of writing-paper at any point of its length between it and the stone, it may be said to be true enough. If any want of truth be found in it, a sheet or two of coarse cabinet paper is to be laid across the stone, and the scraper rubbed upon it, until it is made to touch all across.

The stone and transfer being ready, the latter is to be laid face down upon the former, and where it is a plain, single job, such as a circular, it may easily enough be laid in its place; but as it frequently happens that the transfer has to be laid very accurately to a mark, and that it will not do to shift it about upon the stone to adjust it, it is desirable to handle it in the manner following:—Take a piece of clean, rather stiff paper, and lay the transfer upon its upper left-hand corner, so that about half an inch shall hang over the paper. This, being held in the right hand, can be readily accommodated to any point upon the stone without soiling it ; when in position, place the finger and thumb of the left hand upon the projecting edge of the transfer, and press it to the stone while the plain paper is being withdrawn, after which the left hand can be taken away, and the transfer left *in situ.*

If several transfers have to be laid upon a stone that is warm enough to dry them quickly, they must be pulled through the press singly or in rows of two or three, according to the quickness of the workman, for if all were laid before pulling through, some would be dry, and would not adhere. To prevent this, they may be mounted upon a sheet of paper ; but it frequently happens that the paper used for mounting will expand one way in damping, and the transfers another, causing creases in the latter when drawn through the press.

Now that the transfers are laid upon the stone, lay over them a piece of clean printing-paper, and over that a piece of printer's fine blanket ; pull them through once with a moderate pressure, and increase it a little afterwards until, say, the third pull ; now take off the backing, reverse the scraper in its box, shift the stone a little in the press (to overcome any slight defect that may exist in the tympan or backing), sponge the back of the transfer, and pull through again. Repeat the damping and pressure twice or thrice, and then remove the stone to the trough, and pour *hot* water over the transfer, which may then be peeled off, leaving the ink and composition upon the stone. Some transferrers do not use hot water, but are content to allow longer soaking, and give more pulling through the press, so as to drive the water through the pores of the paper.

The composition may now be washed off, and the stone gummed and allowed to dry.

The student's attention is requested to the great importance of a level stone and level scraper ; when these co-exist much less pressure is required to make a successful transfer, and the risk of spreading the lines is much reduced. It is also facilitated by the use of the blanket. Those who do not employ a blanket for transferring, generally substitute for it several sheets of paper, to form a backing, but these are neither so elastic nor so durable. When the transfer is very large, and the evenness of the stone cannot be relied upon, strips of cardboard or folded paper may be applied to different parts of the stone in succession, both longitudinally and transversely, so as to be sure of applying sufficient pressure to every part.

Independently of getting a true surface, large transfers present a difficulty in their liability to *slur*, by the ink touching the stone when laid down, and shifting afterwards by the stretching of the paper, thus making two marks instead of one. It is therefore desirable that no part of the paper should touch the stone until the instant before the pressure is applied to such part. This presents a mechanical difficulty that might be overcome by transferring with cylinders ; but as they are not in use in litho presses, the difficulty can be got over by the use of the damp stone ; or, better, by damp stone and damp transfer (see par. 112).

The transferring of the autographic transfers mentioned in paragraph 76, comes within this class, and is usually performed as follows :—The paper is sponged at the back with weak solution of nitric acid in water, laid upon the warm stone, and passed once through the press under heavy pressure ; or the back of the paper may be floated upon the acid solution (taking care not to wet the front), and hung up to dry. To transfer, damp the back with plain water, and proceed as before described. If the acid has been somewhat strong, the paper will adhere sufficiently to permit of its being passed through the press several times. To make sure of this point, the paper may be examined after the first pull through, when, if found to be non-adherent, do not attempt a second. A convenient way of floating will be to put a quantity of acid solution on a piece of clean, level glass ; lay one corner of the paper upon it, and push the rest of the paper down gradually.

For another style of transferring such subjects, see paragraphs 130, 131.

111. TRANSFERRING TO A WET STONE can only be successfully accomplished with a transfer-paper that is readily rendered adhesive by cold water. Such paper may be coated with any of the varieties of starch or common glue, mixed or not with gum arabic ; but transfer-paper made with the harder and purer varieties of gelatine does not

answer the purpose, though a little may be added to the starch paste to improve its quality.

The advantages of laying down a dry transfer on a wet stone, when it can be successfully done, are many and great. It is easier to damp the stone than the paper; it is quicker; patched transfers can be put down without creasing them, and all can be transferred without altered dimensions. This last qualification renders it especially useful in transferring for colour printing, which will be noticed in its place.

Everything is to be prepared as for the mode of transferring last mentioned; but instead of damping the paper, the stone is to be made wet with a perfectly clean sponge, linen rag, or wash-leather, the latter being preferred because it leaves less loose material from its surface upon the stone. The quantity of water to be left upon the stone must be determined by experience, but it may be sufficient to say that no more is required than will unite with the composition and cause it to adhere to the stone. Thus, a plate transfer-paper would take up more water than a writing transfer-paper. If the stone be wetted to about the same degree as is required in printing, the water will be found in about the right quantity.

If the transfer consists of several pieces, they should be attached by gum to thin printing-paper. When transfers are patched up for transferring to dry stones, they must be attached with flour paste, gum in this case not being suitable, because it would become so moist in the damping process as to squeeze out in the first run through the press; but in the wet stone process gum will do best, because the transfer adheres to the stone at the first pull, and the gum is more readily made soluble by damping the back of the mounting-paper than paste would be.

The stone being ready, the transfer is laid upon it as in the first process, and as quickly as possible passed through the press under proper pressure, about three times over. By this time the stone should be dry, which may be ascertained by lifting a corner; if not dry, let it remain uncovered until it is so. If the stone is dry, it may be assumed that there is no impediment to its union with the ink, and the back of the mounting-paper may be wetted until the gum is soft enough to allow it to be lifted, leaving the transfers upon the stone.

The transfer may be now considered to be in the same condition as after the first pulls in the last process, and may be damped, &c., and finished in the same manner, the transfer-paper allowing of the subsequent damping without blistering, if the process has been successful.

112. TRANSFERRING BY DAMPING THE TRANSFER AND WETTING THE STONE may be resorted to with great advantage when the transfers are very large, and more especially so tracings on transfer-paper. These latter are very difficult to damp properly, because the varnish by which the paper is rendered transparent fills up the pores of the paper, and prevents the entry of the water for a long time in damping the back of the transfer, both before and after it has been subjected to pressure ; while, if it be put into a damp-book or cloth, the probability is that the composition will either be too damp or not damp enough. If it become too damp, two results will follow in laying it down on the dry stone—

(*a*) If the composition touch the stone in a place where a line or other inkmark subsequently falls, it will prevent its adherence to the stone.

(*b*) If a line first touches the stone, and afterwards shifts, it will attach itself by mere contact to the stone in the first instance, because the composition has become so soft ; and when the job is transferred, the line will probably present a broken appearance, thus : —————— ——— ———, instead of being continuous, as intended by the draughtsman. Now, if the transfer be damped upon the back, so as to render it limp before the composition is softened, the transfer may be shifted considerably on the stone without injury ; and if the stone be wetted to make it adhere, the conditions of success will have been, in a great measure, complied with. After sufficient pressure has been applied, it should be allowed to dry on the stone (which takes a little longer when this process is used), and then treated as before described (par. 110).

It may here be pointed out that in the process described in par. 110, the dry stone absorbs the damp from the transfer, while in the second method (par. 111) the transfer absorbs much of it from the stone; but in the way just treated of, both being damped, the one has no chance of correcting the other, and must be permitted to dry before being taken off the stone.*

CHAPTER XIII.

Proving and Printing.—Rolling up—Cleaning—Etching—Taking the first impressions—Marking the stone for laying down transfers—Mode of printing.

FOLLOWING up what has been explained in previous chapters, we are ready to enter upon the actual printing of drawings and writings on lithographic stones.

113. TREATMENT OF TRANSFERS PREVIOUS TO PRINTING.—This includes the "proving" of the work : by which is meant the rolling up, cleaning, etching, and taking the first impressions to be submitted to the customer; and the instructions equally apply to drawings or writings executed direct upon the stone.

(*a*) Suppose the drawing to be composed of very fine lines, the printer may have some doubt as to all the details being firm upon the stone if rolled up in the ordinary way. He may then take, in a sponge, some gum-water (free from acid) of the consistency of oil, and pass it over the entire drawing, using the left hand, while in his right he has a pad of soft rag charged with a mixture of turpentine, thin printing ink, and stone retransfer ink, which may be rubbed over the drawing upon the still wet gum-water, with a circular motion, recharging the pad with ink and the sponge with gum-water as often as necessary. This should develop every line of the drawing, and render it quite black. By keeping sufficient gum upon the stone, there is little fear of

---

* The transfer-paper may sometimes be very conveniently removed from the stone by covering it with sufficient water to run upon it, and then laying on a sheet of paper, and allowing it to soak for some time. The sheet of paper prevents the water from running off the stone, and will keep wet for hours if required.

injuring the drawing, though it will make the stone very dirty in appearance by reason of the mixture of ink and gum ; this, however, may be removed by a wash of clean water, and the stone gummed in with clean gum and set aside for the ink to penetrate. In this operation the stone may be warm but of course it must be set aside after this treatment to cool.

(*b*) If there be any idea that the transfer is weak, and if the *stone is cold*, it may be rolled up with the roller previous to gumming it, but this must be done cautiously, because the ink will, in the absence of gum, attach itself to the slightest grease upon the stone. It is also very apt to cause the lines to spread, and is to be recommended only in cases when the work is wanted quickly and almost anything will pass muster ; such as some kinds of law and parliamentary work.

(*c*) The common and best way for the ordinary run of work is to gum the stone, after the transfer is made, with fresh gum ; allow it to dry, wash off with clean water, and roll up carefully with ink of medium strength.

Whichever method may have been adopted, the dirt will have made its appearance, and must be removed. This may be done by the conjunctive employment of the following methods :—

1st. Clean the edges and other parts of the stone where there is no work with a water-sponge and piece of snake or pumice-stone, using a small pencil of the same (art. 24) to get between the lines. The principal part of the dirt may thus be taken away ; but as there will most probably be specks among the work that cannot be got at with the snake-stone pencil, use the acid " stump " as now to be described.

2nd. Having a water-sponge in the left hand, dip the acid stump (art. 51) into the gum and acid, and try it upon the edge of the stone, when it will be found to effervesce energetically if strong enough. This will also reduce the quantity on the stump, which may now be applied to the speck to be removed, rubbing it with the wood point. If any acid be observed to spread in dangerous proximity to other lines, the water- or gum-sponge must be quickly used to wipe it off. This is a rapid and effectual method of cleaning, and a person expert in its use will require little else; but the novice had better finish cleaning up his job with the scraper.

3rd. The finishing touches of cleaning between very close work, reducing the thickness of lines, &c., must be done with a sharp scraper, such as a mezzotint-scraper, or a penknife (see art. 85).

The work having been cleaned, must now be rolled up again cleanly, but strongly; and etched in the following simple manner.

Have ready a small basin or other convenient vessel, containing acid and water of about the strength of lemon-juice, or of such strength as to effervesce gently when applied to the stone. Now, with a soft sponge charged with this dilute acid, go regularly and quickly all over the stone with a light hand, and again over the edges and other bare parts. After this gum in and allow to dry.*

If the work is to be printed at machine, or to go into the hands of an inexperienced youth to be printed, it may be treated with powdered resin (see art. 52). Roll up in rather thin ink: dust over the resin when the stone is dry; wipe off what is superfluous with water-sponge, and repeat the operation. Set it aside for a short time for the ink and resin to incorporate, when, on taking it up again, it will probably allow of another dusting without rolling up.

The stone may now be acidulated freely without fear of injury; either the strength of the acid being increased, or the application several times renewed. The acid is best used with gum and applied with a broad flat brush, if considerable relief is desired, but for ordinary work the sponge and ordinary etching-water will be sufficient.

The stone having been gummed, the ink and resin are

---

* When the work consists of narrow surfaces like lines and dots, the etching-water, if used in moderate quantity, is thrown off again as soon as the sponge has passed over, by reason of the greasiness of the work. But if the work contains any broad surfaces of solid black, more care must be taken, because the repelling power of the ink will not be strong enough to throw off the acidulated water, which, standing in patches on such surface, will be likely to find its way through the ink to the stone, and cause a grey appearance when printed. By using powdered resin as next described, this difficulty will be overcome.

now to be washed off with rag and "turps," or the mixture described in art. 25, and again rolled up, gummed, and set aside to dry.

It is desirable, whenever there is time and opportunity, to allow some hours or even days, to intervene between the getting ready or proving of the stone, and beginning to print ; though when work is wanted immediately it may be put in hand at once.

114. MARKING THE STONE FOR LAYING DOWN TRANSFERS, &c.—Before proceeding to lay down the transfers, it should be ascertained whether they are to be printed on the whole sheet or on some part of it. If the job to be printed is to run a small number only, it may be transferred to any convenient part of the stone, because one at a time will be all that will be found necessary to print ; while if a large number is required, resort will be had to multiplication by transferring, and care must be taken to put the transfers properly in position on the stone. Let a few examples be taken.

1st. One or two hundred 8vo. one-page circulars, with fly-leaf. These may be printed on quarter-sheets of paper and then sent to the stationer to fold and cut ; but as he cannot well do it without causing them to set off in the cutting, they may be printed upon ready-folded 8vo. paper. Take the necessary quantity of paper section by section, open it, and "break its back," so that it may lie flat and open. Lay it inner side uppermost. Lay the next section *across* it in the same manner, and so on, to make a heap, in which each section is distinct from another by the long way of one being set *across* the short way of the other. Now lay the top sheet with its under side upon the stone, and when taken off, place the printed side up. When the section is printed and thus laid, as soon as it is complete, it may be easily refolded in the same manner as it was at first, and in like manner the rest may be printed.

This method will answer for any single page, or for first and fourth, or second and third ; but when first and second or first and third pages are required to be printed, they are managed differently.

Let it be required to print first and second pages.—(*a*). Transfer first page to the right and second page to the left, so that an inch more space is left between them than if they were intended for second and third.—(*b*). Or transfer the pages one above the other, with space enough to prevent the paper overlapping. To start printing, lay a piece of waste paper over page 2 and the *first* side of the note-paper over page 1, in proper position and pull impression; now lay *second* side of printed sheet on page 2, and the *first* side of a clean sheet over page 1; cover the printed side (which now lies uppermost on the stone) with a piece of tissue-paper and pull through the press, when one will be completed and the other half-done. By continuing this method the whole may be completed and printed on both sides in as many pulls as there are sheets to be printed, plus two. They may also be printed first on one side only, and then completed by printing the second side. In this case, during the second printing, two printed sides will be uppermost upon the stone, and a larger sheet of tissue must be used, so as to cover both. In each case the quantity of tissue paper required is the same.

To print 1st and 3rd pages, transfer (*a*) 1st page to left hand and 3rd to the right, leaving no extra space, but exactly as if 1st and 4th were to be printed; or (*b*) 1st to right, 3rd to left, leaving no extra space; or (*c*), transfer one above the other. *To print,* (*a*) Lay 3rd page down and then 1st with 4th page overlapping 4th. (*b*). First, lay page 1 and next page 3, when page 2 will fall on page 2. The tissue-paper is to be used as before.

This system of laying the paper on the stone may be illustrated graphically thus :—

To print 1st and 2nd pages lay them on stone thus :—

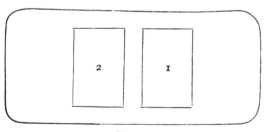

Fig. 1.

Or in this manner—

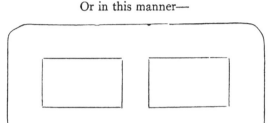

Fig. 2.

For 1st and 3rd pages lay thus :—

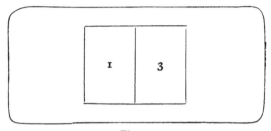

Fig. 3.

These pages may be reversed if the paper be laid in the reverse order also. Fig. 2 will answer the purpose for either 1st and 2nd or 1st and 3rd pages, but it will be found less convenient for laying down the paper.

We have not made any attempt to exhaust the subject of the methods of arranging work upon the stone, but have supplied only a few hints for a starting-point. By first folding and marking the paper, the young printer will soon, by the exercise of his judgment, find out the best manner of setting out his work, so as to save time and trouble.

When a large number is required, retransfers may be taken, and a stone made up in such a manner that both sides may be printed from it by turning the paper over. Thus, four pages of an octavo circular may be arranged thus upon the stone :—

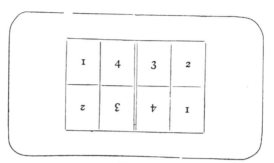

Fig. 4.

And, of course, any page may be omitted, and the same arrangement will do for 1st and 3rd, or 1st, 2nd, and 3rd.

This disposition of the pages is, perhaps, the best possible for the purpose, because in the second printing the sheet of paper cannot be laid for the pages to back each wrongly.

The transfers for headings, invoices, and similar jobs are put upon the stone in this way :—

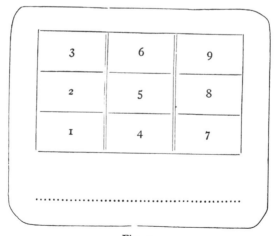

Fig. 5.

The paper is first laid on Nos. 1, 2, 3 ; the bottom of the first piece of paper occupying the position of the dotted line ; then three more pieces are laid upon 4, 5, 6, and three more are then laid on 7, 8, 9. In this manner No. 2 will overlap No. 1, and No. 3 overlap No. 2 ; so also No. 5 overlaps No. 4, and so on. When passed through the press, nine copies will be yielded at one pull.

The printer having his heap of cut paper on his left hand, draws his right thumb-nail over it, with a motion towards the left, which spreads the papers into steps, as it were ; he then takes, as nearly as he can guess, nine pieces in his left hand, and adjusts them with his right to make the steps wider. Next, he applies the projecting piece to the marks on No. 1, holds it with his right fore-finger and thumb, and draws away the rest of the pieces of paper. He then applies the next to No. 2, and repeats the operation until the nine pieces are laid in their proper position.

In examining these sheets when printed, it will be found that the pieces 4 to 9 inclusive will be marked by the pressure forcing them upon the edges of the pieces underlying. This is avoided in the best kind of work by taking a piece of cardboard or stout paper nearly as long as the stone is wide, folding it to the thickness of a florin, and about three inches wide, and then cutting gaps about half an inch wide to correspond to the edges of the pieces of paper. The tympan is now to be taken off, and the notched card-board inserted between the scraper and its leather covering, in such a position as to prevent any pressure being applied to the top and bottom edges of the paper. Put the tympan into its place, and when another set of impressions is taken the marks will be absent.

The foreman or printer who wishes to economize time may make a set of cardboard patterns, with rectangular openings to place upon the stone, to mark it for laying the transfer to, and also a set of " stops " to correspond, to be placed between the leather and its scraper.

115. PRINTING.—In the last few paragraphs it has been necessary, to avoid complexity of description, to assume that the student knows how to use the printing-roller, damping-cloth, &c. ; but as that was an assumption only, it

is proposed now to deal more fully with this highly important subject. If the reader will refer back to paragraphs 11 and 12, he will get some idea of the nature of the varnishes and inks used in lithography, and the theory of using them under different circumstances.

Let it be now supposed that the student has placed at his disposal a piece of work on stone that is in proper condition for printing, and that he desires to take impressions therefrom. He will require a roller, ink, palette-knife, sponge, damping-cloth, and a basin of water. As he is supposed to be as yet unacquainted with the process, he must not begin at once to work, because the stone is not in working condition. The first thing to be attended to is its temperature. If it is warm, the gum may be washed off its surface, and it may be put to soak for an hour in cold water; or it may be set aside in any cold place as long as convenient; the object being to equalize the temperature of the stone to that of the printing-room. If the stone has been put into a cold, dry place, the first thing to be done will be to saturate its surface with cold water. This may readily be done by washing off the gum with a sponge and water, leaving a pool of water upon its surface, and laying a sheet of paper on it. The paper will keep the water from running off or drying in patches, while it is soaking into the stone. The damping-cloth may be used for the same purpose, but after being a short time in use it is usually so full of holes that it would answer the purpose only imperfectly.

While the stone is absorbing water, the ink may be prepared for printing. It has been mentioned in article 13 that the printing ink, as bought from the manufacturer, is much too thick for use; in fact, the ordinary palette-knife is hardly strong enough to remove it from the can, and a short stiff one should be used for that purpose, if at hand. If the weather is cold, and the ink stiff, a thin, flexible knife is very likely to be broken, if used for its removal.

Before the printing can be proceeded with, some of this ink must be reduced with varnish to a thinner condition. The student before proceeding further is recommended to refer to article 13, and read it as a preface to the instructions to be given in the next chapter.

CHAPTER XIV.

Printing (continued).—Preparing ink for use—General instructions for printing—Manipulation of roller as affecting result—Temperature —Paper—Damping—Preparing India Paper for Printing.

PREPARING THE PRINTING-INK FOR USE.—116. With a suitable knife, remove from the can a piece of ink of the size of a nut, and place it upon the slab. From the varnish-can* take as much *thin* varnish as will lie upon the end of the palette-knife, and transfer it to the upper part of the slab. A *small* quantity of this varnish must now be mixed with the piece of ink by means of the palette-knife. At first there will be a difficulty—the ink being very tenacious will not easily separate, to allow of mixture with the varnish ; but by industriously working it with the knife it will gradually yield and be incorporated with it. When this has once taken place, more varnish may easily be added if required. It is to be supposed that our students' first essay at printing will be a simple subject in line-work, a bill-head, circular, or such like. The temperature of the room in which the printing is to be carried on being moderate, the mixture of ink and *thin* varnish is to be such that it will run slowly off the palette-knife when held in a position to allow it to do so. It is better to err in having the varnish too thick than too thin. When the ink has been brought to a proper consistency, it is to be scraped off the slab and laid upon that portion of it farthest from the printer.

A small portion of ink is next taken up on the palette-knife, and spread along or placed in small pats upon the roller, which is now to be rolled over the clear portion of the slab until the ink is evenly distributed over both. To do this properly requires a certain "knack." The roller must be taken by the leather handles which cover the wood ones, one in each hand ; rolled away from the operator and

---

* Cans of varnish are frequently secured by soldering a circular piece of tin over a large hole in the top. A neat and easy way of removing this is to hold the can under an open gas-flame, so that the flame will impinge upon the cover to be removed. In a few seconds the solder will be melted, when a knife may be inserted beneath the edge, and the cover lifted off.

back again to the near edge of the slab ; then lifted off the slab, and by a forward bending of the wrist brought down again to the place whence it was lifted. This motion, which should be made with the elbows fairly close to the body, will change the position of the roller in relation to the slab so that each point on the roller's surface will come in contact with a different portion of it. By repeating this operation several times, accompanied by a change of position laterally, and by turning over the roller so that the handle which was in the right hand may now be in the left, a good distribution of the ink will be effected.

Another way of effecting the same object is to lift the roller off after each push forward, and to set it down upon the near edge of the slab and repeat the movement. The printer may use either or both methods as the object to be gained is an equal distribution by the renewal of the ink-surface.* The inking-roller being now in proper condition for work, and the damping-cloth having been prepared, as described in paragraph 21, the superfluous water that has been lying upon the stone may be removed by the sponge, and the stone then "set" ready for printing, as described for transferring in paragraph 110. See that the stone is marked for the "lay" by means of the lead mentioned in paragraph 55 ; that the scraper is level and in its place ; that the press is oiled in its working parts ; that the backing-sheet is in position ; and that the stone is prevented from shifting by being set against a piece or pieces of wood

---

* It may be mentioned that the ink on the roller in the course of working becomes deteriorated both by absorbing water and gum, as well as by taking up the "fluff" produced by the wear of the damping-cloth. If the stone is a little rough, and the damping-cloth not good, the roller will soon assume a grey appearance, and will part with its ink with difficulty, necessitating the application of more ink to its surface. In this way the roller becomes charged with a quantity of ink, and does not, in this condition, impart much of it to the stone ; but if the same quantity were applied to a newly-scraped roller it would be altogether unmanageable. It is for these reasons that the damping-cloth is replaced by a second sponge in printing from grained stones, on which the wear of a damping-cloth is so rapid that the roller becomes comparatively white after a few impressions. Though the damping material in printing machines is usually of cotton, the action being a rolling instead of a rubbing one this covering of the ink-rollers is reduced to a minimum.

between it and the front end of the bed. These matters being all in proper condition, the student may proceed to try his " 'prentice hand " at lithographic printing.

With the sponge in the left hand wet the stone with a stroke from corner to opposite corner. The damping-cloth must be held in the right hand, so as to form as flat and broad a pad as can easily be managed. Commence at the top right-hand corner, carry the cloth across to the left-hand corner, covering well the edge of the stone. Drawing the cloth downwards nearly equal to its breadth, pass it to the right again, down again, and then to the left, and so on until you have gone regularly over the stone. This will take less time to do than to read a description of it; but what is desired in thus specifying the particulars of the operation is that it may be performed systematically and mechanically, leaving no part to be gone over again. The stone should now be uniformly wetted, or rather damped all over; if any part has been omitted, that part will take the ink in the next operation. If the stone is properly wetted, no part of it will take the ink from the roller except the fatty parts that are intended to do so.

Now take the roller in both hands, holding it by the leather handles, lay it on the stone and cause it to rotate backwards and forwards. If the work be larger than the roller will cover, the latter must be shifted about until every part is gone over. When the roller returns towards the operator it is to be lifted off the stone and rotated while off by the motion of the wrist before described, which changes its position and allows of more equal inking. When from four to six passes of the roller to and fro have been made (or more, according to the nature of the ink, temperature, and hygrometric state of the printing-room atmosphere), the stone, if not sufficiently inked, will require redamping as before, and the roller will require "knocking up" on the ink-slab to redistribute the ink and freshen its surface.*

---

* In rolling it over the smooth stone, the roller will have become glazed, and may be regarded as being covered with an exceedingly thin film of water. When the stone is very damp, the roller pushes the water before it, and unless it is held very loosely will perhaps slip over the stone without rotating, which will take off the ink instead of putting it on. When the roller has thus become smooth on its surface and probably wet, it does not deposit enough ink, and hence the necessity of freshening it on the ink-slab.

The stone must now be inked again with the roller, and will probably be in a fit state to yield an impression.

The next thing to be done is to lay the paper on the stone in such a manner as to prevent the impression being "slurred" or doubled. To effect this the paper must not shift, or be shifted between the time of first laying it on the stone and taking the impression. Let it be supposed that the paper is small enough or strong enough to be handled easily with one hand : the mark to which it is to be laid can then be made *across* the stone and a corner marked either next the printer or away from him at the other side of the stone. Take now the piece of paper in the right hand, with the fingers underneath it and the thumb on the top; keep the fingers a little bent, so that the pressure of the thumb in holding the paper will cause it to assume a somewhat concave surface : apply the corner furthest from you to the mark, and place your left forefinger lightly on it at the corner; adjust the edge of the paper to the line, and when there put your left thumb upon it to keep it so; at the same time let the paper fall from your right hand, and carefully take off your left.

If the sheet is too large or too flimsy to be treated in this manner just described, it must be laid upon the stone by taking it in both hands. Suppose the "lay" to be made along the edge of the stone furthest from the printer. Take the sheet in both hands, holding it between the thumbs and *second* fingers, extend the forefingers so that they will rest upon the corners of the paper; lay one corner to its proper mark and keep the forefinger upon it, while the edge is being adjusted to the line; place the other forefinger to hold down its corner; withdraw the thumbs and second fingers, and the paper will fall into its place. If the sheet is not sufficiently strong to be kept in position by this manipulation, it may be permitted to rest upon the printer's breast until laid to its mark. It is sometimes more convenient to have the line for laying by on the edge of the stone nearest the printer, in which case the paper is held by its near corners between the thumbs and fingers, the thumbs being uppermost. Whatever mode may be adopted, the principal point to be attended to is, that the edge only of the paper shall be properly adjusted before the rest of the sheet is allowed to come in contact with the stone.

The operation of taking the impression is to be conducted in the manner described in the articles on transferring, but the sheet has only to be taken once through the press. Lifting the paper from the stone should be done carefully, because it may sometimes tear or break if the ink is strong and the surfaces are broad.

The impression when lifted off should be examined, to see whether the operation has been properly performed. It will, however, require either an experienced or artistic eye to determine this point, and we now proceed to state what are *the essentials of a good impression :—*

1. As we have been printing in black ink, the lines of the drawing or writing must be black also ; or, in other words, they must *not* be grey.
2. They must not be wider or blacker than they were upon the stone ; such impressions are called "smutty."
3. They must not be "ragged" or broken ; or, as printers call this defect, "rotten."

Greyness and smuttiness are respectively the result of too little and too much ink ; while, if the work is good upon the stone, rottenness of impression is caused by insufficient pressure. The remedy for the latter is obvious ; but as it is possible to produce impressions either too light or too dark without altering the quantity of ink, some observations must now be made on this point.

117. MANIPULATION OF THE ROLLER.—An account of the theory of the inks and varnishes having been given in paragraphs 11 and 12, it will be unnecessary to go over that ground again. Attention is now directed to the different results obtained by varying modes of using the roller, independent of the quality of the ink upon it. It is not to be understood that the quality of the ink is unimportant, far from it ; but the point we are now establishing is, that with the same ink and the same number of passes of the roller over the stone, different qualities of impression may be produced. If the student will fix upon his memory the theories of the varnishes and the methods of using them upon the roller, he will be in a position to profit by the experience that may be gained in printing, his mind being

stored with a knowledge of the principles that must govern the practice.

1. *Bearing heavily* on the roller " feeds " the work more rapidly than bearing lightly on it.
2. *Light* pressure on the roller transfers but little ink to the stone, and also takes off some part of that which has been previously applied by heavy rolling.
3. *Slow* rolling produces similar effects to heavy rolling.
4. *Quick* rolling produces similar effects to light rolling ; consequently—
5. *Slow and heavy* rolling, combined, produce the maximum feeding effect upon the work ; while—
6. *Quick and light* rolling combined has the greatest effect in clearing an already over-inked job, and making the work look sharp.

Passing now to the influence of the ink upon the quality of the impression, the first axioms will be easily understood :

A. *Too little ink* upon the roller will produce grey impressions, under ordinary conditions of rolling.
B. *Too much ink* will, on the contrary, give smutty proofs.

These are matters purely mechanical ; but the nature of the ink has also to form an element in the calculations of the printer. He may use it thick or thin—*i.e.* he may bring his ink into working consistency by the use of " thin," " medium," or " strong" varnish. Now in following out this subject of the ink, we may add to the foregoing axioms the following :—

C. *Thin ink* feeds the work very freely, and if too freely used will cause it to thicken and grow smutty.
D. *Strong ink* leaves the roller with difficulty, and necessitates slow and laborious rolling.

From a study of the foregoing, the two following may be arrived at as being the combined effects of a certain state of the ink and mode of using the roller :—

Slow, heavy rolling with *thin* ink will produce the maximum effect that can be obtained under similar conditions of temperature. And—

Quick, light rolling with *strong* ink will have the greatest possible tendency to bring the ink away from the stone.

118. TEMPERATURE is also an important consideration to the printer. If the weather or the printing-room be too warm, his ink will practically become thinner. If the heat is caused by a fire in the room, that of course may be removed. But if it be impracticable to remove the source of heat (as in summer), thicker varnish can be used with a similar result. In connection with temperature, there is the fact that the stone dries more quickly in a warm room than in a cool one. This is an annoyance that will be intensified by opening the windows with the view of cooling the printing-room, because the draught from an open window or door will dry the stone still more rapidly. Under these circumstances the stone will get dry before the rolling-in has been completed, necessitating two or more applications of water, when under more favourable conditions one wetting would have sufficed.

To obviate these defects, the printer may add some substance to the water used for wetting the stone that retard its evaporation. Sour beer is a very favourite remedy, as, besides not drying so quickly, it possesses a slight etching quality that tends to keep the work clean ; but it must be used with judgment, especially in connection with very minute lines or dots. Glycerine, golden syrup, neutral salts having a deliquescent tendency, &c., have been used with varying degrees of success for the same purpose ; but in using any of them it will be necessary to wash the damping-cloth or sponge more frequently than is required when simple water is used. It may be remarked that the use of these substances is rarely requisite in ordinary black printing, but in colour-work they are frequently resorted to.

119. PAPER.—The choice of Paper is a very important matter in lithographic printing, if the beauty of the work is of any consideration. It is a subject upon which much ignorance exists generally, as every lithographic printer must admit. The clerk or other person who receives the order from the customer, not knowing any better, is quite willing to execute it upon any proposed paper. He is probably afraid to suggest to the customer that writing-paper is not a fit material upon which to execute any kind of printing. He takes so many orders for letter and account headings on it that it does not occur to him that

there is no necessity for adopting writing papers when nothing has to be written. Most circular letters for business purposes would print better and cleaner upon *glazed* printing paper or half-sized plate paper than upon writing paper.

These papers may be obtained of beautiful surfaces at the present day, and we cannot think any customer would object to them for the purposes named, if this superiority were pointed out.

Supposing their *surfaces to be equal* and printed dry, the following papers are arranged in the order of their printing qualities, the best being first upon the list :—*India paper, plate paper, half-sized plate paper, fine printing paper, common printing paper* (containing more size and earthy matter), *common writing paper, best writing paper* (machine made), *hand-made writing, loan, and drawing papers.* Enamel and other surface-papers are not here enumerated, because they are selected not for their printing qualities but for their adaptability to fancy purposes ; exception, however, must be made in favour of a dead enamel paper which is specially manufactured for yielding fine impressions.

It will only be necessary to point out the variety of materials used in sizing papers to show that their influence is sometimes positively inimical to perfect lithographic printing. In various recipes we find mention of potash, soda, soap, resin, alum, gelatine, starch, &c. It is thus clear that the printer will, when he is permitted, do well to select the paper containing the minimum of sizing matter. In selecting one of two papers he may choose that which most rapidly absorbs the moisture from his tongue ; for, by wetting the two samples equally, and then holding them obliquely to the light, he will find that the hardest-sized sample will retain the moisture longer than the other.

120. DAMPING paper is not so necessary an operation now as formerly. It is resorted to for the purpose of modifying the resistance to pressure, and enabling the printer to bring the paper into closer contact with the work. The extended use of steam-driven paper-glazing machines has rendered the damping of paper less necessary, because paper can now be obtained, even in common printing qualities, with so fine a face that it requires but little pressure to bring it

into intimate connection with the drawing or writing.   As, however, circumstances may render the damping of paper necessary, the mode is here given.

To be able to damp paper properly is an acquirement to be gained only by experience.   The quantity of size contained in the paper, and the thickness of the sheets, are the chief matters that influence the result.   Papers may either be damped with a sponge or dipped in water.   The sponge is apt to disturb the surface of plate-papers, and must be used in such a manner as not to go over the same part twice.   If the paper is to be dipped, several sheets must be taken and dipped at a time, to save trouble.   Whether dipped or sponged, the paper is to be set up as evenly as possible in a heap and have a weight placed upon it, so that the humidity may be equally distributed throughout the mass.   When this appears to be effected, the paper will probably present a " cockled " appearance, to remove which the paper should be separated into small sections, and stroked and struck with the hand ; or the paper may be struck on a board, piled in a heap again, and put under a weight again until required.   Be cautious in leaving paper too long in damp in summer-time, or it may become mildewed.

In damping large-sized plate-papers they will not admit of being immersed, as their own weight would then be the cause of tearing them when held by the ends.   They are best damped by sprinkling.   Loan and drawing papers should not be placed under a weight until time has been allowed for expansion.   After an hour's standing in small heaps they may be beaten with the hand and then put under a weight, care being taken to prevent drying on the sides of the heap.

121. PREPARING INDIA PAPER FOR PRINTING.—There is an imitation of India paper that is free from the spots and blemishes of the genuine paper, and though it does not yield so good an impression, its freedom from specks is a great recommendation.   To both kinds of paper the following instructions will apply :—

Take the India paper in full-sized sheet, and brush over the back with rather thin flour paste, and hang it up to dry. Damp the plate-paper in the manner described in paragraph 119.   Cut up the India paper carefully to the size required, and put a piece between each two sheets of plate-paper—*i. e.* one piece for each. The India paper should be about half an inch or more larger each way than the work to be printed upon. The larger the work, the more margin will be wanted. Make a mark upon the stone to correspond with the size of the plate-paper, and another to agree with that of the India paper. When printing, first lay down the India paper *pasted side up,* and upon it the plate-paper ; the paste, being damp, will be found to adhere firmly to the plate-paper, which is always slightly damped, after being submitted to the pressure of printing. It will be seen that this is a combined method of printing and mounting at the same time. In like manner photographs may be mounted, where there are many of them to be done.

CHAPTER XV.

Printing (*continued*).—Defects and Remedies—Advice—Slurring—Setting-off—Proving Chalk-Drawings—Unequal Etching—Soft-backing.

DEFECTS AND REMEDIES. PRINTING.—122. We have digressed to a slight degree, but only to indicate those conditions which more or less influence the result ; and it will now be our duty, aided by the principles we have been considering, to show how certain defects which may appear in the proof may be remedied, if that be possible.

DEFECTS.	REMEDIES.
A. The proof does not appear so firm as the drawing on the stone, yet the ink looks black upon the paper.	Increase the pressure.
B. The print looks altogether too dark.	There is either too much ink on the roller, or it has been rolled in by too heavy pressure, or the roller worked too slowly. The paper, if smooth and hard, may print

C. The impression though firm is pale.

D. White streaks occur in the whole length of the proof.

E. The impression is always too light at one end.

F. The impression has one or more light places that do not show on the stone.

better with less impression, or the ink may be too thin. These observations suggest the remedy.

There may be insufficient ink on the roller. It may also be too thin. The roller may have become covered with gum, or have accumulated a film of dirt from long use without change of ink. Try a good "knocking-up" on the ink-slab, and, if that does not cure it, scrape off the old ink and apply some more. This defect may also proceed from rolling too quickly and lightly.

The scraper is notched or otherwise uneven. Make it level with coarse cabinet-paper or a plane.

There is a deficiency of pressure there: pack the stone at that end.

The stone is hollow, or the tympan or backing-sheet thin at such places. Try a piece of blanket for the backing, and if that is not successful, paste small pieces of paper on the backing-sheet or tympan where it occurs. To do this properly, *tear* the paper into shape; paste or gum one side; lay it on the stone where required, adhesive side up; bring the tympan down upon it, when the paper will be attached at the defective place.

G. The drawing is missing or has failed to print at one end.

The scraper has been set too far on the tympan, or not pulled far enough.

H. Notwithstanding all precautions the drawing yields only pale impressions.

This can only occur when the paper is too wet. It usually occurs when the paper is not only too wet, but also highly sized.

I. The paper tears, and is partly left upon the stone.

This commonly occurs with plate-paper when it is imperfectly damped. Give it more time to lie by. If that will not do, use a thinner ink, as that can be used on plate-paper with success, because each impression clears the stone.

The impression being, it is hoped, what it should be, the printing may be proceeded with. For each pull the stone must be first damped, and then inked; but in these two operations defects may occur which attract the printer's notice before he takes the impression.

J. On the rolling in being r e c o m m e n c e d, black patches may occur.

The stone has not been damped at these parts. Damp again properly; roll briskly and they will go away.

K. After rolling several times the ink begins to "catch" as before.

The stone has become too dry. It may arise either from too long - continued rolling without redamping, or the temperature of the room being too high. Remedy as in the last case.

L. The roller does not turn in the handles, but slips over the work.

The stone is too wet.

M. As the printing proceeds, the close lines or dots join together, or the work becomes darker all over.

The ink is too thin. Wash out with turpentine and a little oil, but be careful to have the stone quite wet at the same time. Roll in again with an ink made stiffer by having less varnish in it, or one of a stronger nature. Gum in and let it lie by for a day or two if possible. This defect is more likely to occur with hard papers.

N. The drawing grows thin and pale.

The roller may have become dirty,—see case C,—or the ink may be too stiff, in which case use thinner ink.

123. ADVICE TO BEGINNERS.—In summer, use medium varnish to reduce your ink ; in winter, add a little thin varnish to it. This will make the printing more slow than the use of thinner ink, but you will be enabled to print without running the risks attendant upon the latter, which you may use with greater confidence when you have mastered the use of the thicker.

Avoid wetting the stone too much at a time, or the roller will not only be liable to slip, but will become so glazed as not to ink properly until it has been "knocked-up" on the slab again, in doing which repeat the operation until the ink is felt to adhere to the roller.

After proper damping, count the number of times that the roller can be passed over the stone before it begins to soil it, then in your printing do not make so many passes by, say, two. This will insure you against too much rolling.

When the roller begins to make an audible sound in going over the work, it is a sign that it is time to leave off rolling. Another stroke or two would soil the stone.

Having inked your work, "knock up" the roller ready for the next inking before taking the impression. This will allow the stone to dry a little, which is an advantage in printing glazed writing-paper. A wet stone deteriorates the polish.

Be careful to keep the edges of the stone clean, avoiding rolling over them if possible. If they are once allowed to soil the backing-sheet, it will be difficult to prevent the edges from becoming again dirty. The edges may be sponged occasionally with gum and acid, and if necessary they must be polished again.

Work with as little ink on your roller as is consistent with obtaining a good impression. Too much ink is apt to produce ragged lines, and to aggravate " slurring," besides the more obvious result of too great blackness of general effect.

The beginner will find it useful to touch the stone occasionally with the gum-sponge, to assist in preserving the coating of gum upon it. In using it, however, for a long number of impressions, the cloth must be occasionally washed to remove what has accumulated in it, so as to prevent as much as possible its mixing with the ink upon the roller, for if that happens, the roller will cease to ink properly, and will require scraping.

Keep separate sponges for gum, weak acid, and wetting the stone. Let them vary sufficiently in size, so as to be readily distinguishable from each other, which will lessen the liability to accident, in mistaking, for instance, the "acid sponge" for the " gum-sponge." Keep also another good-sized sponge for use with perfectly clean water only. This will be useful when washing a stone previously to making corrections.

Have a place for everything, and keep everything in its place, so that you may be able to put your hand upon what you require at a moment's notice. This is not unfrequently of the utmost importance.

124. By " SLURRING " is understood a doubling of the lines or dots composing the impression at some part of it. It is usually found at or about that part of the proof which last received the pressure, and may proceed from one of several causes, though its immediate cause is always the same—namely, the shifting of the paper between the time of its being placed upon the stone and its passage under the scraper. It will happen when the paper is not sufficiently flat, and can then scarcely be avoided. The paper may sometimes be prevented from moving by placing the hand upon it immediately it is laid upon the stone, as it will then adhere to the ink if there be sufficient breadth of it to hold it until the tympan is brought down. At other times it may be obviated by placing a small block

of wood to receive the end of the tympan-frame in such a manner that the tympan does not rest upon the stone until the scraper is brought to bear upon it. The printer must form his own judgment as to which cause the defect owes its origin.

125. " SETTING-OFF " is a transferring of some of the ink before it is dry to the back of the paper of the impression lying next to it. It ought to be avoided in careful work. It is chiefly owing to one of two causes : first, the hardness of the paper, and second, to the use of ink unsuited to the paper. Hard, smooth writing-papers are very liable to it. When the copies are placed one above another until a heap is formed, the under ones receive most pressure and are more liable to the defect. Black printing-ink dries very slowly, but the printer does not like to use dryers in it, because it necessitates the use of some solvent for removing it effectually from his roller, the frequent use of which deteriorates that instrument very materially. The turpentine used, and the amount of time involved in washing the roller, are, of course, items that cost the employer something, so that it is usual to put such works into small heaps, to lessen the weight upon the bottom impressions and to give them more time to dry.

It frequently happens, however, that circulars and other work are wanted for immediate use. The customer may be accommodated at a trifling extra expense, by the application of powdered French chalk.* It is to be applied with a small pad of cotton wool, first dipped into the powder and then rubbed over the impressions, after which they may be handled and folded with impunity. The French chalk being semitransparent, the colour of the ink is reduced in only a slight degree ; and for this reason, and that of its not imparting any unpleasant grittiness to the paper, is preferred to other substances, which—such as *magnesia*— may be used for the same purpose. While upon this subject we may inform the student that a similar use may be made of this material when proving chromo-lithographic work to prevent the last-applied colour " setting off " on the stone.

* This is the common name of the mineral *steatite*, a variety of talc, of granular structure and soapy feel ; hence it is frequently called *soap-stone*.

"Setting-off" also occurs when both sides of the paper have to be printed, unless that which was first done has become quite dry, for which time should be allowed if possible. The "set-off" is found upon the backing-sheet, and when the ink is partially dry may at first very little re-set-off on the work now being "backed," but it soon accumulates and shows upon all the subsequently printed sheets. This may sometimes be avoided by oiling the backing-board and then rubbing as much off as can be removed with a clean cloth. The backing-board thus loses in a very great degree its power of absorbing the ink, because the pores are already closed by the oil. When it is necessary to print on both sides of the sheet in quick succession, a piece of tissue, or other thin smooth paper, must be laid on at each impression, and this paper, if kept, will answer for many similar jobs if time be allowed for it to become dry. When hard, smooth paper is the material which has to be printed on each side, and no time is allowed for drying, the first printing should be rather darker than the second, so as to make allowance for what will be removed by the tissue-paper.

126. PRINTING CHALK DRAWINGS.—If the student has mastered the theory of the inks and varnishes, and applied them in the practice of printing from ink drawings, he will now be able to take in hand printing from a chalk drawing. There are some differences between the ink and chalk printing, which it will be well to point out before proceeding with the instructions for printing. In the first place, the stone being granulated, the dots whose aggregation make up the drawing, do not lie in one plane. This necessitates the use of a roller having sufficient "nap" to reach the bottom of the grain. 2. The grained surface also disposes the stone to remain longer damp than does a polished one. 3. The rough stone so rapidly wears away a damping-cloth that two sponges must be used, one to apply the water, and the other to spread it. (See the second note to par. 116.)*

---

* Where an assistant is employed at the press, it seems to us that a roller similar to the inking roller, but covered with a suitable material, might be used for damping the stone, as is done in machine printing. We think a boy with a little practice would thus damp more evenly

I

4. Stronger ink and more rolling will be necessary in chalk printing. 5. The drawing consisting of an innumerable quantity of points or dots frequently touching each other, is more liable to become smutty than work of a more open character, as are the majority of ink drawings. 6. The chalk with which the drawing is made contains a larger proportion of soap than is used in ink. This necessitates the use of acid in preparing the drawing for the press, and if this be imperfectly done, the drawing is very liable to run " smutty " in printing. If the printer will bear these differences in mind, he will more readily conquer the peculiar difficulties of chalk printing. After all, the most important qualification for a chalk printer is to have a good eye for pictorial effect. There are many printers who scarcely know a good impression from a bad one, whose chief guide, in fact, is to avoid blackness and greyness, and who have no appreciation whatever of the principles that guided the artist in the production of the drawing. A good chalk printer will usually be found to be a man who is fond of pictures, and can probably draw a little himself. Such a person is more likely to produce good prints than a mere mechanic, whose chief ambition is to draw his wages at the end of the week.

Taking the first-proofs from a chalk drawing is an operation of great delicacy and importance, as affecting the quality of the after-prints; and it is an axiom among printers that the particles of chalk composing the drawing require to be removed as early in the printing as otherwise convenient, so as to get rid, as soon as may be, of any superfluous soap which may not have been decomposed in the etching process. Two methods are in use for effecting this object; but as each in the hands of good printers yields equally good results, it is to be presumed that more depends upon the workman than upon the process he employs.

The first way to be described would seem, if there is any real difference, to be that most fitted for delicate drawing. After a good soaking, and carefully removing the surface gum, the stone is to be rolled in with ink of medium

---

than by the use of a sponge. The drawing would suffer less abrasion, and would probably yield a greater number of impressions.

tenacity. If too thin, the dark parts will ink up too fast, and if too strong, the delicate light tints may nearly disappear. If the roller and slab have been newly cleaned, very little ink will be required. Keep as much gum upon the stone as is consistent with the proper working of the roller, and damp and ink up about three times. Take now an impression upon thin, dry plate-paper, and if the operations have been properly managed, the proof will yet be too light; but may be expected to consist partly of the chalk that was upon the stone. Repeat this for several impressions, during which the proofs should become gradually darker by the substitution of printing-ink for chalk, until at last the drawing looks about the same upon the paper as it did upon the stone when it left the hands of the artist; making due allowance for the difference between the colour of the paper and that of the stone. This change from the stone to white paper is often the cause of great disappointment to the inexperienced or amateur lithographer; and the printer should, if possible, submit to him a proof upon paper as near the colour of the stone as convenient. Again, there is not only a difference in the colour, but the granulation of the paper is reversed to that of the stone. On the stone the drawing was on the *tips* of the grain, and the hollows between helped to soften the shade; while on the paper the ink is in hollows caused by the pressure of the same points upon it, and the un-inked portion of the paper is in relief, and catches the light. The paper-impression, from these causes, always seems less satisfactory than the appearance of the drawing on the stone would lead an inexperienced person to expect.

The other method of removing the chalk is not only a more direct one, but much to be preferred when it includes very dark masses of drawing. After the stone has in the soaking process well absorbed water, a little turpentine is put upon a *soft* rag or sponge, or sprinkled upon the damp stone, and the rag applied to it with a light circular motion until the chalk is removed. Put some more clean water upon the stone, and wipe it and the turpentine off together. The drawing will now appear of a grey colour; or will even appear to have gone away if much turpentine has been used. Now use the sponges as before, and roll up gently, endeavouring to keep a little gum upon the stone; in doing which be careful that the gum is not sour, as the drawing may be easily injured until it has fully received the printing-ink. There will be no need for taking an impression until the drawing resumes the appearance it had before it was washed out.

By the careful use of strong ink, good proofs may be taken, even if the drawing has not been properly etched ; but it is likely that it will show an early tendency to run "smutty" from this cause, and the printer will do well in correcting the error, by —

127. RE-ETCHING.—It must be understood by the young printer that when the chalk has been once removed, the print-ing-ink alone has less power to resist the action of acids than the chalk had, and requires some protection, previous to the renewed acidulation of the stone. Inks containing copal-varnish, asphaltum, and similar substances, might be used for this purpose ; but an effectual and simple method, which does not involve the use of another roller, consists in *dusting* powdered rosin over the work after rolling-in, and permitting the stone to dry (see paragraphs 52 and 113). In the absence of powdered rosin, common bronze-powder may be used, but it is not so resistive of the acid, and more resistive of the turpentine in the subsequent process of washing-out ; for which reason it is less to be recommended than the powdered rosin. After the application of the rosin, let the stone remain a little while before applying the acid and water, which may be done in any of the ways described in the chapter on Etching, or in the more "rough and ready" mode generally adopted by printers, with a sponge. The stone having been gummed-in and dried, the rosin is afterwards washed away by spirits of turpentine, as described in par. 126, and the work rolled-in as before. It should now be, in the hands of an expe-rienced printer, in a condition to print properly and cleanly.

128. DEFECTS SOMETIMES ARISE FROM UNEQUAL ETCH-ING, and show themselves in printing as darker spots and patches than the surrounding parts, which were even enough when the drawing left the hands of the artist.

These can only be remedied by etching the parts that are darker, and so bring them to a level tone with the rest, by the application of a camel-hair pencil containing dilute acid, and immediately wiping away the acid with a sponge to prevent its acting further than intended. With a little care, and dexterity in the application of the acid to the exact spot required, this kind of defect may be much improved if not entirely removed. The acid must be quite weak, or injury may result, as its effect is not immediately visible. When the roller is passed briskly over this part, it will remove the ink in proportion to the effect produced by the acid; and by this operation the printer will be able to judge whether the part has been sufficiently etched, and can repeat it until the desired result is gained, after which the part should be gummed and permitted to dry.

129. DEFECTS ARISING FROM OVER-ETCHING.—When the drawing has had too much acid applied in the etching process, the light tints are perhaps so reduced that the drawing has a worn-out appearance, as if a very large number of impressions had been taken from it. Most printers have their own pet way of improving such defect, though sometimes they succeed in quite spoiling the work in the attempt to make it better. We cannot, therefore, give any infallible information on this subject, and will be content to point out some of the methods in use and the principles upon which they are based. The broad principle upon which all these methods are founded is, that the chalk was not entirely removed, but only its hold upon the stone weakened in the etching process. If it were entirely removed, it is clear that nothing but re-drawing could replace it.

1. This defect may sometimes be cured by using a *small* quantity of *thin* ink upon the roller, which will be found to attach itself to any part that has only a slight tendency to greasiness. If the proofs then appear satisfactory, the printing may be carefully continued until the drawing is re-established upon the stone, after which the strength of the ink may be gradually increased, as may seem necessary. In following out this or any other method having the same object, care must be taken that the dark parts do not become too black.

2. If the printing-ink be replaced by a more fatty substance, the latter will tend to strengthen the work. In practice this is done by damping the stone with gum-water, and applying palm oil, green oil, or a similar substance, upon a piece of flannel, until the printing-ink disappears. The stone must then be damped and inked-up as before. A thin scum of ink will probably be found adhering to the whole surface of the stone; but it may be removed by repeated damping and rolling-up with the printing roller.

3. The ink may sometimes be made to adhere to the weaker parts by spreading a little turpentine on the wet stone and rolling-in. The first effect is to blacken the stone all over; but that gradually disappears if the stone be kept damp, and it becomes clear again.

4. Soap and water shaken into a froth may be applied with a pad, as described for the use of palm oil. It is a powerful and dangerous expedient, and one that should not be attempted by the inexperienced printer.

5. Having got up the drawing as strong as may be required, by one of the foregoing methods, roll-up in thin ink and dust with rosin, as described in re-etching. Wash with warm water; finally remove the gum with perfectly clean very dilute acid, and set aside to dry. The parts that are sufficiently dark must be gummed in with a hair pencil, to prevent their becoming darker. If the stone be now warmed in front of an open fire, the light parts will probably spread a little and thus become stronger. Set the stone aside to become cold, after which it may be gummed, dried, washed out with turps, and rolled-up in the usual way. The principle of this method will be better understood by the student if read in conjunction with the instructions for re-touching in paragraph 97.

These methods of repairing the errors of etching must not be relied upon for producing any very marked improvement, or in any way to compensate for errors of drawing. To be successful, they require to be used with judgment and experience, and these qualities employed in the first etching (if the drawing has been properly done) will usually effect a result in which no repairing will be subsequently needed.

If the principles laid down for the use of the roller

and printing-ink be well mastered, they will apply equally to printing any kind of drawing, and we shall consequently not have to repeat what has already been said in regard to printing generally.

In addition to the differences mentioned in the beginning of paragraph 126, it may be added that the backing-sheet should be an elastic one ; and that recommended for transferring—viz. a piece of fine printer's blanket fastened on cardboard, will answer admirably. In default of such a one, two or more sheets of plate-paper will serve the purpose.

If the paper to be printed be a thick plate-paper, the elasticity of the backing will be of less importance, because the paper itself will possess sufficient body, under the influence of the pressure, to enter the grain of the stone.

It is believed that this chapter contains all the instructions concerning plain printing from stone that can be conveyed to the student in words ; and we pass on to another chapter, in which will be given various auxiliary processes relating more or less to the subject of chromolithography, but to which it does not necessarily belong.

CHAPTER XVI.

Miscellaneous Processes—Tracing from Photographs, Pictures, &c.—
Key-stones for Colour-work—Autographic Transfers—Reversing
Transfers—Transposition of Black and White—Other Methods.

WITH a view to avoiding confusion in the treatment of our subject, we here refer to a few processes which do not frequently come within ordinary practice, but which, nevertheless, should be understood, on account of their occasional usefulness. Some of them might have been included in a previous chapter, but it has been thought best to allot them a separate one.

130. TRACING PHOTOGRAPHS AND OTHER SUBJECTS OF INDISTINCT OUTLINE.—It often happens that the lithographer requires an outline tracing of a subject which, though tolerably clear in itself, becomes very confused when seen through the ordinary tracing-paper. There are several methods of overcoming this difficulty.

I.—Very transparent tracing-paper may be made by coating fine *tissue*-paper with crystal varnish. Coat it on one side, and let it dry, and then coat it on the other. The varnish may be made by adding spirits of turpentine to Canada balsam until thin enough to be used with a varnish-brush, the solution being effected with a gentle heat.

II.—French tracing-paper, *papier végétal*, may be oiled, to render it more transparent; but care must be taken to avoid bringing the oiled surface in contact with the stone or transfer-paper.

III.—Ordinary tracing or other thin paper may be wetted with spirits of turpentine or benzoline, and the wetted side applied to the glass or paper photograph. The tracing may then be made in pencil The liquid will soon evaporate; but if the paper becomes opaque in consequence, a corner may be lifted and another drop of the fluid introduced, which will instantly restore the transparency. When the tracing is completed, it and the photograph will dry rapidly, and the latter will remain uninjured.

IV.—Sheets of transparent gelatine may be laid over photographs or paintings, and the tracing made by scratching the outline with a sharp steel point. The scratches thus made are to be filled with powdered red chalk, dusted on with cotton wool : the scratches being rough, retain the powder, which is rejected by the smooth surface of the gelatine. If the gelatine, thus prepared, be laid upon a stone and passed through the press, a red chalk tracing will be left upon the stone. The scratches may also be filled in with lithographic writing-ink, dissolved in spirits of turpentine, wiping it clean off the smooth part of the gelatine. This being laid upon the stone as before, and subjected to pressure, will leave an ink outline that may be rolled up as an ordinary transfer. Or the gelatine may be treated, after filling-in with ink, as an ordinary transfer, by damping it between sheets, applying it to a warm stone, passing through the press, and finally washing it off with hot water. It requires a very slight etching before rolling-up.

V.—If the photograph to be traced is of no further value than furnishing a copy for the draughtsman, it may be treated in the following manner :—With india-rubber, paper-cleaner, or ink-eraser, remove from the surface of the photograph all tendency to greasiness ; outline every detail with lithographic writing-ink, which, after the cleaning referred to, will adhere readily to the photograph, treating it as far as possible as a sheet of transfer-paper. Set a stone in the press, and make ready as for ordinary transferring ; pour spirits of turpentine upon the stone, and spread the spirits all over. Let it stand a few seconds to be absorbed With one stroke of the squeegee (par. 56) remove the superfluous turpentine. Now quickly lay the inked-in photograph upon the stone, lower the tympan, and pass once through the press, under heavy pressure. The stone having been uniformly damped with the turpentine, the latter acts equally in softening the ink, which is then absorbed by the stone. If there should be too much turpentine, the ink will spread ; and if too little (which may happen if the stone is allowed to dry somewhat before the photograph is laid upon it), sufficient ink may not be absorbed to roll up. However, with ordinary care on the part of the draughtsman and the printer, success is certain. The stone having been gummed and rolled up, impressions may be taken. If a key-stone be wanted for colour-work, nothing but the register-marks will require to be added ; but as that subject will be fully treated further on, we say no more about it in this place.

We have successfully used this method in obtaining a correct outline for an architectural subject in chalk. Having obtained a slightly grey impression on *printing*-paper, we put it, face downwards, on the grained stone and passed it through the press, which then gave a faint set-off. The small quantity of grease thus added to the stone was removed by the etching after the drawing was finished, and was found to give no trouble whatever.

As, however, some might prefer a red chalk outline, we may state that it can easily be obtained as follows. Instead of taking a weak impression on printing-paper, take a full one on highly-sized and glazed writing-paper ; place upon it a quantity of finely-powdered red chalk ; holding the paper by opposite edges, raise and lower each hand alternately, until the chalk has been brought into contact with every part of the outline ; pour off the superfluous chalk, and finish by giving it a smart jerk or two to remove the remainder from all parts except the lines. The prepared print may then be laid upon the stone and passed through the press, as before described. This method is very applicable for drawings in ink.

This method of transferring to stone for the purpose of obtaining a mere faint tracing for a guide in the actual drawing, may appear more complicated than the ordinary tracing and retracing; but where the details are minute and numerous, it will be found that time is saved by its adoption; while the artist, being saved the drudgery of the intermediate operation, will approach his task with better spirit, knowing that a more correct trace is before him than would have been obtained by any other method.

131. AUTOGRAPHIC TRANSFERS BY TURPENTINE.—The method of transferring by means of turpentine, described in the last paragraph, is capable of still wider application. Writings in lithographic ink, and recent impressions from stone and type on plain paper, may be transferred successfully in a similar manner; indeed, we much doubt whether they may not be more certainly and better executed by this method than by the Anastatic process.

132. REVERSING TRANSFERS.—Circumstances sometimes arise in which the lithographer desires to reproduce automatically subjects which involve much labour when executed by hand. Of designs which are repeated, like some kinds of borders, a portion only may be drawn upon the stone or transfer-paper, and be completed by taking retransfers of such portion, mounting them in the manner required upon a piece of paper, and transferring the whole to the stone, when any defects may be remedied by the methods we described when treating of *corrections*. It sometimes happens, however, that the design is of such a character as not to contain elements that are often repeated, but which require a duplicate in reverse, in regard to right and left. The design may be an ornamental one, involving much intricate drawing, and the artist may be desirous of avoiding the tracing, retracing, and drawing that would be necessary to repeat the design for the other half of the border. The printer may sometimes save him this trouble by the following process.

Take a transfer from half of the design, and lay that upon another piece of transfer-paper, face to face, and pass it through the press so as to obtain a set-off upon the second piece of transfer-paper. A reverse will be obtained, and the two, being properly cut and mounted in position upon another piece of paper, may be transferred to the stone and the border completed. This process will be found very applicable to borders of show-cards, almanacks, &c.

133. TRANSPOSITION OF BLACK AND WHITE.— It is sometimes desirable to be able to change dark letters, &c., on a light ground to light letters on a dark ground. This will be found of great advantage in some kinds of colour-printing, as in the instance of printing in bronze or silver on dark glazed paper. It may be accomplished by either of the methods following, giving preference to them in the order they are placed.

I.—If the subject be a copperplate engraving, the transfer-ink or letterpress printing-ink may be applied directly to its surface by means of a letterpress-roller, using it lightly and with as little ink as will answer the purpose of transferring. The impression may be taken at the lithographic press, but instead of laying a soft material at the back of the transfer-paper, a piece of very smooth cardboard should be used. If this is properly done, there will be no difficulty in transferring it by one of the methods hereinbefore described.

II.—In this system, any subject that can be printed from a polished stone may be changed from a light ground to a dark one, or *vice versâ*. The subject having been protected by rosin (paragraphs 52, 113, 127), is to be acidulated until it stands perceptibly in relief, the thickness of the resinous coating being allowed for. Wash the ink, &c., away with turpentine, and the whole stone quite clean with water, using clean water, containing about one per cent. of acid, for the final wash. The stone having become dry, cover the work to the extent desired for the ground with lithographic writing-ink, which must be permitted to dry, when the whole may be rolled up in printing-ink. This covering with lithographic ink may, if the operator wishes, be done after the etching operation, allowing the stone to dry. The work and the ground being now equally black, the ink has to be removed from the parts in relief, so that they may be reversed from black to white. Take a piece of snake-stone, make it quite flat by rubbing it upon the margin of the stone; then polish away the surface of the raised portion until the design becomes quite clear. If any part of the ground should be accidentally damaged, it must be touched up with lithographic ink to repair it. Gum the stone, dry, and roll up. It may be again rosined and etched, in the same way as before, if it is thought worth while, to reduce the parts in relief to the level of the ground. Many examples of this kind of work will be found among labels and show-cards,—the uninitiated sometimes thinking they are printed in white, more especially when the sample has first been set up in type.

III.—If an impression of the subject to be transposed be taken in a strong ink, it may be dusted over with finely-powdered dry gum-arabic, or with dextrine, which may subsequently be placed in a damp place until they become sticky. In this state they may be laid face downwards on a damp stone, and the gummy coating transferred to the stone. The margin may now be protected by gumming it round to the shape and drying it. If a roller with greasy ink be applied to the dry stone, it will be covered all over; but on subsequently washing with water, the ink will come away where the stone was protected by the gummy covering transferred to it from the design.

IV.—At least partial success may be obtained by gum-ming the stone all over, drying it, washing it off, and again drying. The transfer in greasy ink is now to be made with care. A *very* weak etching-water must next be applied to clear the stone of gum only, with the exception of that lying under the design. Dry again, and roll in with printing-ink. If the stone be now damped and rolled in with very stiff ink, the parts of the design where the gum was not etched away will probably yield the ink of the transfer and become white, which may then be kept pure and open by another application of the etching-water.

V.—A process similar to the last is the following :— Apply to the surface of the stone a solution of silicate of potash (commonly known as water-glass) ; make the trans-fer; dust with powder rosin, and remove the water-glass with a solution of alum ; ink in, and proceed as before described.

VI.—*Transposition* may be effected by photo-lithography

(*q.v.*).   Take a piece of sensitized photolithographic paper, print the design upon it, and dust it with bronze powder, to make it more impenetrable to the action of light; expose it to light, and treat it as a photographic transfer.

Without any pretence of having exhausted all the methods that are *possible*, it has been shown that Transposition may be conducted on at least six different principles, the fourth and last methods being known only to a few.

CHAPTER XVII.

Miscellaneous Processes (*continued*)—Making-up Labels—Bronzing— Gilding—Dusting—Dabbing Style—Remarks.

MAKING-UP SHEETS OF LABELS, &c.—134. Having determined upon the size of the sheet, or portion of the sheet, upon which it is proposed to print, it must be set out with a pair of dividers, and ruled with pencil into as many squares, oblongs, or other shapes as are to be printed at one time.   By the method already described for taking transfers, pull as many transfers as required, taking notice that each one is good enough for the purpose.   Trim them round neatly with a pair of scissors, a little within the size of the space marked on the paper, holding them in such a manner as not in any way to soil them.   With a small stiff brush, or other convenient instrument, lay a little thick paste at the corners of the spaces marked, and carefully lay the transfer upon it, sliding it or shifting it into position by the help of a pointed penknife, or any similar tool, using the same to press the transfer upon the pasted portion of the paper, so as to maintain it in place.   See that it is right by the help of a straightedge or parallel ruler, and proceed to the next transfer ; and so on until all are done.   When the pieces to be handled are very small, and have comparatively no margin, a pair of spring forceps, such as are used by watchmakers, will be found very convenient in laying the little pieces in position.

When much of this kind of work has to be done, the following simple piece of apparatus will be found very convenient.   Let an ordinary drawing-board be fitted up with a bridge, similar to the hand-board described in paragraph 31, and in such a manner that the transfers and the paper can be just moved about underneath it without being injured. This will be found more convenient than a loose straightedge or parallel ruler, because the paper may be adjusted under the fixed guide without rubbing the transfers, and notice can be taken whether the border line, or any particular line of lettering, corresponds with the pencil line upon the paper.

It is necessary to arrange the transfers in this exact manner, in order that they may run in lines fit for cutting at a machine. Where different sizes of labels are put upon the same sheet, they must be so arranged that they can be divided straight across or down the sheet at intervals, and these strips be cut across again, and so on, until all are cut.

The sheet when complete and dry must be put to damp in the damping-book mentioned in the chapter on Transferring; but if the paper be of such a nature as not to become " sticky " without remaining there a long time, the stone may be damped, as well as the sheet of transfers. Damping the back with a sponge is of no use in this case until the transfers are upon the stone.

In printing labels, every care must be taken in laying the sheet exactly to the mark, so that when carefully " knocked up" they may be exactly over each other. Sometimes the sheet has a cross or other mark printed at each end of it, which forms a guide to *thread* the sheets on two fine wires, so as to get them in exact position.

The subject of " sticking up " coloured labels will, however, be treated of in the chapter devoted to Chromolithography.

135. BRONZING, DUSTING, and METALLING, though more usually connected with colour-printing, will be described in this place, because they are often required unaccompanied with other colours.

The principle of the operation is very simple. An impression having been taken in a suitable adhesive ink, the bronze powder, silver or gold powder, or dust-colour, is applied to the wet ink by means of a pad of cotton wool, proportioned in size to the space to be covered, the superfluous powder being afterwards removed by a soft cloth.

When dry, much brilliancy may be added by rolling the impression on a finely-polished metal plate.

In selecting a paper for this work, regard must first of all be had to the purpose it is intended for. Writing-paper answers very well, because it is, when good, sufficiently sized as not to absorb the ink, and consequently enough of the ink is left upon the surface to retain the powder. Enamelled and plate papers, having an absorbent ground, require more and stronger ink, so that at least some may remain on the surface.

The ink is sometimes of essential importance, though at other times almost anything seems to answer the purpose in a more or less efficient manner. If work be wanted in a hurry, and only a few impressions required, a strong, quick-drying varnish may be added to the ink already upon the slab. A mixture of Canada balsam and copal varnish, or some japanner's gold size, may be used for this purpose. Most colour-printers have a favourite ink of their own for this kind of printing, and no doubt there are many equally good compositions in use ; and where so many answer the purpose it would savour of some conceit on our part to attempt to point out the *best*. The ink should dry quickly, but not so fast as to be a hindrance to the manipulation of the roller, and should be sufficiently adhesive to hold the powder or metal firmly. A preparation answering these conditions may be bought of the printing-ink manufacturer, but for the benefit of those who would like to prepare their own, we give the recipe :—

Middle varnish .... 2 parts.
White wax 1   ,,
Venice turpentine 1   ,,
Patent or other dryers .... q. s.
Burnt umber, or similar pigment .... q. s.

The whole to be ground together to form a dark brown ink, which is found to be about the best colour for the gold ground. If the ink be required for dusting a colour upon it, a suitable tint must be chosen for the ink ; for example, a light blue ink would answer for dusting a blue or green. Many printers grind up a tablespoonful each of stiff flour paste and bookbinders' glue in a pound of ink made with middle varnish, and find it answer their purpose remarkably well. The principles underlying the composition of this ink having been indicated, its composition may be safely left in the hands of the intelligent printer.

Metal is, of course, applied differently to the powders. Dutch metal, Planier metal; and Lane's metal may be brought to a suitable size by cutting through the *book* which holds it. The "laying-on" is performed by a boy, who, removing the printed sheet to a convenient table, takes the book or part-book of metal and lays it upon his left hand, with its joint towards the right; folding back the thin upper paper, he turns it under the book, thus exposing the leaf of metal. Taking the joint of the book between the thumb and finger of the right hand, he dexterously turns the sheet of metal over into its place on the printed sheet. This is repeated until as much as required is applied, by which time the printer will be ready for passing the next sheet through the press. The boy now lays the newly-metalled sheet upon the back of the one about to be printed, and both go through the press together, which brings the metal into perfect contact with the ink. The metalled sheet is now set aside to dry, and the new one treated as already described. When all are dry, as they will be in a day or two, the superfluous metal may be rubbed away with an old silk handkerchief, or other suitable duster. It may be well to mention that this process is unsuitable for work having fine detail, for which the bronze powders, subsequently rolled, will be found to answer better.

Real gold-leaf is more difficult to handle, and, being so exceedingly thin, cannot be applied immediately after printing without the ink coming through; consequently some time must be allowed to elapse between printing and gilding. The recipe containing the wax will be found useful for this purpose. We would recommend those who have not had experience in manipulating leaf-gold to use those books wherein the gold is slightly adherent to one side of the paper, which it easily leaves when presented to a more adhesive surface. There is also a thicker gold in use among illuminators which may be found useful in the best lithographic work. The following is the method employed among gilders for applying the gold :—

The tools are—a CUSHION, TIP, KNIFE, DABBER, and

SOFTENER. The CUSHION is a kind of wooden palette, about 9 by 6 inches, covered with smooth leather, stuffed with wool. The TIP is a peculiar kind of brush, consisting of a thin line of badger's hair placed between two pieces of cardboard. The KNIFE is similar in appearance to a palette-knife, and is made to cut along one edge only. The DABBER is a tuft of cotton wool covered with some very thin silk. The SOFTENER is a long-haired brush, used to remove the superfluous gold.

The manipulation is as follows : The leaf of gold is first removed from the book, and laid upon the cushion by means of the knife, which alone must touch it. This operation requires some experience in order that it may be properly performed. A gentle breathing under the leaf should so lift it as to permit of the knife being inserted under it. It is then lifted to the cushion, and flattened upon it by a similar emission of the breath. The gold is divided into strips, squares, or oblongs of suitable size for the work by the aid of the knife. The "tip" being drawn across the gilder's face or hair, and applied to the gold on the cushion, will lift it off. It may then be laid down on the prepared surface, and pressed gently into its place by the dabber. The whole being covered, it is set aside to dry, when the superfluous gold may be removed with the softener.

136. THE DABBING STYLE of Lithography is one of the processes invented by the pioneers of the art, but, from being practised so seldom, an account of it will be new to most readers of this treatise. Its object was to substitute an easier and more mechanical method of producing fine even tints for the laborious process of laying them in with the point of the crayon.

The tools required are very few and simple. Circular pieces of light wood, varying in size from that of a shilling to a half-crown, or larger, about three-eighths of an inch in thickness, are to have a groove turned in their edge. They are then to be covered with fine kid leather, stuffed between it and the wood with cotton wool, so as to make the surface convex, tied round with thread, and the superfluous material cut away. Across the back a light wood handle, six to eight inches long, should be glued, so as to form a kind of light hammer. A clean ink-slab, a grained stone for trials, some fresh gum-water containing a little ox-gall, a stick of the ink whose composition is described in our Appendix, sable pencils, a bottle of oil turpentine, and a small palette-knife, will equip the artist for this kind of work.

Grind up a small portion of the ink with turpentine, put it on one corner of the slab, and clean the rest. The stone for receiving the tint must be a grained one, and must have received the tracing of the work, as in other kinds of drawing. First gum round the margin of the work, and any part that is wished to remain white; and while this is drying prepare the dabbers for use. Take a small portion of ink on the largest dabber, and apply it as evenly as possible over a portion of the ink-slab. On this, charge one of the dabbers that is intended to be used on the drawing; when it is thought to be fit for use, try it upon the trial-stone, and if found to be so, commence laying in the tint, with light taps, going regularly over the surface to be covered, and avoiding striking twice in one place. When the charge of ink is exhausted, it must be renewed in the same manner. Any kind of extraneous matter must be carefully avoided, as must also every unevenness of the ink-charge, otherwise spots and marks will be created. The first tint being satisfactory, the portion that is intended to remain of that strength may be gummed over to preserve it, and the remainder of the work completed in a similar manner to that described for the sprinkled method, in paragraph 83. Defects may be repaired with the needle-point, and lights may be scraped as in chalk-drawing.

French lithographers, in employing this system, use a different set of tools, which give more mastery over it. The tints are laid in with a small india-rubber roller * without seam. This should be charged very carefully, no ink being allowed upon its ends, otherwise lines of ink will be formed upon the stone. The tint having been laid, any part may be graduated by using the ink upon india-rubber stumps of various sizes suitable to the work.

If only one laying of the tint (which, by the way, may

---

* Probably small seamless typographic composition rollers would answer.

be graduated), and no second gumming, be employed, the drawing may be completed by the crayon, after the stone has been set aside to harden the ink. Drawings of this kind will stand scarcely any etching, and require very careful printing.

137. We have now described all the methods of producing lithographs in one colour, in which the application of suitable ink or crayon to the surface of the stone has depended upon the manipulative skill and knowledge of form possessed by the artist. We have also described the various methods of transferring. There still remain to be treated of—1st. *Engraving on Stone*, as completing our subject as far as lithography in one colour; 2nd. *Zincography*, as an application of the principles of lithography to printing from metal plates; 3rd. *Chromolithography*, as an extension of the same principles to printing two or more colours upon one sheet of paper; and 4th. *Photography*, as applied to producing designs suitable for printing direct from the surface of stone or zinc. Our next chapter will therefore be devoted to Engraving on Stone and Printing therefrom.

CHAPTER XVIII.

Engraving on Stone— Tools—Preparation of the Stone, Red and Black—Tracing—Engraving—Corrections and Filling in—Dabbers —The Printing.

ENGRAVING ON STONE may be said to be connected with Lithography only by the chemical nature of the processes of printing; for in every other respect it is an entirely distinct mode of reproduction. We describe it in this place, however, in accordance with our plan of first describing all those manual methods of Lithography in which one colour only is used.

138. ENGRAVING ON STONE is performed by cutting through a film of gum on or in the surface of the stone, and filling up the incised parts with a fatty ink. The printing is performed by a combination of the *dabbing* method of *copperplate* and the *damping* method of *lithographic* printing. Its advantages are — facility of production;

accuracy of drawing; minuteness of detail; and clearness of impression. It is especially applicable to the reproduction of drawings by architects and civil and mechanical engineers when drawn to a small scale; and being performed by tools analagous to those employed by the architect and engineer themselves, errors due to freehand engraving or drawing can be entirely avoided.

139. THE TOOLS.— These will not involve the lithographer in much extra expense, as he may make some of them himself. A diamond point is undoubtedly a very useful instrument, but it is expensive, and will cost as much, perhaps, as all the rest of the tools put together. Added to this, the beginner will find that it requires more practice to use it properly, and will not equal the precision of the steel points about to be described. From a tailors' trimming warehouse, or elsewhere, obtain a packet of strong needles, such as tailors use for sewing on buttons; their cost is about 3d. From a toy-shop procure a common cane, about as thick as an ordinary lead pencil, and cut it into pieces about three and a-half or four inches long, rejecting the joints. These pieces should be cut square across, and a centre made with a point, as accurately as possible. Having obtained access to a vice, oil the needle and screw it up lightly in a horizontal direction, leaving about a quarter of an inch of it projecting; adjust the marked centre to the needle, hold the cane in a line with the needle, and push it on until it reaches the jaws of the vice; loosen the vice, screw up again, leaving a little more of the needle to project, and push the cane further on as before. Repeat this until nearly the whole of the needle is pushed into the cane. By adopting this method of supporting the needle in the vice, and pushing the cane on to it by degrees, we are enabled to effect our purpose without breaking the needle. The cane may now be cut in the manner of a black-lead pencil, and the point may be shaped upon an Arkansas oilstone. Two conical points will be required, one long and tapering—almost as much as the original point of the needle,—and the other more obtuse, for stronger lines. For shade lines, rub a flat side on the thicker part of the needle, and opposite to it make it round;

this will make the point somewhat spoon-shape, and will be found to have the most useful form for ordinary work. The flat side is intended for the cutting part. When broad points are desired, the eye of the needle may be left projecting, instead of the point. A very good *tracing point* may be made by first breaking off about one-eighth of an inch of the needle, and then rubbing the broken part on the oilstone until it becomes round and without any angle which would scratch the paper. When found to be free from a tendency to scratch, it may be polished on a piece of leather covered with *crocus* or red oxide of iron. The *compasses* for engraving may be the best Lancashire spring dividers. Choose two of each of the sizes suitable for the work. Make one leg a smoothly-pointed cone,—the smoother and more pointed it is the better, as it will then hold to its work, and may be kept to a smaller centre hole than it would otherwise require. The other legs should be brought to a V shape and spoon shape respectively,—the one for fine lines and the other for enlarging them into shade lines. For the smallest circles, a bow pencil with a stiff spring may be used, by substituting a steel point for the pencil. The points for the fine lines will require frequent sharpening in the course of the work, and the oilstone must be constantly kept by the engraver's side. Very nice but expensive tools may be bought suitable for this class of work, but those just described will produce as good a quality of work as any.

140. PREPARATION OF THE STONE.—The instructions usually given recommend a film of gum to be left upon the surface of the stone. This may be regarded as impossible in practice, for the film is certain to be thicker in some places than others, and if any mode of wiping has been used streaks will be left, over which the tool will partially jump, and cause an uneven line when a fine one is attempted. Fortunately it is unnecessary to leave any gum *upon* the surface of the stone, all that is required being to fill the pores of the surface.

The stone should have as perfect a surface as possible. This being obtained, the stone must be dried and then gummed, and dried again. The gum must not be too thin, but it will be sufficiently thick if it dries upon the stone with a good gloss. If a little nitric acid be added to the gum the subsequent coloured coating will be darker, but we think that the acid makes the stone harder to cut. If the stone has been warmed to dry the gum, it should be allowed to cool again. The stone is now to be covered with water, until all the gum has become dissolved ; if the gum was previously strained, this dissolving will soon take place, but if the surface before moistening appeared rough, the hand had better be passed over to feel if any specks are left upon the stone. All the gum being now in a state of solution, the stone must be placed in a slanting position, and plenty of water poured over it to wash off the gum. It is best not to rub the stone with the hand in this operation, because all the gum that is *in* the stone should be kept there. When the stone is dry it will be seen whether it has been sufficiently washed, by its presenting an even appearance ; if it shines in streaks or patches it was not washed enough.

As in executing this style of work the lines are to show up light on a dark ground, it will be necessary to colour its surface. For a black ground rub in some best Paris black until the ground is as dark as it can be made. The superfluous quantity must be removed with a soft cloth, or the tracing will not adhere. A red ground may be laid with *red chalk*, but be sure it is red chalk, as sometimes common Venetian red is substituted for it. Red chalk may be known by being smooth to the touch, and will polish when rubbed with the finger. Anything gritty or abrading must be avoided in laying grounds, and any scratches made in this operation will print. The red chalk may be used dry, but it is preferable to use it in the following manner, which produces a darker and more intense ground.

Take a little powdered or scraped red chalk and a little water, rub it over the stone with the palm of the hand until the stone becomes almost dry, or "dead" looking, but not dry ; it will probably be rather streaky, but that may be removed by rapidly passing the fleshy part of the right hand over the stone towards the left hand, on arriving at which, wipe the right hand quickly upon it so as to remove some of the chalk. Commence at the bottom edge of the stone, and continue regularly to the top, wiping the right hand upon the left at each stroke. By this operation, neatly and quickly performed before the stone becomes dry, nearly all the superfluous chalk may be removed, and the stone left with a beautifully smooth covering. If any specks are left they may be removed by rubbing them with the finger or with a piece of paper.

Some engravers gum and wash the stone as before described, and then lay on a wash of colour containing just sufficient gum, and no more, to prevent the pigment being removed by rubbing; but the previous method is preferable, as there is less material to remove in the process of working upon it.

The advantages of the red chalk ground as compared with the black are, that a better tracing may be made upon the former, and that sketching may be easily seen, if made with a lead pencil.

141. THE TRACING is best made on the black stone with paper prepared with chrome-yellow; but on the red stone it must be done with a paper covered on one side with Paris black, the ordinary black-lead paper not being sufficiently intense. Where great accuracy is required, the tracing may be neatly made in indian-ink, to which a little sugar, gum, and ox-gall have been added. The proportions may be found by trial, and the mixture kept in a small bottle, if a drop of carbolic acid be added. The tracing having been made, is to be placed between damp sheets of paper for a few minutes, so that the ink may become slightly moist. When it is found to shine, it must be laid face downwards upon the stone and passed once through the press, when sufficient of the ink will have set off to enable the draughtsman to see his work very well. This may appear somewhat troublesome, but it must be remembered that the retracing is accomplished at the press in such a manner as to admit of no error of hand or eye, and consequently some time is saved by having to refer less seldom to the original.

142. THE ENGRAVING is so simple as to scarcely require description. It more resembles *etching* upon copper than engraving, but as the term etching is in lithography appropriated to the acidulation of the stone, usage has decided in favour of this mode being called engraving upon stone.

Let it be supposed that the subject to be engraved is a

piece of machinery. Begin by determining the junction of the circular arcs with the straight lines, marking them with a pencil. As it is easier to join straight lines to circular arcs than the reverse, it is preferable, in most instances, to put the curves and circles in first, with the compasses. In doing this care must be taken that in making small circles the stationary leg of the compasses must be slightly longer than the moving one, or it will be apt to slip out when making the cut with the other leg. A sharp point, practice, and perseverance will enable the young engraver to do this without making a large centre-hole. The circular portions having been executed, proceed to the straight lines by the help of the parallel rulers and a point not too fine. The facility with which thin lines may be made in this process generally tempts the student to employ them for outlining the subject. This is a mistake. They should be reserved for tinting and shading, especially in those parts that approach the light. When the whole has been firmly outlined, the compasses having the spoon-shaped point may be used for thickening the shade-lines, and a similar point, with the ruler for a guide, for strengthening the straight lines on the dark side.

The thin, taper, and very sharp point may now be used for the delicate lines of cylindrical and other shading next the light, deepening the lines, and exchanging the point for a broader tool as the darker portions are reached. A little practice, and the study of good examples will teach the student more of this work than can possibly be conveyed by writing.

The engraving having been completed, the centre-holes and other parts that must not be printed may be stopped out with a little acidulated gum-water, coloured with any convenient pigment to enable it to be seen, and applied with the point of a sable pencil.

In working, avoid the condensation of the breath upon the stone, which may cause the gum in the stone to spread, and injure the more delicate lines. For a similar reason, guard the stone against the reception of any kind of mucilaginous matter.

143. CORRECTIONS in this kind of work must be avoided as far as possible. If it be imperative that any should be

made during the progress of the work the part must be scraped out as smoothly as possible, and a new ground laid. This may be done by painting over the place neatly with the ordinary cake water-colours of any convenient tint. Red chalk or light red will do very well, but it must be understood that this, though an effectual "stop," will not be so pleasant to work upon as the original ground.

If the work has already been inked in, the scraping must be deeper, because the ink penetrates the stone below the incised line. Where practicable, it will be best to polish the part with the Water of Ayr stone, which leaves a better surface than the scraper. The stone may then be dried, gummed, &c., as described in the preparation of the stone in the first instance. If the correction consist of an addition only, the stone will merely require to be washed of superfluous gum and the surface coloured previously to the addition being made.

Let it be supposed that the work is finished; it must next be made ready for the printer. Take, upon a soft rag, some thin printing ink, boiled oil, thin varnish, tallow, or in fact any kind of grease, and rub it into the lines forming the engraving. Though any of these substances will answer the purpose, yet, in practice, thin printing-ink will be found most convenient, because it is always at hand, and shows distinctly when the lines have been filled, which is very important. After being sure that every line has received some ink, remove the superfluity from the stone, and cover it with gum-water. The ink has most likely tinted the surface of the stone, but if it be rubbed with a piece of printers' blanket or other woollen cloth and gum-water this will in most part be removed, the more refractory parts usually yielding to the fingers. There is no need for being alarmed, for the lines are below the surface, and the grease will hold firmly only to them, the surface still retaining its preparation of gum. Any specks of grease formed by the dirt from the engraver's hand or other cause having had more time to penetrate, will be more difficult of removal, but even they will succumb to the influence of a little gum and acid applied with the "stump." The scraper should not be used for this purpose if it can be avoided, as any unevenness of surface is apt to catch the ink in printing.

Slight scratches, or a tendency to tint, may be removed by rubbing it with a little putty powder, or rouge, applied with gum-water on a piece of buff leather or flannel.

144. DABBERS are used for inking instead of the rollers used in other styles of lithographic printing, and may be made as follows :—Take two pieces of wood of a convenient size for the stone to be printed, and about two inches thick ; the underside, which must be quite flat, should be covered with the coarsest and thickest printers' blanket, strained over and tacked to the sides. Cover one of them in a similar way, and the other with a piece of fine blanket. Charge the coarse one well with thin ink, and the fine one with stiffer ink, and work it about on the slab until only a small quantity remains on its surface, and it will be fit for use, its office being to clear the stone of superfluous ink.

145. PRINTING.—Damp the stone as if for printing with the roller. Take the coarse dabber, well charged with thin ink, and apply it to the stone, with pressure from the shoulders, at the same time twisting it about until the stone is gone all over, when the dabber may be moved about in circular strokes to remove some of the superfluous ink. Putting this upon the ink-slab, take up the fine dabber, and use that in the circular, wiping manner only. The stone should now be pretty free from surface-ink, but a wipe with the damping-cloth will finish it. If the stone become dry, it must again be wetted. After the dabbers have been got into working order, the fine one will effectually clear the stone without the subsequent use of the damping-cloth, and will do it more clearly and effectually. The position of the printer should be such as to avoid all chance of any dirt falling from the ceiling, &c. If the part of the room over his head be without ceiling, some sheets of paper should be nailed up to form a temporary ceiling, because if any grit get upon the dabber, the stone may be scratched, and the scratch inked in at the same time. This may in part be avoided by the use of gum in the damping-water, which will be found an excellent precaution, because the surface of the stone being submitted to more friction than in the use of the roller, the coating of gum is sooner removed, and the stone more susceptible to the effect of scratches. The stone having been fully inked in, may be etched all over

with weak etching-water, to finally remove any scum arising from the first inking, and afterwards gummed and dried.

The other essentials in printing are an elastic backing of printers' blanket as described under backing-sheets, and some damped paper. The printing, when all is in working order, may be carried on nearly as quickly as when using the roller. The roller is entirely unnecessary in printing from engraved stones, though sometimes recommended for taking off the superfluous ink, in doing which it usually takes a portion of the ink out of the lines as well. This will be understood when it is considered that in rolling, the surface of the roller in contact with the stone is successively lifted nearly perpendicularly, while the action of the fine dabber is almost exclusively a wiping one, and consequently leaves the ink in the lines.

CHAPTER XIX.

Zincography. Its Principles—Scraping, Polishing, and Graining the Plates—Re-preparation of Old Plates—Etching Recipes—Transfers—Printing.

THIS important branch of the art will require only a short chapter, not because we underrate its merits, but because nearly all that has been said on drawing and printing on stone, is equally applicable to working on metal plates, and consequently no necessity exists for extending the previous instructions on those points.

146. THE PRINCIPLES OF ZINCOGRAPHY are almost identical with those of lithography; and all ordinary styles of drawing may be performed upon zinc plates instead of on stone; the chief distinctions being that blacklead pencil-marks are apt to roll up in printing, and that the two- and three-line lettering-gauges used by copperplate engravers may be used to mark direct upon the zinc. The materials used are the same, and the *mode* of printing is identical. Zinc plates have the advantage over large stones, in being less in first cost, and being much more portable. Hence, they are used very extensively in many printing establishments for a variety of work; the

chief among which, it may be mentioned, are large plans and wall-advertisements. As neither ink, crayon, nor gum penetrates the zinc in the same manner as they do stone, the printing is more liable to accident, and requires great attention and skill on the part of the printer. One very marked difference between the zinc and stone, is that the former is subject to oxidation by contact with a moist atmosphere. For this reason, great care must be exercised in drying the plates off quickly after their preparation for drawing, and during the printing, to prevent the gummy preparation from being actually removed. The principal difference in the treatment of the zinc plates by the printer, as compared with lithography, is the substitution of infusion of nut-galls for nitric and hydrochloric acids.*

147. PREPARATION OF THE PLATES.—Zinc plates may be obtained ready polished or grained, of the dealers in lithographic materials; but as their subsequent preparation will in all probability have to be done at home, it will be as well to describe how they may be made ready for use after being purchased, as they may sometimes have to be, of the metal-dealer.

GAUGES.

18   17   16   15   14   13   12   11   10   9

Zinc plates may be had in almost any size and thickness, but our illustration shows the strengths most frequently in

---

* In a note to par. 91 we gave Mr. M. Hanhart's view of the nature of the drawing in combination with the stone. He holds a similar view in regard to the drawing on zinc. The theory is shortly this :— That the drawing-ink and chalk form a metallic soap with the zinc plate. That this metallic soap has a great affinity for the zinc, so that the ink on the roller has little influence in pulling it off the plate. That the brown insoluble compound produced by the action of the nut-galls upon the plate, resists the printing-ink in a similar manner to the gum upon the stone. That these two opposite forces acting at the same time enable the printer to take a larger number of impressions than could possibly be the case if the only principle involved was that of the antipathy of grease and water.

use, and the numbers by which they may be ordered of the dealers in litho materials.

The zinc must be of the quality known as "best rolled Vieille Montagne." It may be made into convenient sizes, by cutting a groove with a V-pointed chisel and hammer, in the direction required, but the cut must be quite straight across the whole. It is only necessary to cut about half through, when, by bringing the groove just over the edge of the table, the plate may be broken through by a sudden pressure on the part overhanging. The rough edges and corners may now be taken off with a file. Next, place it on a stone in the press, smoothest side uppermost, lay on a few sheets of paper, and pull through under heavy pressure. If the plate is found to be generally flat, it may still further be tested by drawing some pencil-lines across the plate with an HB lead pencil. If the plate is fairly level, these lines will show on the paper when pulled through again. Convexity may be remedied by putting some blanket or soft paper on the stone, and pulling through the press with convex side up, with light pressure first, increasing it gently until the effect sought is obtained. If there should be any bruises in the plate, it may be sent to a coppersmith to remedy them.

The surface of the plate as it comes from the rolling-mill and as usually sold, is contaminated with scale and oxide, which must be cleared off. This is done by removing the surface of the zinc by means of a sharp scraper. The scraper used by the cabinetmaker will answer the purpose. It should be set in wood to get a convenient "grip" upon it, and may best be sharpened by burnishing its edge, holding the burnisher in such a manner that it may be at a right angle to the scraper. This will, if properly done, produce a good scraping edge on each side. A tool that will answer still better may be made of an old smoothing-plane, the face of which has been somewhat removed at its front part, so as to bring the knife more upright. The knife must be ground at a very obtuse angle, so as to produce more of a scraping than a direct, cutting action. If the surface be removed by this tool, it will be done more evenly than by the other kind of scraper, because the wood of the plane prevents the knife sinking into any hollow places.

The plate having been scraped level all over, is to be

treated as described for stone with pumice and snake-stone. However, unlike stone, all drawings on zinc, whether in ink or chalk, should be executed on a *grained* surface, to produce which proceed exactly as in graining a stone, substituting, however, a muller of zinc for one of stone. A plate about 24 by 18 inches will take a man an hour or more to grain, because the zinc is less easily abraded than the stone. When the plate is done, wash it well, finish with hot water, and rear it up to dry off quickly, so as to prevent corrosion.

If a plate has been used already, it may be prepared anew in the following manner. 1st. Remove the ink with spirits of turpentine. 2nd. Wash it with a strong alkali, such as pearl-ash or caustic soda. 3rd. Wash with water. 4th. Pour over the plate for two or three minutes some of the following dilute acid :—

Sulphuric acid (oil of vitriol) ... 1 part.
Hydrochloric acid (spirits of salt)... 1 ,,
Water ... ... 24 parts.

5th. Wash in plenty of water. And 6th, Regrain.

Some persons prepare the plate by washing with turpentine, followed by a sharp acidulation with sulphuric or other acid, and then wash the latter well off.

148. PRINTING FROM ZINC.—The drawing having been done precisely in the manner described in our chapters on drawing on stone, is handed to the printer, who etches it by applying the following mixture with a flat camel-hair brush :—

Decoction of nut-galls ... ... ¾ pint.
Solution of gum (thickness of cream) ¼ ,,
Solution phosphoric acid ... ... 3 drachms ;

letting it stay on half a minute or more according to the nature of the work. To make the decoction of nut-galls, steep 4 oz. in 3 quarts of water for 24 hours, and then boil up and strain.

To make the solution of phosphoric acid, put some sticks of phosphorus into a bottle, taking care not to handle them with the fingers. Pour water upon them, but not quite sufficient to cover them. Close the bottle with a cork having a notch cut out of its side to admit air. Set the bottle aside for a few days, and the air will oxidize the phosphorus, making phosphoric acid, which will be dissolved by the water, and the solution in that time will be strong enough for use.

Another etching solution which is in use in Germany may be made thus :—1¼ oz. of bruised nut-galls is to be boiled in 1¼ lb. of water until reduced to one-third ; strain, and add 2 drachms of nitric, and 4 drops of acetic acid.

Though these solutions are, no doubt, well suited to the purpose and well recommended, we prefer in our own practice the most simple formulæ when we find them answer the purpose as well. Thus in this case we use the simple decoction of nut-galls, and do not think there is any need of complicating it by additions of other acids.

After etching, wash off, gum in, dry by the application of heat, and then proceed as follows.

Wash off with turpentine without removing or moistening the gum, and roll in the plate until quite black. Now sprinkle it with water, and continue rolling and throwing on water until the plate becomes clean and the work rolled up. We find this is safer in the first instance than washing out in the ordinary way.

If the work rolls up weak, it may frequently be much strengthened by rubbing up with thin ink and plenty of gum. The lay for printing may be made on the zinc plate by means of the edge of a silver coin. It will be remembered that a piece of lead was recommended for stone.

The plate may be supported during printing on any convenient surface, but perhaps the most convenient is a block of rather hard wood, such as beech (made quite level), to which the plate may be screwed.

The transfer method may be applied to zinc in precisely the same manner as to stone, but after washing off the transfer-composition the plate must be etched as before described. It is not necessary in the transfer process to grain the plate, as a polished one will do equally well. The polishing may be begun by pumice-stone and water, and finished when dry with No. O emery-cloth, or it may be finished with emery and turpentine, which must be well wiped off and then washed with benzoline.

In washing out subjects on zinc, add a little oil to the spirits of turpentine.

Printing from zinc is conducted in exactly the same way as from stone, only greater precaution must be taken to have every appliance and material in good working order.

In consequence of the adhesion of the ink forming the drawing being less complete than in lithography, where the stone is more porous, it is not allowable to use ink containing strong varnish. The thinner the ink can be worked, consistently with a good quality of impression, the better; but at the same time it must be understood that the gum does not adhere so firmly to the metal, and judgment must be used in preventing the spreading of the ink.

CHAPTER XX.

CHROMOLITHOGRAPHY. General Conditions—The Key-stone, how Prepared — Set-off, or Feint; Different Modes of Preparing — Order of the Colours—Bronzes—Dusted Colours.

IN treating of Chromolithography, we propose first to point out those conditions and processes which are common to all the various methods of producing coloured effects; then we shall give a description of simple colour-work, suitable for plans, labels, show-cards, &c.; next, of tinted lithography, which is used in subjects of more artistic character; and, finally, that combination of the former methods which is usually denominated Chromolithography or Oleography, when applied to the reproduction of artistic subjects. In this manner we shall have occasion to introduce some things in the first part which it will not be necessary to repeat in the other two, of which the methods of making sets-off and registering the sheets may be cited as examples.

149. GENERAL CONDITIONS.—It may be stated generally that all lithographs in two or more colours are printed from two or more stones. That being so, it will be seen that some method must be employed, first, to get a correct trace of the subject on the first stone made upon the second; and, second, of being able, in printing, to lay the sheet so correctly in position that the second printing may fall exactly into its place upon the first. To attain the first of these conditions we must have what is called a key-stone.

150. KEY-STONE.—In the ordinary run of show-card and

label-work this stone is used for finishing, but in work of more artistic character it is usual to employ this stone as a means of getting all other colours in their place, and generally to omit it in printing. It is necessary, in making this key-stone, that there should be lines to indicate either the junction or separation of every colour from each other, wherever any kind of distinction has to be observed. In show-cards it is usual to edge nearly all the colour with an outline, and this is then all that is necessary for the purpose of a key-stone; but circumstances may occur in which it is necessary to bring two printings into juxtaposition without the intervention of a separating line of black or other colour.

To make our meaning more clear, we will cite a familiar and simple example. Suppose it to be required to have a line of letters in which the upper half is red and the lower half blue, with a stroke of white to divide them. In this case it would be almost indispensable to make in the key-stone a black line, to represent the white one in the finished print; but for this purpose it would not be necessary to make a distinct key-stone, because such a small matter as the line we have been describing might be taken out of the stone after the sets-off were made. If the colours were intended to soften into each other, or to overlap each other to produce another tint, the line would then be used as a mark whereat to stop the solid colour, the softening effect being continued beyond it on each side.

The case we have cited involves nothing that cannot easily be comprehended; but when we come to an example of a key-stone to be used for the imitation of a landscape, the uninitiated will encounter nothing but a hopeless mass of confusion, as even the sky will, if cloudy, be found to contain a number of lines that only tend to render the complexity greater.

In our chapter on "Miscellaneous Processes" we have given methods of tracing which may be adopted in making key-stones, and it is unnecessary to repeat them in this place. We may, however, take this opportunity of informing the student that he must on no account attempt to make a key-stone in a *hurry*, such a course being certain to end in confusion. He should take every possible care to make the key-stone thoroughly trustworthy, studying each

L

bit as he proceeds, so as to find out the best mode of producing the imitative effect required.

151. THE SET-OFF, or FAINT.—By this is meant the *trace* produced when an impression from the key-stone is laid down upon another stone and pulled through the press. Now, the one essential condition of this is that the trace, set-off, or faint impression, shall be exactly of the same dimensions as the original from which it is made ; for if it be not, it is quite evident that impressions from the two stones will not fit each other when printed upon the same piece of paper. To ensure this, attention must be given to the following :— 1st. The impression from the key-stone must be pulled upon dry, well-rolled paper. 2nd. The key-stone should be allowed to become dry before the impression is taken, so that the chances of the sheet absorbing moisture, and thereby expanding, may be reduced to a minimum : and 3rd. The impression when taken should be laid down upon the stone as soon as possible, so as to prevent the sheet either expanding or contracting by any change in the state of the atmosphere.

We think that a sheet of good, thick, cream-wove letter-paper, that has been well rolled, is as suitable as anything that can be used for this purpose, because the hard size which it contains prevents in some degree the absorption of damp from the stone. If the set-off should, for any reason, be required to be very strong, the print may be treated in the style described in the fifth part of par. 130. In a general way, however, it will be necessary that the set-off shall not be liable to roll up among the new work, to prevent which several expedients may be resorted to ; but the following one possesses every advantage in practice and is so simple that we need give no other. Take the strong impression upon well-glazed paper ; place on it some finely-powdered *red chalk ;* then take up the sheet by the two hands, and alternately raise and lower each hand until every part of the ink has been brought into contact with the red chalk, which may then be run off and set aside for future use. Now hold the sheet by one corner, and tap the back of it, to shake off the non-adhering powder. The sheet thus prepared may be laid upon the stone and passed through the press, when sufficient of the red chalk will remain upon the stone to answer the purpose of the artist ; but when it is passed over to the printer it will wash away, much in the same manner as a red tracing. It is essential that red chalk should be used for this purpose, because no other substance that we are acquainted with adheres so well to the stone.

152. THE ORDER OF THE COLOURS. — The order in which the colours should succeed each other in the course of printing is a matter of much importance, not only as regards the effect of the finished print, but as regards economy of time. In a case in which bronze powder, metal, or any dust colour, is used, this ought to precede the other printings. The reason of this is obvious ; viz., that an ordinary printing may succeed a dusted one almost immediately, but if it were required that a dusted one should follow an ordinary one, it would be necessary that the latter should be so thoroughly dry that there should be no tendency in it to hold the bronze or other powder colour. When the bronze must be introduced after other printings, it will be found almost imperative to prepare the sheets with some semi-transparent powder, such as talc, rubbed on and well dusted off, to prevent the adhesion of the bronze, which would otherwise attach itself to any part that might not be thoroughly hardened.

There is another order of succession, which is based upon the fact that while some colours are opaque others are transparent. As a rule, the transparent colour should succeed the opaque one, because the former allows the latter to be seen through it, and is modified by it, for which reason the transparent colours are usually reserved for the finishing ones.

Further, it may be stated that another order may depend upon the hue of the colour desired ; thus, for instance, a Prussian blue over a chrome yellow might make a dark, cool green, but the reverse order would give a warmer and lighter green. For the same reason a crimson-lake over a blue yields a richer purple than the opposite order would give.

For positive colours it may be stated, as a general rule, that they should succeed each other as follows :— 1st, Bronzes or Dusted Colours ; 2nd, Blues ; 3rd, Reds ; 4th, Yellows ; and, 5th, the Outline or Finishing Colours.

In the matter of transparency, the student may observe that those colours which are dark in the mass are *usually* transparent and fit for finishing with, while those which appear much the same in the lump as upon the paper are opaque. But there are some exceptions, notably raw sienna and emerald-green. In this connection it may be stated that though the opaque should generally precede the transparent colours, there are instances in which the reverse order is to be preferred.

Having indicated the general principles upon which the order of colours may be arranged, we must leave the skill and judgment and the experience of the lithographer to find out and master the rest, as the circumstances of each piece of work vary so much that no precise rule can be given. In another place we shall have more to say respecting the pigments most suitable to the purpose, and will now dismiss this part of the subject and pass on, in the next chapter, to the different modes of *registering*.

CHAPTER XXI.

REGISTERING. By Lay—By Needles—By Fixed Points—By New Method — Registering-Machines — Influence of Paper — Dry Paper—Damp Paper—Drying-room—Surface of Stone—Dusting to prevent Set-off.—Application of Principles.

REGISTERING.—153. By this term is understood the adjustment of an already printed sheet to the stone, in such a manner that the further work about to be printed on it shall coincide with the spaces intended for it.

This is one of the most important matters that can engage the attention of the chromolithographer, for it is quite clear that all the care of the artist, having this end in view, will be thrown away if the printer fails to make the colours fall into their proper places.

There are several methods more or less adapted to obtaining this important object, but it must be observed that in each case, the key-stone must have applied to it appropriate marks adapted to facilitate the subsequent operations. and that this preparation varies somewhat in each method. To facilitate reference, we will number these methods, commencing with the simplest :—

I. *By Lay.*—This, in many hands, is a very effectual means of obtaining register, and is the simplest possible ; but the size of the paper to be used should be determined before the set-off is made. It is true that this is not absolutely essential to the method, but it greatly facilitates it in every way. The size of the paper having been fixed upon, a "lay," corresponding to the edge of the paper, is made on the stone, by which the subject is brought into proper position upon the sheet, and this lay is then drawn with fine lines in lithographic ink in such manner as to print upon the sets-off and to remain all through the printing. A set-off is now to be made for each colour, and this "lay" mark is to be made permanent. If the colour to be printed be a dark one, the mark may be carefully inked over at the same time that the rest of the work is done ; but if the printing is to be a light colour, some method must be devised of making this mark not only indelible, but dark, so as to be readily seen by the printer ; and this may easily be accomplished as follows.—Cover the place with gum, through which, when dry, make scratches to coincide exactly with the marks they are intended to replace. With a pen and common writing-ink, go over these scratches, and when dry, if the gum be washed away, well-defined marks will be left that will last all through the printing.

In using this system all that is necessary is to accurately adjust one corner and edge of the paper to these marks all through the printing ; but care must be taken that the paper possesses well-defined corners and edges. If the paper should be found to expand a little, a good workman will, by laying the sheet a little over the mark in the direction required, be able to make the necessary allowance to preserve the register. In many kinds of work this system will be found all that is required, and indeed in many houses scarcely any other is used.

II. *By Needles.*—In this mode sufficient marks are usually to be found among the work to answer the purpose of registering ; but occasions may arise in which a small dot or cross may be made near the centre of the shorter edges of the paper on opposite sides of it.

To take an example : let it be supposed that the border line of a subject be chosen for registering by : make, with a sharp-pointed scraper or other convenient tool, fine *holes* in any two opposite corners of the set-off upon the stone. Some registering-needles must now be provided, and may be made thus :—Two pieces of wood or cane about $1\frac{1}{2}$ inch long, of the thickness of a blacklead pencil, are to have inserted in each of them a moderate-sized sewing-needle, with about an inch of it projecting.   If the point be inserted in the wood and the eye end broken off and repointed, the tool will be better.   Another similar piece should be provided with a needle of the same size having its point preserved.

Thus equipped, the printer may proceed.   The sheet printed first must be pricked through exactly at the corners which are intended to be used, and which correspond to the holes in the stone.   Through these holes in the sheet the needles are to be inserted *from the back*. The printer now takes the sheet, contriving to hold the needles and the paper at the same time, and, inserting each point into its proper hole, allows the sheet to drop from his fingers on to the stone.   He then holds the sheet in position with his little fingers, while he withdraws the needles, and afterwards carefully withdraws his fingers ; thus leaving the sheet, if the operation has been carefully performed, in its proper position upon the stone.   When it is required to make allowance for expansion of paper, the needles may be inclined in the direction necessary to correct the error.

Though this system is, perhaps, the one most generally employed, we regard it as little superior, in point of accuracy, to the one first mentioned, while it is certainly much slower ; but when, as is sometimes the case, the paper is larger than the stone, it is a very useful method.

III. *By Fixed Points.*—The previous method may be varied by setting the two needles in a lath of wood, so as to correspond with the holes in the paper and the stone. With a lad to assist, this way will be found a quicker one than that of using the needles separately, but will possess the disadvantage of not permitting them to be inclined in opposite directions, as is sometimes necessary.

We have an opinion that a perfect method of register should admit of the following conditions :—*a*, That it should depend for its exactitude upon the sense of touch : *b*, that the guides should be attached to the stone itself : *c*, that the guides should be capable of being moved so as to accommodate any expansion of the paper subsequent to the first printing : *d*, that there should be no necessity for pricking holes in the sheets by hand, as that introduces an element of error.

We are happy in being able to describe two methods by which this can be accomplished.

IV. *By Points in Stone.*—Get the following materials and tools :—Some lengths of lead such as is used for balancing ivory and bone-handled table-knives ;* a drill that will make a hole of the same diameter as the lead ; a brace for rotating the drill ; some steel music wire, about 22 of the Birmingham wire-gauge ; a small chisel or a broken palette-knife ground off square and sharp ; a small wood mallet ; and a fine flat parallel file, about one inch wide, with safe edges, but no handle.

Thus equipped, the lithographer may proceed. We will for the present suppose that the stone and sheet to be printed are about equal in size. The case of a stone larger than the sheet will be treated of subsequently.

At the centre of each end of the key-stone, about half an inch from the edge, drill a hole about half an inch deep ; cut off a piece of lead five-eighths of an inch long, and with the mallet slightly taper one end. This must now be driven into the hole, and the projecting part cut level with the stone by means of the chisel. A piece of the wire is to be slightly pointed with the file, and then a notch made about one-fourth of an inch from the point at which it may be broken off. Drive this into the lead until only one-six-

---

* If there is any difficulty in obtaining these pieces of lead, they may be made in the following manner :—Procure a piece of straight brass tube, ¼ in. in diameter, and about 3 in. long. With a fine saw cut it entirely through, lengthwise, and carefully remove the burr from the inside where it has been cut. Holding this piece of tube in a pincers or hand vice in such a manner as to close the slit, rest it on something to close the bottom end, and pour into it some molten lead. When set, the tube may be loosed, and will by opening a little at the slit, permit of the lead cylinder being pushed out.

teenth is left projecting. Over this place a bit of stout writing-paper, and with the safe edge of the file resting upon the paper, bring the bit of wire to a fair point.

In the same manner treat each end of each colour-stone, as far as the insertion of the lead goes, but put in a point at one end only.

In taking the impressions of the key-stone for the set-off, simply lay the sheet to a mark ; but *before it is lifted from the stone*, press the finger on the points so as to make them puncture the paper. Each set-off will thus be pricked exactly in the same manner. In laying these upon the stone, one hole is to be placed over the point, and the other hole over the lead without a point ; near which end a little strong gum should be placed, so as to temporarily hold the sheet. The set-off sheet having been submitted to sufficient pressure (taking care that the scraper only acts upon that part of the stone between the points), a hole must be accurately pricked into the lead *through the hole in the paper*. This having been properly performed, the stone is ready for the artist, as the insertion of the second point may be omitted until the stone is placed in the printer's hands for proof, when it may be inserted as previously described.

In the actual process of printing the first impressions are laid to a mark, and the sheets punctured as described for taking the set-off impressions. The subsequent ones are obtained by laying the holes over their proper points, the printer being able, with very little experience, to feel the points through the holes with his *forefinger*. Any expansion of the sheet can be provided for by driving a small dull punch into the lead alongside the point, which is thereby shifted in the opposite direction, and will so remain until again moved by similar means.

If it be necessary to use stones larger than the sheet of paper, it is clear that it will not do to drill a second hole far up the stone, as that would probably spoil it for future use : in that case, the mark, instead of being made upon the lead, must be made upon the stone, and a cross scratched through it with lines about one inch or more long. For a point, get a piece of thin brass, about three-fourths of an inch square, and let the tinman tin it at the back, and drill a hole to match the wire near one corner, and solder it (the wire) in, letting it stand one-sixteenth high, as before. By means of a blowpipe and a piece of shellac this may be firmly attached to the stone, the point being set at the junction of the cross scratches. This point may be slightly moved at any time by warming it by means of the blowpipe. When done with, it may be removed altogether by setting a square-edged punch or dull chisel against it, and giving it a sharp tap with the mallet.

Some of the few drawbacks to this method of registering may be got rid of by drilling the holes in the side edge of the stone and using only lead foundations for the points. If they are put, say, $14\frac{1}{2}$ in. apart, they will serve for crown, post, royal, and demy folios; and larger stones may be similarly treated for larger sizes.

Where the cardboard or paper is too small, pieces of paper to carry the point-holes may be gummed to the edge. These pieces of paper can be torn off when the printing is completed.

V.—We have used with considerable success the following method, which enables the printer to see as easily what he is doing as in the simple way described first. Where there is sufficient margin, it is not only the easiest but much the quickest system.

Two pieces of brass, about three-fourths of an inch long, and shaped like the letters ▌ and ⌞ respectively, are to be tinned at the back as before described, and fastened to the stone with shellac, corresponding to the edge and corner of the paper in the following position

the ⌞-shaped one being towards the tympan. The scraper must be set in its box in such a manner as to avoid these brass register-marks when the impression is being taken. A pair of these having been fitted to the keystone, the set-off sheet is to be carefully set in the corner of one and against the other, and the impression taken. Similar marks must be put to each stone, and the set-off sheet being laid against them exactly as at first, an exact register must be the result when the paper is applied to them in a like manner in the printing.

With good paper, having clearly-cut edges, and a fair margin, this method is simply the perfection of registering.

In some of the processes now described, it not unfrequently happens that in the attempts to lay the paper *in situ*, it becomes slurred. This may be avoided by getting an assistant to keep the paper from the stone by means of a lath of wood, which is to be drawn away when the sheet is adjusted.

Registering-machines have also been employed by some lithographers with success, and though they are not usually on sale by dealers in lithographic requisites, they may be had to order. The annexed figure shows one of these contrivances adapted to a stone. The mode of using it will easily be found out on examination, but it may be as well just to point out its general principle.

It consists, in the first place, of a frame adapted to the stone by means of set screws, which answer the double purpose of securing the frame to the stone and adjusting it in position. To the frame which surrounds the stone is hinged a lighter one, upon which two adjustable slides carry points, which can be covered up by thin flaps of brass. While the stone is being rolled in, the lighter frame is thrown back out of the way; in which position the sheet may be laid upon the points and the flaps placed over them to keep the sheet upon them. The inking having been completed, the frame with the sheet upon it is turned down upon the stone, and the paper held in position with one hand while the frame is thrown back again with the other. The tympan being then lowered, the operation is completed by taking the impression.

We cannot say that these machines will not work properly, but the other methods being so much more simple and applicable to all sizes of stones, machines are very rarely to be met with in use.

154. THE INFLUENCE OF THE PAPER UPON THE REGISTER is frequently very great, and we will point out some of the conditions necessary to success in registering.

I. *Paper for colour-printing must be well rolled*, so as to stretch it as much as possible. This is very important, because printing-paper as received from the mill, under ordinary pressure used in litho-printing, will stretch sufficiently at the first pull to make " slurring " almost inevitable.

II. *The temperature and hygrometric state of the printing-room must be maintained as equal as possible*, as it is no uncommon thing to find the sheets printing in register one day and out the next, in consequence of a wet day succeeding a dry day, or *vice versâ*. This effect is sometimes set down by the printer to the action of the press in stretching the paper ; but where that has been well rolled, such is not the case. Paper that has been subjected to the rolling machine sufficiently to glaze it, will not stretch under the lighter pressure of the lithographic press. The influence, however, of the damp stone and a moist atmosphere is very considerable. It sometimes happens that the sheets expand in width instead of in length ; in which case it cannot be the action of the press, and the cause must be sought elsewhere, and will be found to be due to expansion by the absorption of moisture, either from the air or the stone, or both combined. If a sheet of writing, printing, or drawing paper be taken, and a strip be cut from its length, another from its width (both being of one size), then dipped in water for a second or two and laid upon the table, it will be found that one will become larger than the other, without any pressure being applied. If replaced to where they were cut, it will be found that while one has scarcely moved at all, the other has expanded from one-hundredth to one-fiftieth of its length.

It will sometimes be convenient to print views and other similar work in one or more tints, on damp paper; in which case care must be taken, by keeping them in a heap, to prevent their becoming dry at the edges, which causes them to cockle, and slur in the printing. It will be well, then, to remove them from any current of air, and to keep them covered over when they are left for any length of time. Damp paper will do very well for black, and one or two tints ; but when more decided colours are employed and they are of greater body, the ink must be dried between each printing, a proceeding which is incompatible with the use of damp paper.

In these cases it is therefore necessary to commence the printing upon dry paper, and to allow free access of air to the sheets between the printings, which can most easily be accomplished by setting the impressions in a pile, and keeping each separate from the other by means of laths of wood, printer's reglet, or strips of cardboard. For the thinner varieties of paper, however, some kind of perforated shelves, placed in racks, similar to case-racks, will be found most suitable. These shelves may be framed of thin wood, and pieces of small twine may be laced across them as a support for the paper.

This provision for the drying of the ink has the disadvantage, however, of exposing the paper to all the alternating influences of heat and cold, and dry and damp. To reduce these to a minimum, it would be well to make provision for maintaining the room in which the impressions are dried at a sufficiently high temperature to keep it and the paper dry. To insure the full effect of this arrangement for the attainment of good register, it will be requisite, in most instances, to thus dry the paper *before commencing* the first printing, and so make sure of the paper going to the stone always in the same condition.

To moderate the absorption of water from the stone, it is usual with some printers to apply a coating of zinc-white and varnish to the paper by means of the printing-press ; but in much of the work done this is hardly necessary, as the first printing of a warm tint over the paper, to give tone to the subject, answers almost the same purpose.

155. OF THE SURFACE TO BE GIVEN TO THE STONE. —In ordinary colour-work it is customary to employ polished stones whenever the pen or brush is used for producing the required effects. When it is necessary or desirable to use chalk, or employ tints, grained stones must be used. Grained stones are employed in tints, even

though there may be no gradation of colour required, because it is found by experience that they carry the ink more evenly, and produce more level printing than do polished ones. The nature of the grain to be employed will depend upon that of the work ; but as a general rule, a somewhat coarser grain is given to stones for colour than to those for black work.

156. SETTING-OFF OF COLOURS UPON THE STONE may be prevented by dusting the previously printed sheets with powdered talc, magnesia, powdered chalk, or other similar substances ; but the process should be avoided as much as possible, as it somewhat injures the brilliancy of the colours. (See paragraph 152.)

157. APPLICATION OF PRINCIPLES TO PRACTICE IN THE PRODUCTION OF A SIMPLE COLOUR JOB.—For an illustration of this subject we will suppose that a show-card is to be printed in the following colours : gold or bronze, a warm tint, emerald-green, vermilion, and black.

The first thing to be done is to make a coloured sketch, in which the arrangement of colours must be definitely settled, because it will not be advisable to deviate from it during the making-up of the stones. When this has been done, the artist must draw a keystone, in accordance with the principles laid down in par. 150, not forgetting to make such provision for registering as may be necessary, according to the particular method to be adopted, which in this instance we will suppose to be that of the fixed points upon the stone. With this in view, the drawing must be placed upon the stone in such a position as to accommodate it in regard to the place of the fixed point.

After the printer has rolled up the work, he must affix a second point to the stone, as described in par. 153, and then prepare four other stones to receive the other colours. Four impressions having been taken on well-rolled paper, *three* of them are to be dusted, as mentioned in par. 151, and laid upon polished stones, while the black one, not dusted, is put upon a grained stone. These set-offs, having been pulled through the press, are to be marked for register, in accordance with one of the methods previously given.

The grained stone is intended to receive the tint, which may be prepared in the following manner:—The margin, and all other parts which are to remain white, should be stopped out with gum, as explained in pars. 81 and 82. This will be found to be an easier method than painting in, with lithographic ink, all those parts which are to remain as tint.   If there should be time to permit of the drying of this tint thoroughly before the next stage, it will be as well to allow the tint to be underneath the bronze, more especially if the paper or card has an absorbent surface.   If the tint be a light one, it may underlie any other colour which may be intended to be dusted on.   The reason for having the tint thus to underlie the dusted colour is that the paper shall be less likely to absorb the ink, and weaken its power of holding the dusted colour.   Another advantage it would have would be that of not showing any little inequalities of registering.   When the gum-ink is dry, the stone may be covered with drawing-ink and turpentine, or in fact almost any kind of greasy matter free from water.   Some time should then be allowed for it to penetrate the stone, after which the gum may be washed off and the work rolled up. The other stones may be drawn upon with lithographic ink, care being taken to keep each colour to its proper stone; but where two colours can be kept sufficiently apart to be applied by the dusting-on process, they may be drawn on one stone.   Thus, in the instance before us, as we have to use an emerald green, the varnish for it may be coloured to pale blue, and that will take also a blue dusted colour, so that, if not too near each other, both may be employed on the one printing, with a little care. In filling in the stones the artist should observe that by covering his outline with each colour he will improve his chances of good register; and where there is a broad black line he may carry his colour considerably beyond its edge, because the black printing will effectually hide the under-colour.

When those colours which are dusted are applied to the show-card, the vermilion, and then the black, may be printed next in order.   In making up the red stone, it will be as well to so arrange it that the colour may underlie the black, which will thus have a greater richness.   Care should at the same time be taken that the red is kept well within the outline of the black, so that it may not show when a little out of register.

It must be borne in mind, that as the colours are to be printed over each other, they should have *dryers* in them to facilitate the work. Under the ordinary circumstances of one printing, the absorption of the ink by the paper will hasten the drying, but where one colour is superimposed upon another this does not take place, and it becomes necessary to add dryers to the ink. (See par. 171.)

CHAPTER XXII.—TINTS.

CHROMO-LITHOGRAPHY (*continued*). Different Methods of Making Tints—Tints in which white Chalk is imitated—Tints of several gradations of One Colour—Washing Out Tints—Etching Tints—Various kinds of other Tints.

AT the end of the last chapter we described the manner in which to a simple job in colours might be applied the methods previously detailed for making keystone, set-offs, and registering. In the practice of Chromo-lithography it is, however, very necessary to become acquainted with the methods of making tints which imitate more or less effectually light washes of colour, as seen in water-colour drawings, &c. These methods we proceed now to point out.

158. OF THE DIFFERENT METHODS OF MAKING TINTS. —The method of producing a tint given in par. 157, though the simplest one, is only adapted for producing one uniform colour, and therefore is very limited in its application. If the student will examine some of the subjects frequently to be met with, which are printed in black and one or two tints, he will notice that each colour or tint consists of more than one gradation. If he will study also those imitations of chalk drawings on tinted paper which are generally imported from Paris, he will find that the lights appear as if they had been laid on with white chalk. To obtain these effects in a more rapid manner than could be done by the methods of drawing previously described, is the object of tint-making, though all of them are frequently introduced in one work in the higher branches of the art. Tints, as understood by the lithographer, usually mean masses of somewhat light colour spread over large spaces. They con-

sist of two or more gradations, though the term is equally applicable when variety of light and shade is not attempted.

The modes in common use of producing tints depend upon the principle of laying some fatty matter on the stone in such a manner that, if left in that state, it would roll up of full strength all over, unless part of it had been removed by etching with dilute acid or scraping, or both combined.

159. TINTS IN WHICH WHITE CHALK IS IMITATED.—For this method a somewhat coarse, but very sharp-grained stone must be employed, and the set-off of the drawing must be made upon it in such a manner that the subject can be distinctly seen during the several subsequent stages. As this imitation of white chalk is to be produced by scraping, it is desirable that the artist should have his ground colour sufficiently dark to enable him to estimate properly the effect he is producing. A dark ground would, however, obliterate an ordinary set-off, but if it be laid down with turpentine, as described in the fifth part of par. 130, it will show through the ground. If the ground for the tint is, on the other hand, so dark as to obscure even this kind of set-off, a dusted one may be laid on the top of the ground after the latter has been put on.

The practical treatment will be as follows :—On the grained stone make the set-off. With gum and acid stop out the margin and high lights. Then lay the ground. If the set-off do not now show sufficiently, an impression dusted over with red chalk or vermilion may be registered upon it, and passed through the press with light pressure, provided the ground is hard enough to permit of it.

The ground forming the tint must possess the following properties :—It must be hard enough to allow of the scraper removing it in parts without smearing. It must resist the action of the acid sufficiently to roll up solidly, after an etching which is strong enough to keep the scraped parts clear. Thus it must not be too greasy, but must be soluble in solvents that dissolve fatty matters. There are several substances which can be used for this purpose, but perhaps the most convenient are asphaltum or Brunswick black, and copal varnish, the latter of which will require some colouring matter added to it to enable the artist to see what he is doing. The coating must be even, but not too thick, and may be best applied by means of either a letterpress or glazed litho roller, both of which can be more easily and effectually cleaned with turpentine than can an ordinary leather one.

The ground, having been laid evenly, must be left until dry enough to permit of the use of the scraper, by which the lights may be put in so as to imitate the stroke of the white crayon as closely as the circumstances will allow. Thanks to the grain underlying the varnish, this may be accomplished more easily than would at first sight appear possible. The scraper must be quite sharp, and should be held lightly in the hand, so as to obtain the necessary freedom in manipulating it.

The scraping having been done, the stone will require to be etched, in order to preserve the lights. The strength of acid necessary for this purpose will depend a good deal upon the thickness of the varnish. Though the exact strength cannot be stated, little difficulty will be experienced if the following expedient be resorted to. Select a portion of the tint for experiment that is to remain solid or of full colour, and commencing with very dilute acid, try it upon that portion of the stone until, by the addition of more acid, the ground is attacked. Then by diluting the acid it will be brought gradually to such a condition that it will not attack the ground, but will be efficient in keeping the scraped parts open. The solid part that has been used for the acid test may be restored by rubbing upon it a little soap, which will effectually restore it to a full tint when rolled up. Any of the methods described for etching chalk drawings may be used in this process, after which the stone may at once be rolled up by the lithographic roller in black ink, until the lights become clean and the dark parts quite solid. It may, previous to the rolling-up in black, be washed with a mixture of turpentine and oil.

After rolling up in black, if the tint is found to be satisfactory, it may be dusted with very finely-ground rosin, and acidulated until a perceptible depth is reached. In this way relief will be imparted to those portions representing white chalk when the tint is printed in its proper colour on soft paper.

160. TINTS OF SEVERAL GRADATIONS. — Any of the

M

methods employed in making drawings on stone may be used for the purpose of producing tints of various gradations, and are, in fact, so used where exactness and definition are essential in the practice of Chromo-lithography. The method about to be described is, however, best adapted when two or three tints are required to be added to a drawing in black, or in the broader tinted effects in landscapes, &c., in colours.

The stone must have a sharp grain, as in the last-described method, but as this is a more complicated one, special attention is requisite to the subject of set-offs.   If an ink which will permit of a black set-off being seen through it be used for rubbing in the ground, as described further on, such set-off may be made with a good drying ink and allowed a day or two to dry.   If, however, the ground be too dark, or time cannot be allowed for the set-off to dry properly, the parts of the stone required to be defined in the various gradations are usually scratched with a sharp point through the lines of the set-off.   Sometimes a very fine gum outline will be found preferable, or common black writing ink, if not too gummy, may be used for a dark outline.   The white parts should then be determined upon and stopped out with gum and acid, and the stone, when dry, will be ready to receive the ground, which, however, must not be laid in with the roller, as in the last method, but as follows :—

Set the stone before a fire, and get it hot equably all over. Now rub over its surface a piece of rubbing-in ink,* and

---

* This ink may be obtained of the dealers, but as its composition is not of any great importance, most printers who are conversant with the process described above have their own favourite recipe.   Beeswax alone is a very good substance for this purpose, but is better when made dark by the addition of some black pigment.   Tallow may be added to the beeswax to make it softer and more easy to rub in on a moderately hot stone.   Wax, tallow, and cuttings of lithographic chalks, also make a very good ink, the latter ingredient rendering it sufficiently black to enable the artist to see the effect of his scraping.   These different compositions will be found to vary in their power of resisting acids, and we would consequently recommend the student to keep to one kind as soon as he finds it to answer the purpose, as he will thus be able to know what degree of etching he has to give to obtain any wished-for effect.

continue rubbing until the grain of the stone is filled in. Experience will soon determine the degree of heat necessary for this operation, and it will vary according to the nature of the rubbing-in ink. The superfluous ink is next to be removed by rubbing the face of the stone with a large piece of an old coat or other woollen fabric, changing the dirty part of the cloth for a clean one, as may be necessary, and continuing until a perfectly even surface is obtained.

The stone, having become cool, may be washed with water to free it from the gum, so that the effect of the scraping may be more distinctly seen.* This washing should now be done.

The next thing to be determined is, how many gradations of tint are required. For many purposes, what is called *full-and-half* tint will be sufficient in conjunction with the scraping; it will do very well for ordinary fine-weather clouds, and is thus performed :—After the scraping is done, the parts intended to be full tint must be filled in with thick litho ink, Brunswick black, or copal varnish. It must be observed, however, that gradation between full and half tint may be attempted by the use of crayon laid on in the usual way, or Lemercier's stumping crayon, applied with the stump ; but it must not be relied upon for producing the same effect after etching as is seen upon the stone. The margin and any broad white parts should also be covered with varnish, but not with litho ink, which might penetrate the gum. The reason for so covering the margin is this :—In the process of etching it will be found that the acid will recede from the edges of the tint, when there is a space of clear stone alongside it ; consequently, such part of the tint is less acted upon, and prints darker than is required. If, however, such margin or other broad spaces be stopped out with a resisting varnish, the etching fluid will act more equably where it is required.

---

* The inks we have indicated in the previous note will permit of washing, but it is quite possible that one bought from the dealer in these materials may have so much soap in its composition as to render washing a dangerous operation ; if so, it must be deferred until the tint has been once etched, but the *scraping* must be done previously.

The ink or varnish used for stopping out having become fairly dry, the stone may be etched by any of the methods described in treating of etching chalk drawings, but the acid should be used in a less diluted condition. The strength of the rubbed tint will determine how strong it must be used; but, speaking generally, the acid may be employed sufficiently strong to produce a brisk effervescence. If the method of etching with gum and acid, applied by a brush, be adopted, it will require dexterous management, on account of the tendency of the greasy ground to throw it off. Some parts, in consequence of this, will receive less etching than others, and the tint will become "spotty." This unequal biting of the acid may be much modified by setting the stone quite level, and applying plain gum-water to its surface until there is sufficient liquid upon it to lie there without receding from the greasy ground-tint.

A large flat camel-hair brush is now charged with gum and acid, and boldly swept over the stone, mixing it well with that previously there, until an effervescence appears all over the tint. The action having been continued a few seconds, the fluid must be washed off. It ought to be borne in mind that, by reason of the stone being covered with plain gum-water at the outset, the etching preparation must be used proportionately stronger.

One of the methods of flooding the stone before described will afford a better chance of even etching if it be thought worth while to set up the necessary apparatus. In any case, however, good work will ultimately be accomplished by noting the amount of effervescence taking place upon a ground of known resistive power. A little fresh gum, free from acid, may now be applied, and the tint washed out with turpentine and oil. It is then to be rolled up in black ink to test whether the process of etching has been successfully carried out. If there is not sufficient distinction between the full and half tints, the etching may be repeated with more dilute acid applied by flooding. If, on the one hand, it seems to be overdone, a thinner ink used in printing will tend greatly to restore the half tint without increasing the strength of the full one.

Tints of more than two gradations are produced in a similar manner. The parts desired to be of full strength having been preserved by the stopping-out varnish, the stone is then etched for the next lighter tint. This will need, in proportion, less etching than for half tint, but it must be borne in mind that more acidulation is required to produce the first than subsequent gradations. The stone is next washed and dried, and if only acid and water containing no gum have been used for the etching, it should be gummed in with weak gum-water. It is then stopped out with varnish, and the same operations repeated for the next gradation, continuing the process until the number of tints necessary to the effect sought have been obtained. Theoretically, there is no limit to the number of gradations that may be got by these means, but in practice it is usual to limit them to two or three between the deepest tint and white paper.

TINT-PRINTING requires considerable experience and judgment. We may point out, as a general rule, that thin inks produce soft and wash-like tints, while stiff inks make the tints look more granular, and keep them in better condition while being printed. The lighter the tint is, the less easily can any defects be seen while they are being inked; but as light tints show the grain of the stone less distinctly than darker ones, it follows that stronger ink may be employed for the purpose of keeping the work clear. The colour which needs most attention in this respect is *yellow*, which, on account of its lightness, is very apt to catch unobserved upon what should be the clean parts of the stone. The commencement of this defect is best detected by occasionally looking obliquely across the stone towards the window, or other source of light, when the stone will be seen to be distinctly greasy where it should be clean. The best preventive of catching is strong ink. A little stale beer may also be used in the damping water. When necessary, it must be washed out, and rolled up in black to better examine the condition. If the tint is found to have extended itself, it must be etched with very much diluted acid. This will require great care, and had best be performed for the student by some one more experienced, as it is next to impossible to give verbal

directions. The student may, if he has mastered the principles we have already laid down, be successful in re-
storing the stone to its previous condition, by a careful
etching, after it has been dusted with rosin. Previous to
applying the rosin, it will be well to take an impression
in black, to see if the full tint prints quite black; for if it
does not, there will be danger of further reducing it in the
deepest parts.

161. WASHING OUT TINTS AFTER THEIR FIRST PRE-
PARATION. — Care must be taken when washing out
these tints if they have been stopped out with varnish
made with turpentine. This solvent sometimes dissolves
the ink used in laying the ground, and when the whole
comes to be washed out with turpentine alone, there is
a likelihood of those parts of the tint not rolling up
properly. This difficulty may easily be overcome by
adding a little grease or oil of any kind to the turpentine used for washing out. After it has been once
successfully inked in, turpentine alone will usually be
sufficient for washing out when removing the black ink
to prepare for colour. It must be borne in mind, however, that the mass of ink is so much greasy matter,
and that when the dirty rag is changed for a cleaner one,
the quantity of grease is reduced with the next dose of
turpentine. If, then, the cloth, or sponge, or water should
be slightly acidulated, mischief may be done to the tint in
the last stage of washing out. Having due regard to these
matters, we may recommend the following mode of proceeding. Let the stone be gummed in with thin fresh gum-
water, or if the stone has been previously gummed, apply
water until it (the gum) becomes thin upon the stone.
Now apply the turps, and rub it with a soft rag until all
the ink dissolves. After absorbing as much as possible
of the dirty matter, a cleaner rag must be taken, and
a fresh application of turpentine applied, the stone being
still kept wet. If the stone now looks fairly clean, but
yet requires a final washing, a little oil may be added to
the turpentine to obviate any danger that may otherwise
arise from the use of too much. Though not actually
so, yet it will be well to act upon it as a principle, that
it is possible to wash the grease out of the stone with

turpentine. The printer will then add grease or oil to this solvent to prevent any ill effects consequent on too much cleaning.

162. THE ETCHING OF THESE TINTS may be facilitated by the following operation :—After the ground has been rubbed in, the gum used in stopping out must be thoroughly washed away and the stone dried. Set the stone in the press ; lay upon it a sheet of paper of the thinnest and evenest substance procurable ; upon this place a thin smooth sheet of metal, such as is used for paper-glazing, and pass the whole through the press with a light, even pressure. The result will be that some of the ink will be removed from the upper points of the grain, leaving them in a better condition for the action of the acid. The stone must then be stopped out, and treated just as described in par. 160. This brings us to

163. ANOTHER METHOD OF PRODUCING A TINT of several gradations with one etching. Any kind of set-off is first put down, so that the margin may be neatly and accurately gummed out. An impression is then taken upon tracing-paper, or an impression upon ordinary paper is laid upon grey or somewhat dark paper, and passed through the press so as to get a reversed key. If the corners of the margin be cut away exactly to the corners of the work, the impression may be accurately registered to the corresponding corners upon the stone and fastened to the margin, after the tint has been rubbed in with a soft ink. The tracing-paper impression, being turned over, will give the same results as the reversed impression upon the grey paper, and be equivalent to a set-off. If the desired effect be now worked up with hard white crayon upon the paper, a proportionate amount of ink will be removed from the stone by the back of the paper. It may here be mentioned that a more absorbent surface than the tracing-paper will effect this object better, and consequently the grey paper is to be preferred. In drawing in this manner, the hand-board or bridge must be used to rest the hand upon, because, if the hand rested upon the paper it would have a similar effect to the pressure of the crayon, and remove the ink where such is not intended. The tint ink is thus removed in proportion to the pressure of the crayon.

These tints may be etched by either of the methods
previously described, but perhaps the most effectual is
putting on a bordering of wax, pouring on the dilute acid,
and pouring off again, when the bubbles of gas have become
as large as pins' heads.*

164. ONE OF THE MODES INVENTED BY SENEFELDER
FOR PRODUCING INDIA INK EFFECTS may also be employed
for tint-making. A grained stone is first prepared with
soap-water, which, when dry, is removed from the surface
by washing with turpentine. The drawing is then made
with washes of hard ink, containing a considerable proportion of soap. When completed and dry, the drawing
must be rubbed over with a piece of flannel or other
woollen cloth, so as to better expose the points of the grain
to the action of the acid. Even the deepest shades previously laid will now be assailable ; therefore those parts
which are to remain quite black must be laid in after the
rubbing-in has been finished. We think that the principal
difficulty of this process consists in making the drawing.
In practice it is found that the working of the lithographic
ink on stone is so different to that of India ink on paper
that other modes are resorted to in preference, even though
they may be more laborious. When these drawings are
completed, they are best etched by surrounding the work
with banking wax, and pouring very dilute acid on the
work, letting it remain on until bubbles of gas arise and
attach themselves to the points of the grain. When the
work is thus covered with gas-bubbles the acid is poured off,
and these bubbles are thereby broken up. Another application of dilute acid is made, and the same action permitted
to go on again. This is repeated until sufficient etching has
been given, according to the subject. It is necessary that

---

* This method seems to be based on one of Senefelder's. He first
prepared the stone with gum, as for engraving, and then covered it
with soft ink. He then drew with *black* crayon upon *white* paper
placed over the soft ground. The stone was then etched with acidulated water without gum, and consequently the gum was removed from
the stone only in proportion to the manner in which the action was
regulated by the quantity of ink left upon the stone. The stone being
then washed and dried, would receive most ink where it had been most
etched.

the bubbles should be broken, or they would become enlarged, and prevent further action at those points. The acid would then seek new points to attack, and the consequence would be that the effect would be less brilliant than when the same set of points are repeatedly etched.*

165. STUMPED-IN TINTS.—The set-off having been made on a sharp finely-grained stone, the high lights are to be stopped out with gum. Take a piece of soft wash-leather, strain it over the finger, and charge it with some of Lemercier's lithographic stumping crayon. Now go all over the stone for the light tint, with a light circular motion of the wash-leather, re-charging it with the stumping crayon as often as necessary. The nature of the work will determine the precise method to be employed. Rolled wash-leather stumps may be used to lay in forms of clouds, &c. The scraper may be used to give precision in lights, and the crayon or ink for the deepest parts. If it be desired to imitate repeated flat washes of colour, it may be done in the following manner.

The light tint having been laid, as before described, the parts that are to remain of that tint are to be stopped out with thin gum, to which a little ox-gall has been added. When this is dry, the stumping crayon is again used to give the next gradation, which is in turn stopped out to preserve it. For each gradation the same process is gone through. When the whole is complete, the stone is to be flooded several times with hard water, until the gum is all removed

---

* In the year 1840 Mr. C. Hullmandel took out a patent for an improvement upon this method of producing effects upon stone in imitation of Indian ink drawings, which he called Lithotint. The drawing having been made in washes upon the stone was subsequently covered with a solution of rosin 4½ oz., pitch ¼ oz., and strong spirits of wine 1 quart. When dry it was etched with one part of nitric acid in six parts of gumwater. Some of the drawings done in this style were remarkably fine; but the process, like that of aqua-tint on copper, has gone out of use. In 1855 Mr. J. Aresti patented a different means of attempting to secure similar results, by subsequently transferring a granulated ground over the drawing, and then etching it. The results were inferior to Hullmandel's, and little was afterwards seen of it beyond a book of samples and description, called "Lithozographia."

without injury to the work.   It should then be permitted to
dry spontaneously, when it will be seen, from the absence
of shining patches, whether the gum is equally removed.
It may then be gently etched by any of the modes previously described, and further treated as if it were a chalk
drawing.

166. TINTS FORMED BY TRANSFERRING LINES, &c.—
In par. 82 we treated of transferring lines, in connection
with ink-work.   The same system may be pursued in
getting light tints in colour-work with good effect, and for a
simple light tint in conjunction with full colour the mode
there described will be all that is necessary.   These lines from
plate, however, may be used very effectively, and four distinct gradations obtained with one printing, by following the
instructions about to be given.

The plate to be used should, of itself, form what may be
denominated a quarter-tint.   The parts which are to be of
full strength are drawn in with litho ink, and those which
are to be white are to be gummed out.   The lines from the
copper or steel plate are then to be transferred, in a horizontal direction.   When this first transfer is complete, the stone
must be washed as clean as water will make it.   It must
then be prepared, either by an acid, such as acetic acid, or
a salt, such as the mixture of alum and sal ammoniac (see
par. 86); the latter being what we prefer.   In this process
it is necessary that particular attention be paid to this preparation of the stone.   To make the process more certain,
it is well to wash off the salt with a small pad of soft
cotton, covered with prepared chalk or whiting, which,
by a gentle friction that does no harm to the work,
removes the scum formed by the wash.   When the stone is
dry, those parts which are not to receive the second series
of lines are gummed out.   The direction of this second
series of lines is very important, and must make an angle of
60° with those first transferred.   A piece of cardboard may
be cut into an equilateral (equal-sided) triangle of any convenient size,—say six inches on each edge.   One edge being
applied to the lines already on the stone, a pencil line
should be drawn along one of the other sides.   The new
transfer is cut along one of the lines at or near the edge, or
is marked similarly on the back, and is then laid upon the

stone, so that the lines will run in the direction previously marked, that is, forming an angle of 60° with those first transferred. After transferring, the stone is to be prepared a second time, and a line put upon it to complete the triangle. The third transferring is then done, and the result should be that the lines coincide in direction with the three sides of the triangle :—thus △.

The reason for putting the lines so exactly in this direction is, that the production of any set pattern is thereby avoided. During the operation this may be verified on an unused part of the stone. Let the first two transferrings be crossed at right angles, and the third divide them equally. A kind of striped pattern will now be produced that would look very much out of place in a sky, for instance. Practically, then, if we want three transferrings, we must put them in in the manner before explained. For the same reasons, we are *limited* to three transferrings. This number answers very well, and will produce a very fair sky effect in subjects having a small number of colours, or in views having two tints.

At this stage of our work it is hardly necessary to remind the student that the process just described is best suited for polished stones, and that it will print more easily than the rubbed-in tints previously treated of. The same may be said of the next method.

167. TINTS FROM STIPPLED PLATES.—In paragraph 74 we spoke of a paper prepared by rolling it on a stipple-plate. In stipple or similar colour-work upon polished stones, where it is small, a sky or other effect may be chalked upon this paper and transferred in. Where the surface is large, the plate itself may be inked in, as for copperplate transfers, and transferred to produce a tint. This method may be also further utilized by chalking upon the transfer and adding ink to produce darker effects, the lights being scraped out previous to transferring. This, however, is scarcely applicable where there is more than one colour in the sky, as it then becomes necessary to work to the set-off on the stone so as to secure register. In the pursuit of the art it is almost imperatively necessary to be practically acquainted with all these methods, so as to be able to employ the one best suited to the work in hand.

168. We have now gone through all the usual methods of making tints. They certainly play an important part in the production of a chromolithograph or oleograph. It will easily be conceived that all the methods adopted in lithography are more or less used in the production of a chromolithograph. Chalk, ink, and scraping are frequently employed on one stone, and the artist must have taste and experience to know where to employ each to good effect. It may be well, therefore, to give a few hints to the young student upon the best manner of proceeding, leaving it to his further experience to show to him where he may depart from rule.

The picture must be first well studied, and the number of printings approximately determined, before proceeding to work. To this end, a scale of tints and colours should be prepared of the full strength it is intended to work them, and this should, if possible, be rigidly adhered to until the work is completed, as far as these patterns permit. A similar series, of a square form, may be put upon the stones so as to print side by side upon the edge of the subject. As it is difficult to judge of the precise hue and tone of a colour when it is surrounded by others, a small hole may be cut in each of two pieces of white and black paper. The printing colours can thus be fairly compared with that of the picture ; for if they appear exactly similar when viewed by means of the white paper and also by the black, it may fairly be assumed that, practically, a perfect match or facsimile has been attained.

In going through the colours of the subject to be copied, the pure hues of the primary colours must have especial attention, as they cannot be produced by over-printing, like the secondaries and tertiaries. Thus, the yellows, blues, and reds should first be determined, especial notice being taken whether any very deep bit of colour cannot be got by dusting powder-colour on the print, so as to save a working. Assuming that some of the secondary colours, green, purple, and orange, may be produced by printing two primary colours over each other, we may next seek for any special pervading hues of citron, russet, olive, grey, or brown. If any of these occupy a prominent place in the picture, they must have printings to themselves. This is usually the case with greys and browns, and often, also, with green. As there is a limit to the intensity to be obtained in printing some of the colours, it is often necessary to have two printings of full strength of the same colour, not, however, from the same stone. For a finished picture we may require something like the following list :—A pervading warm tint is generally required to tone down the rawness of the white paper in landscape and other artistic work where brilliancy is not the first requisite. This tint may in some cases be deepened towards the foreground by adding more colour to one part of the roller than to another. Of course this tint may be omitted in parts requiring great purity of colour. Then we may reckon upon two yellows, three blues, three reds, a green, two greys, and two browns, besides a finishing brown. We thus reach fifteen printings, which circumstances may modify by requiring less or demanding more, the presence or absence of important figures making considerable difference. Thus, if there were no figures at all, some of the blues and reds might be modified or dispensed with. The varying requirements of softness and texture will often determine where ink or chalk must be used, and whether it is to be used neatly, or delicately, or coarsely. Wherever chalk is used, it should, if possible, have a solid colour underneath or over it, so as to soften and modify that harshness which would result from contrasts with other tints of a solid or lighter colour. The effect of granulation in producing intensity and depth is very important, and is thus more effectively obtained than by printing one solid colour over another. This may be got by using either ink or chalk, or both combined, the one colour showing between the other.

CHAPTER XXIII.

CHROMOLITHOGRAPHY — PRINTING.   Pigments employed for
coloured inks—Treatment of colours—Dryers—Ink for tints—Oleographs—Roughing—Decalcomanie—Multiplication of colour subjects.

THE two last chapters treated principally of the different
modes of putting the chromolithographic subject
upon the stones, and the means of securing their proper
register.   We come now to the printing of these stones, and
shall first of all refer to the qualities of the colours without
entering into the question of their harmonies, a subject
which has been fully treated of by more competent authors.

169. THE PIGMENTS EMPLOYED IN LITHOGRAPHY embrace nearly the whole of those produced by the
colour-makers, but they are not all equally suitable for
lithographic printing.   The two necessary qualities are
permanency and ease of working, but these are possessed in quite different degrees by the different pigments.
The following inexpensive works may be consulted
with advantage :—" Hints on Colour and Printing in
Colours," by P. B. Watt.   London : Wyman & Sons.
" Colour," by Professor Church.   Cassell, Petter, & Galpin.
" The Principles of Colouring in Painting," by Charles
Martel.   Windsor & Newton.   Fortunately nearly all the
most trustworthy pigments can be successfully used in
printing, but some of the most brilliant ones are not only
unpleasant in use, but fugitive in colour.   This question of
permanency of colour is either much misunderstood or not
sufficiently attended to by many among the colour-printers of
the present day.   The demand for cheap inks is probably one
great reason why so many of our productions fade so rapidly,
and it is not in lithography alone, but in typographic block-
printing as well, that this defect frequently exhibits itself.

There are three enemies to permanency of colour
that are found to act inimically on colour prints.   They
are, light, impure air, and the chemical action of one
colour upon another.   We shall mention the pigments

which are more or less affected by the first two causes;
but detailed treatment of the third will be beyond the space
we can afford, demanding as it does almost a treatise to
itself. The works of Field* may be consulted if fuller
knowledge is desired. The following are the pigments
which are most suitable for making lithographic inks, but
the list does not comprise all that may be employed.

Reds	Vermilion. Indian red. Red ochre. Venetian red. Madder lakes. Crimson and scarlet lakes. Red lead. Chrome lead.	Oranges	Burnt sienna. York brown. Mineral orange. Orpiment. Orange lead. Chrome orange. Laque minerale.
Yellows	Yellow ochre. Raw sienna. Cadmium yellow. Yellow lake. Chrome yellow. Mineral yellow.	Blues	Ultramarine (dusting). Cobalt. Oriental, Chinese, and Prussian blues.
		Greens	Scheele's greens. Green lake.
Browns	Raw and burnt umber. Vandyke brown.	Purples	Mauve ink. Mixtures of blues with reds.

The following selection of pigments may be regarded as
permanent, under all the ordinary circumstances to which
a chromolithograph is likely to be subjected :—

Reds	Vermilion. Indian red. Red ochre. Venetian red. Madder lakes.	Oranges	Burnt sienna. York brown. Mineral orange.
Whites	Zinc white. Baryta white.	Blues	Ultramarine. Cobalt.
Browns	Raw and burnt umber.	Yellows	Yellow ochre. Raw sienna. Cadmium yellow.

* "A Grammar of Colouring," by G. Field. London : Lockwood & Co.

The following colours may be used, in addition to the above, *when they are more or less protected from light,* and are, therefore, useful in book illustrations :—

Reds	Crimson lake. Scarlet lake.	*Purples*	Mauve ink. Purple lake.
Yellow	Yellow lake.	*Blues*	Oriental blue. Chinese blue. Prussian blue.
Orange	Orpiment.		

The following colours withstand light and pure air, but are liable to injury by *damp, shade, and impure air :—*

Reds	Red lead. Chrome red.	*Blues*	Cobalt blues.
Oranges	Orange red. Chrome orange. Laque mineral.	*Greens*	Mineral green, or green lake. Scheele's green.
Yellows	Chrome yellows. Mineral yellow.	*Whites*	Flake-white and other lead- whites.

The following pigments *should not be used with flake-white* or other *lead colours :*—Indian yellow, yellow lake, Italian pink, orpiment, red lead, crimson and other similar lakes, carmine, and indigo.

Colours which should not be used with others *containing iron :*—Silver white, King's yellow, patent yellow, Chinese yellow, carmine, scarlet lake, blue verditer.

From the following pigments may be selected the colours for *finishing printings,* on account of their transparency :—Raw sienna, Indian yellow, Italian pink, yellow lake, madder lakes, crimson and scarlet lakes, cobalt, Chinese and Prussian blues, Mars orange, madder purple and purple lake, Vandyke brown and burnt umber.   Black ink, or other opaque dark colour, is used for finishing, on account of its cutting-up quality.

Many colours are kept in stock as inks by the ink-makers, but even if they are bought ready-made, the pigments should be kept by all who have not the advantages of carrying on their business in the metropolis.   Another point to be attended to is the quality of the colours, which should be obtained usually from the dealers in lithographers' materials.

It is unfortunately a fact that some of the most brilliant colours are not permanent, and this fact ought to be carefully kept in view by the conscientious printer. His first consideration should be whether the work to be done demands permanency. Much colour-printing is of a kind in which present brilliancy and prettiness are the qualities chiefly sought after. Among this sort of work may be enumerated, valentines, season cards, box tops, playing-card backs, &c. For these any colours may be used that are brilliant and work well. When, however, colour is to be applied to chromos for framing, show-cards, and subjects of permanent character, the pigments ought not only to be the best of their class, but they should be selected according to whether they will stand the test of time, and this should be done even at the sacrifice of a little present brilliancy. For copying pictures this will not be found difficult, because artists rarely employ pigments of a fugitive character. In the case of show-cards, brilliancy is frequently considered a *sine quâ non*, but if it cannot be had by the use of one colour, it can be got in another ; thus we may usually substitute vermilion for scarlet and crimson lakes. In doing so, we may not at the time obtain so pretty an effect, but if the two were compared after six months' exposure to the light of a window, the one printed in good vermilion will be found to have retained its hue and brilliancy, while the other has lost much of its force, and its colour has become dirty.

170. TREATMENT OF COLOURS.—The proper management of colours is only to be acquired by study, experience, and observation. We may be able, however, to give a few hints on this subject, but would premise that it is only by practice that the practical details can be adequately fixed upon the printer's memory. We have previously (par. 13) explained the manner of grinding colours, but in this place there are some special details of the subject which ought to be mentioned.

Colours differ in their physical qualities : some are bad dryers, while others dry so quickly that they print with difficulty. The obvious remedy for this latter defect is to add some substance which will retard the drying and render the ink more easy to work. We find this desideratum in the animal fats and other similar natural products. A little of any of these added to mineral orange, orange and red lead, &c., will make them manageable. The like addition is also frequently of advantage when enamel paper or card is found to break away and leave some of its composition adhering to the ink upon the stone. The fat, without reducing the stiffness of the ink, weakens its tenacity, and enables its particles to separate, so as to readily leave the stone. This is a secret much treasured by some printers, and jealously guarded from the knowledge of outsiders.

Colours differ also in the manner of their grinding. Some, such as carmine, emerald green, and ultramarine, can scarcely be used at all for litho printing-inks, and require to be dusted upon lighter inks of suitable colour. Some others, like the cochineal lakes, print better when first ground in water or turpentine, though their brilliancy is thereby somewhat reduced.

Some pigments may be ground more easily than others, some being soft and unctuous, while others are hard and gritty. Much, however, depends upon the previous preparation of the pigment by the manufacturer. Thus, there are natural colours, like York brown, which are ground easily ; while others, like Vandyke brown, are difficult to reduce to the necessary fineness. These and other colours may be bought after having been ground by steam power, by which much time is saved. A much better colour may sometimes be bought at one place than at another, and such apparently little matters must be learned by experience. The ink-maker will make ink of any colour to order, but some colours are constantly kept in stock, so that they can be had at a moment's notice. All these are important items of business knowledge, and can only be adequately gained by years of experience. Several of the large country colour-printers who employ many machines on chromo work, have small ink-mills, by which they grind their own inks. In this there is the advantage of knowing precisely of what pigments the inks are made.

It is advisable to pay a reasonable and sufficient price, in order to secure good materials. We have seen red ink which printed well and was fairly a good imitation of ver-milion, at three shillings per pound, but when exposed to light, in the course of a few days it showed a perceptible fading, and finally deteriorated to the hue of a poor orange.

171. DRYERS.—We have spoken in the last paragraph of certain colours which dry too readily. Some colours, on the other hand, have the opposite quality, and dry with difficulty. It is now necessary to refer to the substances which may be added to the ink to obviate this latter disadvantage.

What is known as "patent dryers" is a preparation of litharge, ready ground in oil, and it may be added to those colours for which it is suitable. "Patent dry dryers" is a white powder, which requires very little grinding to incorporate it with the ink. *Acetate of lead*, or, as it is commonly called, *sugar of lead*, is one of the most useful dryers, and does not injure the brilliancy of the most delicate colours. *Sulphate of zinc*, or *white vitriol*, or *white copperas*, as it is variously called, is less powerful than lead acetate, but better suited for some colours. These two substances should not be used together, as if so used they would probably decompose each other, producing *sulphate of lead* (which is an opaque white), and *acetate of zinc*, which is a bad dryer. Japanner's *gold size* is oil boiled upon *litharge*, and may be used as a dryer for lakes. These various dryers properly used will generally completely answer the printer's purpose. Too much of the dryers defeats the object of their application, and renders the inks saponaceous.

The following may be taken as good rules, for the general use of dryers. 1. Not to employ them too freely, as they then retard drying. 2. Not to use them in inks which dry fairly by themselves. 3. Not to add them to the ink too long before it is used, which would make them "livery." 4. Not to use more than one dryer at a time. 5. Not to use secret mixtures recommended by others ; but those simple dryers with which you are acquainted.

As dryers, we may use oil boiled upon manganese, or verdigris, in a similar manner to that boiled on litharge. These will do for dark colours. Some of the fast drying pigments may also be used as additions to dark colours, such as verdigris, or *acetate of copper*, red lead, massicot, and manganese-brown.

It will be seen that the printer has a variety of dryers at his command ; but were it not for rendering the colours too liable to dry upon the slab during printing, he might use in addition some of the quick-drying varnishes, such as copal or Canada balsam. A mixture of these two may be kept at hand for occasional use, where a few impressions in bronze, for instance, are wanted in a hurry. The mixture may be added to the ink upon the slab, and used even with common black ink, upon an emergency.

Dryers usually require well grinding at the same time that the ink is ground, but the patent dryers in powder, the patent dryers, and the drying oils, such as japanner's gold size, may be well mixed with the ink by means of the palette-knife.

172. ON INK FOR TINTS.—Tinting inks are those which are employed to produce light gradations of colour, such as those found in skies, clouds, flesh, &c. They are produced in two ways, each of which has its own advantages and defects.

The reader will easily understand that the greater the quantity of varnish used, in proportion to the colour, the paler and more transparent will be the resulting tint when printed. In this state it should be used in nearly all cases where the under printing is intended to show through it. There are occasions, however, when it is desirable to have the tint of an opaque character. It is then usual to grind some kind of white pigment with the ink, and as the whites made from lead possess the best covering qualities, they are frequently employed for this purpose. These whites, however, are so subject to change from various causes, more especially from their union with certain other pigments, that it is generally preferable to use zinc-white.

The use of white in tinting ink should be confined to the early printings. Whites are, indeed, very useful in obtaining effects in imitation of water-colour painting. This appearance is sometimes enhanced by the subsequent use of a dusting colour of a very light similar tint, or the ink may be dusted with white only. Another advantage of the use of white in the ink is that, on account of its requiring to be printed in greater body, its effect when on the stone is more easily seen than that of light transparent colours.

In the production of chromos, many of our best printers almost entirely discard the use of white, which they consider inimical to softness and brilliancy. For economical con-

siderations it is desirable to reduce the number of printings
to the minimum in producing the desired effect, and this has
been found to be more easily done by employing only transparent inks ; those colours being printed first which are in
themselves opaque, such as chrome-yellow and vermilion.
These are followed by the stronger colours of blue, red, &c.,
and they are glazed over by transparent printings of the
lighter tints, which, having no white in themselves, will
deepen and soften the previous ones without hiding or
dulling them.

The kind of varnish to be used for tinting ink will depend
upon the nature of the tint to be printed. If it be quite a
plain tint, the varnish may be of the thinnest, but if it be an
etched tint, or one which possesses much fine work in it,
the varnish should be stronger. An ink made with thin
or tinting varnish will lie soft and even on the stone, while
too strong an ink will give too great a disparity between the
light and dark parts.

173. OF PRINTING TINTS.—After what has been said of
the nature of tint ink in the last paragraph, little remains to
be told as to the method of printing with it, for all the principles previously laid down, in regard to printing in black,
apply to the printing in colours or tints. A great help to
printing tints well and quickly is the use of proper rollers.
These should be quite even on the face, of a fine texture,
and the seam quite invisible. It will save much time, and
add to the probability of clean work if five rollers be
employed :—one each for the blues, reds, and yellows ; one
for light tints, and another for the dark, broken colours.

Especial attention must be paid to the thorough cleaning
of the rollers, both by scraping, and washing with turpentine.
This is essential to printing pure colours, for if it be not
properly done, the previous colour, if different, will be found
to soil the new one. The darker the colour previously used,
and the greater its contrast with the one to be used, the
more likely will it be to injure the latter. The light pink
will be most injured by the dirt from a previous dark green,
and orange by a dark blue, so that the same roller should
not be used for these opposite colours.

On account of the difficulty of cleaning the ordinary
roller, the glazed roller (see paragraph 50) is sometimes

used, because, its pores being filled up, the ink lies entirely on the surface, and can be removed by a wash of turpentine. The use of glazed rollers, however, is restricted almost entirely to colours which print of full body, and in conjunction with polished stones.

Many attempts have, from time to time, been made to make a roller applicable to lithography, which should possess the qualities of good surface, elasticity and impermeability to printing ink. Those made of treacle and glue, which are used by letterpress printers for block or type printing, possess these qualities, but in lithography, the water used in damping the stone rapidly destroys the surface of such a roller, so that eventually it will not hold the ink. Some additions to these substances have been tried to obviate this difficulty with a certain amount of success, and rollers made which seem to answer very well as long as they keep in good condition, but they are liable to crack on the surface after a few months' use. These cracks hold the dark colour, which gradually contaminates the newly-applied delicate ink when such is used upon it. Were it not for this defect, these rollers would be of much service. These defects are overcome by a recent invention —Lanham's Patent " Victory " Rollers,—which are formed principally of india-rubber, and possess all the good qualities of the glazed roller, while they are permanently soft and elastic on the face, and possess a certain amount of nap in which the ordinary glazed roller is deficient. They are in use by some of the best houses in the trade, and are highly appreciated.

174. OLEOGRAPHS.—The distinction between oleographs and chromolithographs is only one of name, the real difference consisting merely in making the print imitate an oil painting as much as possible. To this end the finished print is mounted on canvas, sized and varnished. Sometimes the imitation of canvas is produced in the press by the finished print being pressed in close contact with what is technically known as " a roughing-stone."

In our opinion the oleograph is a mere vulgarity, which possesses no superiority to the ordinary chromograph. It is simply an imitation of the accidents of painting, and one in which these accidents are intensified, and thrust prominently forward. Attempts are frequently made to imitate even the thickly laid-on pigments used by some painters, and the canvas is shown coarser than any painter would care to use it. The embossing is as frequently as not out of register; the effect on an educated eye is far from producing an agreeable impression. It affords, in fact, a proof, the most convincing, that the picture is *not* a painting.

The lithographer is called upon to produce these effects, however, and it becomes our duty to record how they may be obtained.

175. ROUGHING.—Some of the most successful copies produced by chromo-lithography have been those of water-colour paintings. Among the advantages claimed for water-colour paintings are the even granularity of the paper and the absence of glaze. There are no patches of thick colour to suggest that it is paint we are looking at, and this grain of the paper is useful in preserving those aërial effects in which water-colour paintings excel all others. It was soon seen that the lithographic imitation was wanting in some important particulars, viz. ;—that its surface was too smooth, and lacked the atmosphere seen in the original. The defect once observed, the remedy was obvious—to give the picture the necessary granulation, by subjecting it to pressure on a rough stone.

The roughing-stone may be surfaced by using very coarse sand under the levigator; but if this is not thought to be rough enough, it may be intensified in the following or a similar manner. After the stone is dry, it may be rolled over with a glazed or letterpress roller until all the points of the grain are covered with ink, the bottom of the grain remaining bare. Brunswick black may be used instead of ink; but if the latter is adopted, the stone may be wetted, rolled up, and dusted with rosin. These points will now resist the action of weak nitric acid, so that the interstices may be bitten until the desired effect is attained.

A similar result may be obtained by applying stumping-chalk to the tips of the grain with wash leather, subsequently rolling it up and treating it as before mentioned.

If it be desired to have an exact imitation of rough drawing-paper, the latter may be sent to the stereotyper, who will furnish a cast of it which may be used instead of the stone. In the same manner a cast may be taken from a piece of canvas, if it be first well sized with starch.

When it is more convenient to use the stone for this purpose, the canvas can be first stiffened with glue thin enough to be absorbed by it. When quite dry, this will become stiff enough to stand considerable pressure. The stone may then be rolled in with a thick coating of transfer ink, the prepared canvas laid upon it, and pulled through the press with a light pressure. The ink will take the impress of the canvas, and the stone being subjected to the etching process, will be bitten in where the ink is thinnest. Another convenient way of applying a ground to the stone, is to roll it up in ink, and then dust over it some powdered rosin before applying the canvas. If the stiffened canvas be brushed over with gum, it may be applied to the stone with very light pressure, and some of it will set off on the stone in the form of the canvas. When dry, the stone may be covered with grease, rolled up, dusted with rosin, and etched. A reverse effect will be obtained by rolling the canvas with transfer ink, and transferring that to the stone.

When it is required to introduce embossing, a set-off from the key stone is put down, and the forms to be in relief are pencilled in gum, with a little nitric acid added. The stone is then inked and the canvas impressed upon it as before. When it is etched, the forms in gum will come away and will be bitten somewhat deeper than the rest.

If stone be used for this embossing, or roughing, it may be damped when the print is applied, to prevent its sticking, and the print will not need to be so dry as when an un-damped stone or plate is used, because the water on the stone prevents adhesion.

176. CHROMO TRANSFER PRINTS OR DECALCOMANIE.— These are chromographs which are intended to be transferred from the paper on which they are printed, to some other surface.

Take some thin plate-paper, and brush it over with flour or starch paste. When this is dry, the paper may be again treated with a strong solution of gum, or gum and starch. When again dry, it is to be well rolled. The printing is done on this paper, but the colours are worked in the reverse order to what they would be in ordinary work.

The transparent colours must be printed first, and the opaque ones last; so that when transferred the two will stand in their proper order. If these transfers are intended for being transferred to glass, the natural order must be observed, because they will be seen *through* it.

The mode in which these pictures are transferred is very simple. Either the surface they have to be applied to, or the back of the print, is brushed with a varnish, such as copal. When this becomes tacky, the two are rubbed into close contact and allowed to dry. If the paper now be sponged upon the back, it may be pulled off after soaking for a few seconds, leaving the printing firmly attached to the other surface.

177. MULTIPLICATION OF COLOUR SUBJECTS BY TRANS-FERRING.—No doubt most of our readers have seen sheets of chromos in which the subjects are repeated so as to make a sheet-full. These are not drawn so many times, but are transferred. The ordinary process of transferring will not do for this purpose. To insure success, means must be taken to prevent the expansion of the work.

There are two methods in use for this purpose. In the first, what is called "unstretchable varnish" transfer-paper is used. Register corners are put to each subject in each colour. In pulling the transfer, care must be taken to have the stone dry for each impression. The principal colour, or the key, is printed upon paper that has been well rolled, or it may be printed upon a thin sheet of zinc. The transfers are cut accurately at the register corners, and are gummed or pasted exactly to the corresponding corners on the sheet of paper or zinc. The stone having been adjusted in the press, the sheet is laid upon it and pulled through *once* under good pressure, when it will be found to have absorbed most of the ink from the pieces of transfer-paper. It is afterwards treated as an ordinary transfer.

When paper is used as the medium of carrying the transfers, it will be found a great convenience to have a framed piece of thick glass which can be set nearly upright or sloped to any convenient angle. The paper key is secured to the glass by pasting at its corners. The glass being set against the light of a window, a piece of white paper or other reflecting surface is used to throw the light through the glass. The register-marks can be plainly seen through the transfers, which may thus be placed in position with great accuracy. This instrument is called the "sticking-up" frame.

The second method is perhaps used more extensively than the one just described, on account of its possessing some advantages peculiarly its own. The transfer-paper is transparent, or nearly so, being prepared on one side with a transfer composition which will easily adhere to a wet stone. Paper coated with a solution of gum-arabic will answer. The transfers are pulled on this paper and trimmed round, but not so closely as in the other method, because to do so would be unnecessary. They are now fitted over the key (which can be sufficiently seen through them to insure accurate adjustment), and the corners gummed to keep the transfers in their places. The gum being dry, they are ready to be transferred, which is done in the manner described in paragraph 111. Zinc may also be used to attach the transfers to in this, as in the other method, but the cement used must not get dry, because it is important that the transfers shall adhere to the stone, instead of the zinc. They may be temporarily attached to the zinc by means of a little stiff varnish, golden syrup, and strong gum, or other similar adhesive matter that will hold them in place, and yet allow them to separate from the zinc when necessary. Thus when they are transferred to the damp stone they must adhere to it sufficiently for them to be pulled away from the zinc plate.

If opaque paper be used, the transfers may be accurately set up to register in the following simple manner. Corners are drawn in the key-stone, which are inked over in each succeeding colour. In each label of the stone first made

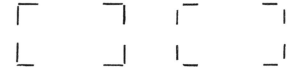

up, the corners are allowed to remain; but in attaching the transfers of the other colours, part of each corner, the extreme angle, is to be cut away, so that when one is laid over the other it can be seen plainly whether the lines correspond. The diagrams will show more completely what is meant.

The breaks in corners of the second diagram show what is cut away. This figure is to be laid over the first, so as to complete the corners accurately. Scotch transfer-paper well rolled can be used for the transfers in this way, and the sheet, when completed, transferred to a wet stone.

178. We have now described the processes of lithography in colours, with sufficient explicitness and accuracy, we hope, to enable those who have mastered the printing in black, to start upon the road to success. To those who have not advanced so far we do not address ourselves. For this reason we have made our descriptions as concise as possible. It would have been easier, perhaps, to have written more fully, but we are desirous of keeping our treatise within reasonable limits. We believe we have omitted nothing of importance, and that we have in many instances written what has not been in print before. Our object all through has been to make our "Grammar" a trustworthy guide, and we have not been intentionally unmindful of anything essential to success.

With the subject of colour-work we conclude those operations which are concerned in drawing on stone or transfer-paper, and printing from them or transfers of engraved plates or type blocks.

Our next chapter will treat of those modes of producing subjects for printing from stone which depend upon the action of light, and are known by the name of Photo-lithography.

CHAPTER XXIV.

PHOTO - LITHOGRAPHY. General Principles—Lenses—Cameras—Negatives—Sensitive Paper—Inking and development—Transferring—Modified processes—Gradations—Direct processes—Albertype—Heliotype.

IN treating of Photo-lithography we do not intend to describe the various general photographic processes, as there are many cheap and good treatises on the subject already published. Most of these photographic manuals, however, address themselves to portrait and landscape work, and we shall briefly point out the specialities of certain instruments which are best adapted to the technical purpose in view. Before doing so, however, we must give our readers an idea of the complete process of photography, so as to enable them to understand the details afterwards. to be presented.

179. Photo-lithography is a method of producing a copy of a print or drawing in line of the same or altered dimensions. This print is of such a nature that it can be multiplied from stone or zinc at the ordinary lithographic press or machine. It is necessary that the subject to be copied should consist of visible lines or dots to insure distinctness in the reproduction. The copying is done by photography upon glass. What is technically called a "negative" is first of all produced. If this negative is viewed by transmitted light, it will be seen that those parts which correspond to the white ground of the original drawing or engraving are more or less dark and opaque, while the copy of the drawing itself consists of transparent lines.

This negative is put into a photographic printing or pressure frame, and a piece of chemically prepared paper is placed face downwards upon it, in contact with that side of the glass upon which the picture has been produced. The back is then secured in its place, and the glass side exposed to the light. After it has been sufficiently exposed, it is carried into a dark room and covered all over with transfer-ink. Upon subsequently washing it, the transfer-ink will be removed from those parts upon which the light could not act, that is to say upon the parts corresponding to the white paper, but it adheres to those parts upon which the light has acted; namely, the lines. We have now a photographic transfer, which may be applied to a stone or zinc plate and printed from in the usual manner.

After this general outline of the process it is necessary to explain the chemical nature of the paper as it was exposed to light under the negative. Certain salts of the metal chromium, notably the bichromates of potass and ammonia, possess the property of extreme sensitiveness to light, when combined with various organic matters, such as gelatine, albumen, gum, &c. Being rich in oxygen, they quickly yield up some of it to the organic substance under the influence of light, and render it insoluble in water.

Not only is the organic substance rendered insoluble, but it is to a certain extent resistive of water, so that the ink applied holds to it tenaciously, while the part not so acted upon by light may with proper care be washed away. This effect also occurs spontaneously even in the dark when the paper is kept for some time, so that it is best to prepare it as wanted. Further, the solution itself will keep for a considerable period without undergoing a similar change; it is only when it becomes dry that the change takes place. This is a peculiarity which, in practice, is found to be very serviceable. We thus perceive that the prepared paper must be dry, not only to prevent staining the negative, but in order to be properly influenced by the light. We are enabled to coat the paper in ordinary daylight, but it must be dried in the dark.

We think we may now glance at the instruments and other requisites for this process.

180. THE LENS.—This is the optical arrangement which produces the image on the sensitive glass plate. The ordinary lenses used for taking portraits and landscapes are not adapted for this purpose. It is necessary to have lenses that will give in the negative straight marginal lines corresponding to or reproductive of the similar lines in the original. Suppose, for instance, a very large map is to be copied by this process. It will have to be divided into rectangular portions, each one of which must be suitable for copying to the required size, according to the lens used. It is imperative that the marginal lines of each negative be straight, or they will not join each other. Now the picture produced by the ordinary portrait and landscape combinations is somewhat barrel-shaped at its edges, and it is obvious that these would not correctly join together. A map is a crucial test; because not only is accuracy imperative, but any defect is at once visible. We cannot divide it into sections without cutting through portions which would at once show any error when the sections came to be put together. Ross's "Symmetrical," Dallmeyer's "Rectilinear," Steinheil's and Voigtländer's "Aplanatic" lenses fulfil these conditions; and such lenses give a

large-size picture in proportion to its focal length, whereas, before these and similar lenses were invented, the photo-lithographer had to use a lens of long focus, and use only the central portions of such picture as it was capable of yielding.

As much of the success of the photo-lithographer will depend upon the quality of his instrument, we advise him to buy direct from the maker, and explain to him the purpose for which he requires it. He may then expect that he will be well served, and that, should any failure occur, it is not an imperfection in the instrument which causes it.

181. THE CAMERA.—This is the dark box in which the plate is exposed while the subject is being copied. We shall not describe it, because that will be done in the work on photography that may be selected as a guide-book. As it is not every lens that will suit our purpose, so it is not every camera which can be rendered available.

The camera should be one of the expanding kind, as it will then be adapted to take two or more lenses, and work can be executed in enlarged or reduced dimensions as well as of the same size. The camera must be proportionate in size to the range of the lenses used, so that we cannot recommend anything definite. The student may also, in this instance, depend generally upon the advice given by a practical manufacturer.

182. THE NEGATIVE.—After the student has acquired sufficient photographic knowledge to take a negative, we may proceed to point out to him the qualities which his materials and apparatus must possess. A negative for portraiture or landscape is best when it is more or less translucent in every part, but that for our present purpose should be uniformly dense or opaque all over, with the exception of the lines forming the picture. These should be quite transparent. It is not easy, and not always practicable, at first, to obtain these qualities; but they should be the aim of the worker, because, after a little experience, it is comparatively easy to produce a good result in photo-lithography with a suitable negative. For first essays in photo-lithography, we should advise that a negative should be obtained from some photographer friend, so that the student may feel sure he is working with something suitable to his purpose.

183. THE PREPARATION OF THE SENSITIVE TRANSFER-PAPER.—It has been stated that gum, albumen, and gelatine are the principal organic substances employed in photo-lithography. The chemical differences between the bichromates of ammonia and potass are in this connection so slight, that it will be sufficient to select one of them,—say the bichromate of potass. Gelatine, albumen, or gum may be used separately or in conjunction; but to simplify the manipulation we shall confine our attention at first to the gelatine.

Set 1 oz. of the purest gelatine to soak in as much water as will cover it. While this is soaking, dissolve 1 oz. of bichromate of potass in 5 oz. of water, and filter. After the gelatine has swollen, pour upon it sufficient boiling water to make 11 ounces, and add the 5 oz. of bichromate solution to it. If put away in a cool place, this will keep good for a considerable time,—many times longer than will the paper that is afterwards prepared.

When used, this bichromatized gelatine should be poured into a dish, and the temperature raised to about 100° Fah. Some positive photographic or other fine-wove paper is taken by the corners and lowered upon it in such a manner as to exclude air-bubbles. Let it remain for two minutes, and then hang it up by one corner to dry in a dark room. When dry, it may be again floated upon the same solution, to insure it being uniformly coated, and hung up by the opposite corner to dry again.

A piece of this paper is placed in the pressure-frame as described in paragraph 179. It will be found upon examination that the back of the frame is divided into two parts by hinges, so that one compartment may be lifted and the progress of the action of light watched from time to time. The exposure may be for a minute or an hour, and will depend upon the intensity of the light and the quality of the negative. The appearance of the paper, however, will be a good guide for ascertaining the proper length of exposure. When the picture shows a deep tawny colour upon the yellow ground of the paper, it may be considered to be exposed enough.

184. INKING AND DEVELOPMENT OF THE TRANSFER.—A stone or metal plate having been adjusted for pressure in the press, is now inked up in transfer-ink. The photo-

graphic print is taken out of its frame, laid face downwards upon the stone, and pulled through the press, by which it is uniformly covered with transfer-ink. It is now laid with its back upon water warmed to the temperature of 100°. After soaking for a few minutes, it is laid upon a slab, and the inked side of the paper sponged with gum-water, until the picture becomes quite clean, after which it is washed repeatedly by pouring warm water over it. When dry it is ready for transferring.

185. TRANSFERRING.—As a basis upon which to transfer the print, we may use either stone or zinc. To guide us in our choice there must be taken into consideration the peculiar nature of the print. For all ordinary work, we have found stone to answer every requirement. It may be stated generally, that a polished stone will take finer work than a grained zinc plate; and that a polished zinc plate will take finer work than a polished stone.

The transfer is placed in the damping-book until it becomes limp, it is then pulled through the press upon the stone or zinc plate. If newly prepared, one pulling through will be sufficient; but if the transfer is two or three days old, it should be passed through the press several times.

When transferred, the subject is treated exactly as if it were an ordinary transfer from stone. If transferred to zinc, it will require the usual preparation of nut galls as for ordinary zinc-printing.

186. A MODIFIED PROCESS.—Some of the most successful operators use an addition of albumen to the sensitizing solution. The most available source of albumen is the whites of eggs. The white being carefully separated from the yolk, is beaten up, until it becomes entirely a froth. It is set aside, when the chief part recovers the liquid form, becomes very limpid, and may be filtered, which before would have been impossible. If only the white of one egg be operated upon, an equal quantity of water may be added to it, so as to render it more easily beaten. As the photo-lithographer does not require much of this albumen at a time, he will find Thomas's dried albumen a very convenient preparation. It can be easily weighed, like the other materials, and therefore can be exactly proportioned to them. It will readily dissolve, by

being soaked in cold water, stirring it occasionally, and it can immediately be filtered, as it requires no beating up.

A little albumen having been mixed with sensitized gelatine solution, the paper is prepared as before ; but care must be taken that the solution is not heated enough to produce coagulation of the albumen, which happens at a temperature above 140° or 160°.

This paper is treated precisely as the other, so far as exposure and inking are concerned, but it must be floated inky, side upwards on nearly boiling water. To do this with safety, the edge of the paper may be turned up a quarter of an inch all round and then dropped flat upon the hot water. This will prevent the water flowing over the surface, which would be fatal to that part so wetted. The object is to coagulate the albumen before the surface of the paper is wetted. This will take a short time, which the experience of the operator will determine. The paper is then washed with a sponge, as in the other process.

The chief use of the albumen is to improve the transferring. The ink entirely leaves the paper, which adheres to the stone sufficiently to permit being passed through the press any required number of times.

187. A PROCESS WITH GRADATIONS.—If an ordinary photograph be printed upon the sensitive paper, it will, upon development, be found to possess considerable gradation of light and shade. It may be transferred to a grained stone, and with careful etching will be found to yield a characteristic impression.

In this state, however, it is neither reliable as a printing surface, nor does it possess the necessary artistic qualities. By regarding it merely as a tracing, it can be made available, and, indeed, valuable. Instead of treating the transfer at once with acid, it should be thoroughly washed in warm water, and then set aside for a day or two. The stone may now be wrought upon with chalk, the work strengthened and granulated, and all deficiencies made good. If an artist be employed upon it, it is even possible to produce an effect superior to an original photograph, unless the latter happens to be of great excellence. The finished drawing must be treated exactly as if wholly executed in chalk.

188. A DIRECT PROCESS UPON STONE.—It was in working in this direction that some of the most valuable processes have been discovered; and though we cannot say that any of them remain as practical modes of operating, yet there is so much that is good in one of them, that we cannot refrain from mentioning it.

A solution of water, 1 quart; bichromate of potass, 160 grains; gum - arabic, 4 oz; and sugar, 160 grains, is spread upon stone and dried. Upon this is placed, not a negative but a positive picture on glass, and the whole is exposed to light. After the necessary exposure, it is carefully washed, first with plain water, and afterwards with a solution of soap, which, sinking into the denuded parts, is allowed to dry. The gum having been rendered insoluble by the action of the bichromate of potass under the influence of light, resists the adhesion of the soap to the stone, so that when it is rolled up, it is only the parts of the stone affected by the soap which yield an impression.

189. ANOTHER DIRECT PROCESS.—A solution of bichromatized gelatine is applied to a warm stone, and when dry a negative is superposed upon it and exposed to light. This negative may be one either of gradations or lines, it is immaterial which kind. After exposure to light, it is washed with sufficient cold water to remove the soluble salt of chromium, when the unexposed parts will be found to possess a little relief; but that is not what is wanted. What is more important is, that the parts most acted on by light should show a greasy tendency; and it will be found that when the inking-roller is passed over the negative, the ink adheres to the gelatine in proportion to this action. Hence we can roll up a most beautiful picture; but, unfortunately, few impressions can be obtained, because the gelatine is not hard enough to resist the united action of rolling and taking impressions. This, however, may be considered the parent of the next process, which has been worked with considerable success by many printers.

190. LICHTDRUK or ALBERTYPE. — The inventor of this process, Herr Albert, observing the defects of the last-mentioned one, substituted glass as the basis for the gelatine, because it gave him the opportunity of hardening the film from the back, by exposure to light. By a preliminary

coating of bichromatized albumen, also hardened by exposure from the back, he was enabled to effect his purpose more completely, so that a large number of impressions could be produced of very great beauty, and hardly distinguishable at a little distance from silver prints from the same negative.

One characteristic of this and similar processes is that a thick and a thin ink are alternately used. The strong ink being first applied, inks up the parts which have received the most light; while the thinner ink adheres to the more delicate gradations of colour. Very thick plates of glass are used, and are cemented to the lithographic stone by plaster of Paris, to enable them to withstand the pressure necessary in printing.

191. THE HELIOTYPE. — In this process the film of gelatine is made portable. A glass plate having the slightest possible film of wax upon it, is levelled, and the mixture of gelatine and bichromate of potass with a small quantity of chrome alum is poured upon it to the thickness of cardboard. When this has dried hard, the film can be removed from the glass, and exposed under the negative in the same manner as a piece of paper. After exposure, the soluble salt is washed out, and the film again dried. For printing from, the film is secured to a metal plate by a solution of indiarubber run round the edge. It is then treated precisely as the Albertype plate, but with this difference, that the inventor, Mr. Edwards, prefers an Albion or similar letterpress instead of the lithographic one.

Though some of these processes seem to be very easy when read of, they will require much patience and perseverance to master them. Had it not been for the similarity to lithography of their mode of printing, we should not have touched upon them at all. As it is, our sketch is necessarily a meagre one, because to have treated it more fully would have occupied too much space, and carried us beyond the limits of the lithographic system which we set ourselves to elucidate. The Woodbury type, and the processes for obtaining relief blocks are so much beyond our scheme, that we cannot do more than mention them.

There are also other lithographic processes in which the bitumen of Judea dissolved in ether, benzine, or chloroform, is spread upon the stone. When dry, the negative is laid upon it, and the whole exposed to light. When sufficiently exposed, the bitumen is no longer soluble ; so that when treated with the same or similar solvent, the part unacted upon is washed away. This process is very uncertain, and requires very bright light: hence, we cannot recommend it as a practical process.

APPENDIX.—RECIPES.

1. SOAP AS A LITHOGRAPHIC MATERIAL.—Soap consists of an alkali in combination with a fatty acid. The alkalies used in soap-manufacture are soda, potash, and ammonia; the acids are chiefly oleic, stearic, palmitic, and margaric. Soda forms the "hard" soap; potash the "sweet" or soft soap; and ammonia the kind of soap used in medicine, technically called liniment. Soda soaps will vary in hardness according to the acid employed. Stearic and margaric acids yield harder soaps than the oleic and palmitic. Soap, although it is of so much importance, is one of the least reliable compounds which the lithographer has to use. The only advice that we can offer in regard to obtaining an article fit for his purpose, is to apply to a respectable shop, and ask, and pay, for the best. Best white or yellow is what we employ. Seeing that soap may by dexterous management be made to contain 80 per cent. of water, that 20 per cent. may be considered a minimum, and 40 per cent. an average amount, it is no wonder that various results are obtained from apparently the same material. Supposing that it is desirable that soap for lithographic ink should consist of stearate of soda only, there is little chance of obtaining it of pure quality, when various samples of commercial soap are found to contain the following substances: glycerine; silicate, sulphate, chloride, and carbonate of soda; rosin; gelatine; fuller's earth; Cornish clay; ground flints; potter's slip; farina; dextrine, and other substances.

The principal object of the soap in lithographic ink is to render the other ingredients soluble in water; and any considerable quantity beyond that will be of doubtful benefit, because the more soap the ink contains the more liable it is, when dissolved, to pass from the state of a liquid to that of an emulsion. It is desirable, then, that the soap should maintain a proper proportion to the other ingredients, to effect which it must have the water removed from it by drying.

Cut the soap into thin shavings or scrape it with a piece of glass ; set it upon a dish before the fire, or on the hob, until quite dry. A cleaner way will be to put the shavings into an earthenware jar ; set that in a saucepan of water, and allow it to boil, and maintain it at that heat until the soap is quite dry. It may then be preserved in corked bottles for future use. Soap for chalkmaking may be treated in the same way.

2. LITHOGRAPHIC WRITING AND DRAWING INK.—Many recipes for this ink have been published from time to time, but the one to which we give preference is one of the oldest of them, having been published in France about sixty years since :—

Take of Tallow.............................. 4 oz.
Wax .... 4 ,,
Soap* .... 4 ,,
Shellac .... 4 ,,
Fine Paris Black .... Quant. suff.

This recipe makes the best ink we have ever used for drawing on stone, though for transfer-paper we have thought we have improved it by adopting the following proportions :—

Tallow................................. 4 oz.
Wax .... 5 ,,
Soap .... 4 ,,
Shellac .... 3 ,,
Black............ About half the quantity used for stone.

For re-touching the latter ink is excellent, as it will frequently hold firmly to the stone, if only well washed, without any acidulous preparation ; not that this course is to be recommended, it being mentioned only to point out the quality of the ink.

Recipes are frequently of very little use unless accompanied by a description of the precise manipulation ; and we think we shall be able to point out a mode of making lithographic ink, that, if followed, will lead to success.

---

* We have found this quality, as bought at the oilman's, quite sufficient to make the other ingredients soluble, notwithstanding the water it may have contained.

Take a small saucepan (one that will hold a quart will do for the above quantity) and fit a handle of wood inside its iron one, so that it may be about a foot longer. This will enable the operator to have command of it when its ordinary handle becomes too hot. Make another wooden handle 12 in. long, and fit it to the handle already upon the lid in such a manner that it may, when on the saucepan, project horizontally. If the flame in burning the ink should become too high, it may be removed from the fire, and by means of the handle last described the lid may be put on without fear of burning the fingers, and the flame extinguished by cutting off the source of oxygen—the external air—without which it does not burn. These simple contrivances will render the operation a safe one with persons of ordinary care and intelligence, and will enable them to devote their attention more satisfactorily to the ink-manufacture. Put any kind of oil or rough fat into the saucepan and heat it until its tin lining becomes melted, when it and the oil may be poured away together; or the saucepan may be gradually brought to a red heat and the tin burned away. We prefer the first method.

The fire for ink-making should be a clear one, yet not low, as the operation will require a considerable time; putting on new coals would perhaps cause a flame to play round the saucepan and set fire to its contents at an inconvenient moment.

Put into the saucepan the tallow and wax, and when melted throw in the soap a little at a time. Contrary to the teaching of some manipulators, we can assure the student that it is not at all essential to have the soap previously dried, if caution be observed in putting it in. The principle is this: Common soap, as shown in the last paragraph, contains a considerable quantity of water, which is readily parted with at its boiling-point. The tallow and wax in the saucepan soon exceed this heat, and when the soap is thrown in, its water is violently expelled; and if too much be added at a time, the whole may boil over into the fire and cause mischief; but if it be thrown in in small pieces, and time be allowed for each piece to part with its water (which may be known by the cessation of the ebullition it at first causes), its solution in the wax and tallow may be safely performed. When this has taken place, the heat must be continued until the dense light-coloured fumes passing off can be ignited upon the application of a light. If the flame be two or three inches high, the saucepan may be removed from the fire, when the burning will most probably be continued without further application of heat to the bottom. Stirring with a rod will facilitate the passing off of the vapour, and will raise the flame higher. If the quantity herein named be used, it may be burnt perhaps for half an hour; but whether a longer or shorter time be involved, it must burn till the twelve ounces are reduced to nearly eight. This may easily be found by weighing the saucepan at starting and afterwards making an allowance for that weight during the burning. Arriving at this stage, put out the flame and add the shellac a little at a time, taking care that it does not boil over. Add now the black.

We do not allow the mixture to ignite after the shellac and black have been added, because it is apt to form a carbonaceous crust on the top. If afterwards it is found, as it probably will be, that the burning has not been continued long enough, it may be again heated, and the effect estimated by observing the density of the light-coloured vapour passing off.

It is important that the black should be ground. This cannot be easily done with any of the ingredients used for the ink, but if it be ground in turpentine and cautiously added to the ink, the heat will vaporize the turpentine, whose place will then be taken by the other molten ingredients; whereas, if it were added in the state of dry powder, there would be considerable difficulty in properly diffusing it throughout the mass.*

Considerable difference of opinion appears to exist as to the amount of black to be used. On reference to formulæ in our possession, we find it variously stated at from one-sixth to one-twentieth of the whole. The following considerations may decide the matter :—1. All blacks are not equally powerful. 2. Ink for use on stone may have more than that for use upon transfer-paper. 3. Ink with little

---

* Good lithographic printing-ink, in the same condition as bought from the maker, may be used for this purpose if an allowance be made for the small quantity of varnish with which it is ground.

black makes purer and finer lines with the ruling-pen than that which has much. 4. Ink for transfer-paper should show a gloss when it becomes dry in the saucer, and the colour of a thin solution should be brown rather than gray. In practice, it is better to err on the side of putting too little than too much black, because the former can easily be remedied.

The ink having been brought to this stage, requires now to be tested to determine whether it is sufficiently burnt, and we believe we can claim the credit of being the first to draw attention to, if not to discover a simple method for determining this important point. Ink that is not sufficiently burnt becomes thick and slimy on standing for two or three hours after mixing with water, but our method shows at once whether it is burnt enough. Place about a grain or so on a saucer, and drop upon it a little distilled water; watch it for a few seconds, and notice whether the ink appears to become lighter in colour : if it does, it is a sign that the burning has been insufficient. Heat again, and allow the white fumes to pass off for a few minutes without catching fire. Try the ink again. When it retains its blackness upon the addition of water, we have found that it will also keep in a good working state, and have made it for law-writing, by the pint, as described in paragraph 68.

The ink having been proved, may now be cast into sticks for convenient use. The method we adopt we can recommend for simplicity. Cut six or more pieces of printers' furniture into equal lengths of 3 or 4 in. and two pieces of 8 in. long, and thoroughly oil them. Take a piece of glazed tracing-cloth and well oil that also. Place it on a stone and arrange upon it the pieces of wood thus :—

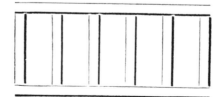

Pour out the ink into each division successively, until the saucepan is empty. Allow the ink to set, but while it is yet warm, slide away first one long piece of wood and then the other. As soon as cool enough to handle, the tracing-cloth may be raised from the stone with the sticks of ink, and then peeled off; the wood pieces separated from the ink, and the latter wrapped in tinfoil and put away in a dry place.

Other substances, such as gum-mastic and Venice turpentine, may be used in making ink, as the following table of the various inks used by Senefelder will show. The list might be much extended, but whether with any improved result, we cannot say.

No.	Lamp-black	Soap.	Wax.	Tallow.	Shellac.	Mastic.	Venice Turpentine.
1	1	4	12	4	—	—	
2	1	4	12	—	4	—	
3	1	4	—	8	8	—	parts.
4	1	4	8	—	4	—	
5	1	4	8	4	4	—	
6	1	4	6	2	4	3	1
7	1	4	2	6	3	5	

It will be noticed that in all these recipes, the soap and black bear an unvarying proportion to the total of the other ingredients.

3. TYPE RE-TRANSFER INK—OR INK FOR STONE-TO-STONE RE-TRANSFERS.—Melt two ounces of lithographic writing-ink in a saucepan over the fire. While this is melting mix two ounces of litho-printing-ink with two ounces of varnish, add it to the writing ink, and well mix the whole while it is hot. This may be set aside for use, and will keep indefinitely. It must be tempered with a little ordinary printing-ink if too stiff for use, which addition will prevent the soap contained in the ink from tinting the stone. When used for type transfers it may be thinned with a minute quantity of turps.

4. INK FOR THE DABBING STYLE. See par. 136.—This may be made as the last, with the varnish omitted.

5. PLATE TRANSFER INK.—The making of re-transfer ink for taking impressions from copper plates is conducted in the same manner as that for writing and drawing. Taking either of the following recipes, it is preferable to burn only the first three of the ingredients by setting them on fire after they attain sufficient heat to do so. For the quantities first named they may burn for 15 minutes. If after the other ingredients are melted the ink is yet too soft, it is best not to set them on fire, but to keep up the heat until the necessary degree of hardness is arrived at. Melt the ingredients in the order they are set down. The first recipe is the one we use ourselves.

No. 1.	Oz.	No. 2.	Oz.	No. 3.	Oz.
Tallow	4	Varnish	2	Varnish	8
Wax	4	Tallow	$1\frac{1}{2}$	Tallow	10
Soap	4	Wax	4	Wax	16
Shellac	4	Soap	3	Soap	8
Pitch	4	Shellac	5	Shellac	14
* Stiff Litho printing ink at 3s. per lb.	4	Pitch	5	Pitch	7
		Lampblack	$2\frac{1}{2}$	Lampblack	2
Tallow	8	No. 4.			
Soap	4	Wax	8	Venice turpentine	8.
		Shellac	4	Burgundy pitch	8
		Lampblack	1		

Where varnish is employed that should be burnt also.

6. LITHOGRAPHIC CRAYONS. — These are made in precisely the same manner as the ink, and may even be made of the same materials if they are burnt sufficiently hard for use in drawing. A good useful chalk that will keep well can be made from equal parts of wax and dry soap. By judicious burning it may be made of various degrees of hardness. The various recipes given from Senefelder will yield a great variety of crayons by burning them

---

* By this is meant the unreduced ink, just as bought from the ink-maker.

more or less. Each one has also its own peculiarity in working, and will yield different grains from each other, which may be found useful to the artist. Crayons almost invariably contain such a large proportion of soap that etching is imperative to correct its tendency to spread, but if they are made with little soap, they do not work freely, and are liable to be more affected by variations of temperature.

Crayons may be cast in the flat cake and then cut up with a saw or hot knife into square pencils, but they are better cast in a grooved box similar to a druggist's pill-machine, and pressure applied while hot. This box may be made as follows :—

Obtain a plate belonging to a pill machine containing about twelve grooves. By cutting this in two across the grooves a length suitable for a crayon will be obtained. Make each half equal to the other and mount it upon a piece of wood a half inch or more thick.

Have these cast in iron and the grooves afterwards smoothed. Around one piece screw strips of iron about one-fourth of an inch in height to form a box into which the composition may be poured. To use this take the tympan away and place a stone in the press, and upon it the mould, previously warmed, and pour in the composition, upon this place the other piece and bring down the scraper-box until the superfluous material is squeezed out. The mould having been previously oiled, the crayons may be removed, care being taken to keep them straight.

Crayons may be well kept in wide-mouthed bottles tightly corked.

SENEFELDER'S COMPOSITIONS FOR CRAYONS.

No.	Black.	Soap.	Wax.	Tallow.	Shellac.	Spermaceti.	
1	2	6	4	–	–	–	
2	2	4	8	–	–	–	
3	2	4	4	–	–	4	parts.
4	2	4	8	–	–	4	
5	3	5	8	–	4	–	
6	3	5	8	2	4	–	
7	3	6	8	4	–	–	

7. LITHOGRAPHIC VARNISH.—Put two quarts of the best linseed oil into a saucepan large enough to hold a gallon. The lid should have a long handle, so that it may be put on the vessel with safety while the contents are burning. Set it on a clear fire until white fumes arise. Apply a lighted paper occasionally until these fumes catch fire and burn. It must now be watched carefully so that the flame shall not become unmanageable. If the flame goes down a little it may be increased by stirring with an iron rod. If it shows a tendency to rise too high it may be removed from the fire, when it will still continue to burn. If it rise too high, and threaten to become dangerous, the lid must be put on, when the flame being deprived of the access of air will be extinguished. If the flame has been very high, the lid should be kept on long enough to allow the whole of the oil to cool down a little, for if it were merely extinguished and reopened, it would take fire spontaneously and flare up nearly as much as before.

The oil is burnt until it becomes one-sixth less. A thick slice of bread is now put in, and moved about with a fork until it is browned. It is then allowed to burn a little more, it being set on the fire again to revive the flame if the latter has become dull. A second slice is now put in and cooked in a similar manner. This proceeding is said to free the oil from its more greasy particles.

One-fourth of the oil may now be taken away. If on becoming cold it is of a syrupy nature it may be set aside for *thin* varnish.

The rest having been burnt again for a short time, a third part of the rest is to be taken away. This is *medium* varnish.

The remainder is again burnt, and one-half of it set aside for *strong* varnish.

The fourth portion is again burnt, and when cold it should be thick and ropy.

If these varnishes are not as strong as expected, they may be burnt again until they become of the required consistency.

It is necessary to take every precaution to guard against accident. The operation should not be carried on in an ordinary apartment, but in a back kitchen or other place where there are few things about likely to catch fire, or be spoiled by an accident. If the oil be neglected, the flame may rise several feet, and become unmanageable ; it is well, therefore, to provide wet sacks, or something equivalent, to use in case of accident.

8. TRANSFER PAPER.—In par. 7 of our Grammar we explained the general nature of transfer paper, but now we give a few recipes.

Transfer Paper for Warm Stones.—Make a size by boiling parchment-cuttings. Let it be so strong that when cold it will be firm jelly. Grind dry flake-white with water, add it to the size after warming it, well mix, and rub through a sieve. The proportion of flake-white may vary with circumstances. If too much be used, pens will not work upon it properly, and probably the finest lines will fail in transferring. Coat the paper with the composition with a full brush, or use a sponge, and give two coats—the second when the first is dry. If for writing, the paper may be thin ; if for drawing, it should be thicker, using drawing-paper for very large subjects. The stone for this paper should be quite warm. Similar paper is made from gelatine, or even from the better sorts of glue instead of parchment-cuttings. Other substances are also used instead of flake-white,—such as chalk and old plaster of Paris. Flake-white is best, because it grinds up so finely.

Paper for Cold Stones.—Take four ounces of starch, and one ounce of best pale-coloured glue. Break the glue, and put it in cold water over night to soak. Mix the starch with a little cold water, and then pour boiling water upon it until it thickens, stirring it all the time. Now put in the glue, and boil over a slow fire or gas-jet, brush over the paper while warm. This may be used on tracing-paper, printing-paper, or writing-paper. For ordinary use printing-paper is preferable, because the water penetrates more quickly through the back of it in transferring. Some persons add a little flake-white to this paper. If a more adhesive paper is required, a commoner kind of glue may be used, and its proportion increased, or gum-arabic or even dextrine may be added.

Colouring Transfer Paper.—The addition of colouring matter to transfer-paper is for the more ready determination of the coated side. Gamboge is generally used, but any kind of colouring matter will answer the purpose. We somewhat prefer a light pink tint, because that is distinguishable by artificial light, while a yellow is scarcely visible. Rose-pink, or a solution of cochineal in ammonia, answers this purpose.

Glazing Transfer Paper. — The paper may be pulled through the litho press, face down, on a smooth stone ; but it is much better to send it to a hot-presser to have it properly rolled. Many law-writers prefer it when it is merely pressed between smooth and clean glazed-boards.

Hanging Transfer Paper up to dry.—Put lines across a room, about nine inches apart. Lay the wet paper over a T-shaped piece of wood, and place it on the lines neatly and cleanly. The piece of wood being drawn away may be used for another piece, and so on until all are done.

The formulæ for transfer paper might be multiplied, and no doubt the student will meet with many in the course of his studies, but we have purposely avoided giving them empirically. What we have given, we have proved in a somewhat extensive practice, and can vouch for it that they answer the purpose intended as well as any. We always prefer a simple recipe to a complex one, when we know it will do equally well. Thus, we prefer the starch and glue paper and a cold stone as being the simplest and quickest, and find it quite efficient for the most elaborate and minute work. The starch forms the main body of the composition and makes it adhesive to a cold stone. By itself it hardly bears out the writing-ink upon the surface sufficiently, and the gelatinous matter is added to compensate for this defect. If the gelatine is very good, the addition of a greater proportion will reduce its adhesiveness to cold stones, while common glue or gum will increase it. Bearing these principles in mind, any kind of transfer paper may be made, but too sticky a quality has the drawback of requiring greater care in damping for transferring, while it is not so pleasant to write upon.

It is recommended by some persons, to put a certain quantity of alum into the composition. This proceeding we cannot recommend, because the alum has a tendency to render the composition insoluble.

9. Scotch Re-transfer Paper.—The recipe for this paper has been given in many works treating of lithography, but so far as we are aware, always unaccompanied by the details of manipulation, without which the formula is comparatively worthless.

Take of plaster of Paris and best seconds flour equal parts by weight, to which add sufficient colouring matter to be able to know one side from the other either by daylight or artificial light. We recommend something of a red or green hue, because that can be more easily distinguished by gaslight than a yellow tint.

To prepare the Plaster.—In this lies the secret of success, and the method is believed to be here for the first time published. Obtain the *best fine* plaster from the manufacturer of plaster of Paris images, &c. That to be found in country towns in use by plasterers and others is usually so coarse as to be worthless for this purpose. Put half a pound of plaster into a basin that will hold about two quarts ; pour upon it a little water and mix it up with a wood spatula until of the consistence of cream. If it were now let alone it would soon set into a hard stone-like mass, but this must be prevented by constant stirring, and the addition of small quantities of water whenever the plaster shows a tendency to thicken. This constant stirring and watering will occupy half-an-hour, by which time the "setting" quality of the plaster will be destroyed, and may be left while the paste is made from the flour. Mix half a pound of flour into a smooth paste with a little water, then add sufficient water to make it into paste of ordinary consistency when boiled. Set it on the fire while cold, stir it constantly until it boils, and let it boil for five minutes. The saucepan should be large enough to hold twice as much, and the fire a slow one, or the paste may be expected to boil over. If this should happen, some will be lost and the proportions destroyed, when it will be better to make a new lot than to run the risk of spoiling the transfer paper.

The paste is now to be added to the plaster and well mixed, after which it must be passed through a piece of cloth or fine sieve (the 120-hole sieve for sifting graining sand will do admirably) by putting in a little at a time and rubbing it through with a stumpy hog-hair brush. When all has been passed through, the composition may be applied to the paper with a large flat camel-hair brush about four inches wide. If any difficulty is experienced in spreading it evenly, it may be too thick and can be diluted with water to a proper working consistency, a matter to be determined by experience. Our practice is to brush it on in one direction, and then to lightly brush it at right angles until it presents a uniform layer of about the thickness of thin cardboard. We recommend the beginner to use a tablespoon or other similar convenient measure for measuring an equal quantity for each sheet; by adopting this method sufficient composition may be applied at one operation. Some recommend two coatings to be given with a sponge, but a sponge is not at all suitable for laying it on, something is required that will glide over the surface and leave a body underneath. If some suitable colouring matter be used it will materially assist the beginner by enabling him to see whether the composition is laid on evenly. The sheet having been coated is to be hung on a line to dry as in making other transfer paper. A thin demy *printing* paper about 15 lb. to the ream will be good enough for this purpose. It will appear very much stouter when dry.

If these directions are faithfully followed, we may venture to say that the best possible paper for re-transfer purposes will be the result.

Be careful that the composition does not dry in the brush. Let it lie in water if inconvenient to clean it at once.

10. RED AND BLACK TRACING PAPERS.—The preparation of these is very simple. Tissue paper is a much better foundation than tracing paper, the varnish of which is apt to unite with the colouring matter and prevent its transference to the stone. Lay out the paper upon a smooth board, sift upon it some powdered red chalk or black lead, and rub it in, being careful not to tear the paper; when the paper is well covered, the superfluous colour may be first removed with a hard brush and finally wiped with a cloth. Its effect may now be tried on stone or paper. If it is too dark, more colour may be removed with a cloth. The colour should not come off by leaning the hands upon it, but should give a nice smooth clear line under the tracing point.

P

Red chalk paper should be used for lithography ; and blacklead paper for designs, &c., on paper, because the, blacklead can be removed with indiarubber, though the red chalk may be removed by bread crumbs.

Chrome yellow may be used for paper employed in tracing on black grounds in engraving on stone ; when the colour of the ground is red, fine Paris black makes the best tracing paper (see Engraving on Stone).

11. Transfer Papers for re-transferring Colour-work.—The Scotch transfer paper will answer almost every purpose for re-transferring where correct register is not required, as in the multiplication of colour subjects (par. 177). For this purpose thin foreign post paper may be coated with starch-paste and afterwards well rolled when dry, so as to restore its semi-transparency and render it in other respects suitable for the purpose. Stout tracing paper may be employed with the same treatment where a more transparent paper is required. Copying letter paper may also be employed. When the main object, of seeing the work sufficiently well through the paper, is secured, it only remains to give such a coating as will take a good impression and stick sufficiently to the wet stone.

Those who do not like the transfer upon wet stones may employ the varnish transfer paper. Paper is varnished by the method given in our article on Collodionizing, &c., and after being thoroughly dried, it is coated with the gelatine sizing material or with starch paste. This paper requires a transparent frame to patch up the transfers by, but it may be modified so as to do without it. If thin foreign post or similar paper be varnished without previous sizing, the varnish will render it transparent. When dry, give it another thin coat of varnish. When thoroughly dry, give it the coat of gelatine or starch as before. This paper may be employed exactly as the other varnish transfer paper.

12. Transfer Paper for Chalk Drawings.—Stout printing-paper is thickly coated with the Scotch transfer composition, to which a little glue has been added. After drying, it is rolled on the stippled plates mentioned in par. 74, or pulled once through the press under heavy pressure on a grained stone.

Almost any transfer paper may be employed for this purpose, when properly grained, but the above possesses the advantage of permitting lights to be scraped with facility,— an important consideration in chalk work, whether on stone or paper.

13. PORCELAIN OR ENAMEL PAPER.—This paper is employed in printing where brilliancy of effect is sought, whether for colour or bronze work. Although we do not wish to recommend its manufacture by the printer, it will be as well for him to understand something of its make and properties.

Ordinary enamel paper is prepared by brushing over common printing-paper a mixture of flake or Kremnitz white with fine light-coloured glue and a little alum. The glue must be only sufficient to prevent the white from peeling off the paper during printing. If too much were used, the paper would be hard and non-absorbent. If zinc-white be used instead of the lead-white, it will be less liable to change colour in impure air. The mixture may consist of 4 oz. of Russian glue dissolved in 3 quarts of water; in this grind $1\frac{1}{2}$ lb. of zinc-white and pass through a sieve. Apply two coats. When dry, the paper may be polished by brushing with a somewhat hard hairbrush, and subsequently further glazed by rolling on polished metal plates.

We believe that sulphate of baryta is sometimes used instead of zinc-white, and that a mixture of white, turpentine, and oil-varnish is also used for a similar purpose.

Enamel cards are damped by placing them between sheets of damp paper.

14. COLLODIONIZING, GELATINING, AND VARNISHING.— Coloured lithographs on box-tops and other similar articles are frequently found to possess a very high degree of gloss, which may be obtained by one of these processes.

COLLODIONIZING or ENAMELLING.—This is the most troublesome process, but it is that which gives the highest finish. A level glass plate, of a size suitable for the work, is first well cleaned. It has then rubbed over it a little white wax, the plate having been made hot. It is then rubbed off again with a clean new linen cloth. The wax may be dissolved in a solvent such as sulphuric ether or benzoline. It is then wiped off, as before described. The object is to leave a very slight film of wax upon the glass, so as to permit of the subsequent applications being removed. A bottle of enamelling collodion (which may be obtained at the dealers in photographic materials) is then taken in the right hand, while the glass plate is held by one corner by the fingers and thumb of the left hand. The collodion is poured upon the middle of the glass and allowed to run towards the edges of the plate. When there appears enough to cover it, cease to pour from the bottle, but run that on the plate towards one corner ; then let it run along the edge to another corner, and so on, until the plate be covered. Resting the last corner at which the collodion has arrived upon the mouth of the bottle, pour the superfluous collodion back into the bottle, observing while doing so to rock the glass plate from side to side, so as to avoid its running into crape-like lines. In a few seconds the collodion will be set. Now pour upon it a solution of gelatine, prepared by dissolving an ounce of fine bright gelatine in ten or twelve ounces of water. Lay the plate in a level position to set the gelatine ; effecting which, it may be placed on edge to dry in a place free from dust. A number of plates may be thus prepared. The print to be enamelled must be quite dry. It is then coated with a similar solution of gelatine, to which a little solution of ox-gall has been added. The print is then dried. The gelatine-print is now laid in water to become limp. The coating on the plate is wetted with a sponge and the two brought in contact, the superfluous water and all air-bubbles being, as far as possible, excluded. The whole is then allowed to dry thoroughly, after which the print may be carefully raised from the glass, when it will be found that the coatings of gelatine and collodion will be brought away with it, and the surface will be equal to that of the glass.

This process may be simplified by omitting the coating of gelatine upon the glass and laying the print down upon the *dried* coating of collodion.

15. GELATINING.—The description of the foregoing process will explain this one, as the principal is identical. The glass plate is waxed or covered with a thin film of ox-gall, then coated with gelatine and dried. The prints are then coated with gelatine, and the two brought into complete contact as before. After drying, they may be separated from the glass.

16. VARNISHING.—This, when well performed, is but little inferior to the foregoing processes, and is more quickly done. The dry prints are carefully brushed over with a sizing solution of the finest glue or gelatine, of such a strength as to impart to the print, when dry, a little gloss in the parts uncovered by printing. If, on trial, the varnish is found to penetrate this coating of gelatine in patches, the coating must be renewed. The prints, being satisfactorily prepared, are submitted to the glazing effects of the rolling-machine. Any kind of clear quick-drying turpentine-varnish will do for the next operation, but special paper-varnish may be bought for the purpose. A good varnish brush must be employed, and the varnish must be employed with decided, steady, regular strokes of the brush, so as to avoid any working up of the previously applied varnish by the subsequent strokes. The showcard or other work should be placed in a sloping position during the application of the varnish, and should be kept nearly upright until dry. Great care must be taken not to pack them up until they are thoroughly dry.

17. COLLODION VARNISH.—Thirty-two parts of collodion and one part of castor oil make a varnish which can be applied with the brush, and which dries very rapidly. It is very durable, glossy, and waterproof.

18. PRESERVING THE DRAWINGS ON STONE AFTER PRINTING.—It is too often the practice in lithographic printing-offices to take but little notice of the stone when the first order from it has been executed, but if there is only a remote chance of its being required again, means ought to be taken, as far as possible, to insure that the stone be in fair printing condition when another edition is called for. The stone may not be wanted again for months, or even years, but the ordinary printing-ink may become so dry in a few weeks as to become insoluble in turpentine, and to have lost its power of resisting the adhesion to it of water. Hence the necessity of preparing it in some manner that will permit of the removal of the ink by turpentine, so that the stone will be in a similar condition as when first printed from. Drawings may be preserved by using the following ink.*

---

* Some recommend the addition of soap to this ink, but it is not only quite unnecessary, but positively mischievous.

Ordinary printing-ink, as bought from the ink-maker, 2 oz.
Tallow   ...   . 2 ,,
Bees'-wax   ...   . 4 ,,

The tallow and wax are to be melted over the fire, and the printing-ink added a little at a time until dissolved.

When about to be used, a small quantity must be ground with turpentine until of the consistency of ordinary printing-ink. Wash out the drawing with the washing-out mixture (par. 25) or with turpentine only, and roll in with the above ink until the drawing shows clearly, using a small quantity of gum on the stone to keep it quite clean. Set the stone aside for a few hours until the turpentine has quite evaporated, and then gum in with gum-water containing carbolic acid (see note to par. 14).

Another Method.—Roll the stone with ordinary printing-ink. Dust with powdered resin and allow time for the ink and resin to incorporate and become hard. Take a spoilt impression of the job, and brush over the back of it with gum-water; lay its gummed side to the stone and pull through the press. Gumming the paper instead of the stone will more effectually exclude the air, and thus prevent " oxidation " of the ink, for which " drying " is only another name. The resin, having no tendency to dry, will very materially assist the preservation of the ink in such a condition as to be soluble in turpentine.

If the stone is to be laid by in a very dry place, the addition of a little glycerine to the gum will prevent its cracking. It is better than sugar, molasses, &c.

19. ROLLING-UP DRAWINGS THAT HAVE BEEN LAID ASIDE FOR A LONG TIME.—First try the effect of turpentine mixed with a little oil after the gum has been moistened. If this does not remove the old ink, gum the stone again, dab it over with the damping-cloth so as to prevent the gum overlying the ink, and allow it to dry. Turpentine may now be permitted to lie upon the stone until the ink be dissolved. If turpentine is ineffective in softening the ink, benzoline or oil of tar may be tried. It must be understood that no water be employed, so that the gum remains undissolved, and so thoroughly to protect the uninked portion of the stone from receiving any greasy matter. If the ink still resists the action of the solvent, friction may be employed.

The solvent may be employed with coarse flannel, and may even be assisted by the addition of some abrading material, such as chalk, tripoli, rouge, or Indian red. These will have little or no effect on the gum, and when sufficient ink is removed, the stone may be washed with oil and turps, the gum dissolved with water, and the stone rolled up in the usual way. The main points are to keep the gum undissolved during the action of the solvent and to use clean sponges and cloth during the rolling-up.

20. TRANSFERRING FROM MUSIC-PLATES. — Music is usually engraved by *punching* the forms of the notes, &c. on soft, white, metal plates, which will not stand the heat employed in taking transfers from copper and steel plates. As the music contains no fine lines, it is unnecessary to employ the hard ink used for finer work. The music-plates may be filled in while cold with the ink used for pulling re-transfers from stone, and wiped from the surface with rags in the usual way. The scum left on the plate will be considerable, and if the impression were pulled upon the ordinary transfer paper, would give much trouble when transferred to stone. If, however, the impression be taken upon ordinary printing-paper, the scum will, in a great degree, be absorbed into the surface, while there will be sufficient ink in the engraved parts to transfer to the stone with one pull through the press. It is sometimes necessary to take off a little of the superfluous ink by previously pulling it through the press with light pressure upon another piece of plain paper.

21. TO PREVENT SET-OFF ON STONE.—ANTE-DAMPING FLUID.—When it is necessary to print two or more colours in succession without time being allowed for drying, the colour first printed sets off-upon the stone. If it be a black or similar colour followed by a delicate one, such as bright red, the black set-off will be taken up by and soil the ink upon the roller. This may be much modified or altogether prevented by adding to the damping-water some substance which retains moisture a long time, such as sugar, common salt, glycerine, chloride of lime, &c. These may be used separately or in combination with each other, or with gum.

These substances are also useful in hot weather for preventing the too rapid drying of the stone, and mixtures have been introduced to the trade under the designation of ante-damping fluid, as more than one impression could be taken with one damping. For this purpose the following may be tried :—1st. Glycerine, 1 oz. ; chloride of lime, 1 oz. ; water, 2 oz. 2nd. Glycerine, 4 oz. ; tartrate potass, 1 oz. ; gum, 1 oz. ; water, 4 oz.

22. THE ANASTATIC PROCESS.—This process at one time attracted great attention, and much time was devoted to it by experimenters. It is now very little used, because the process of photo-lithography can be much more effectually applied to the same purpose. As originally employed, it consisted in reproducing by zincography the recent productions of the printing-press of our own and other countries. The print to be reproduced is wetted at the back with a weak solution of nitric acid in water. It is then laid face downwards upon a clean sheet of polished zinc and passed through the press. It is afterwards treated as described for zincography and printed from. The same process may be employed upon stone of a close texture if it is first treated with turpentine, the turpentine being allowed to become nearly dry.

Many attempts, but with little success, have been made to newly charge the old ink of a print with greasy qualities, but we cannot recommend any one to try it : the print is pretty sure to be spoiled, and nothing can be done that cannot be better performed by photo-lithography, which does not in the least injure the print to be copied.

BACKING STONES.—When stones less than two inches thick, or even thicker ones when large, are used in the press, they are apt to break when much pressure is employed. Such stones are best "backed" with slabs of slate or other lithographic stones. It is performed as follows :—

Mix up ordinary plaster of Paris to the consistency of very thin paste, spread this upon the slab, and place the stone upon it. Move it about until it is felt to rest pretty firmly upon its seat. By this time much of the plaster will be squeezed out from between the stones, and should be neatly plastered round the base of the upper stone, so as to better secure it. If the plaster is new, the stone may be used in the press in about an hour.

When it is required to separate them, it may be done by driving a thin blade between them. A broken palette-knife, ground off square, is very useful for this and other purposes.

23. ENLARGING AND REDUCING PROCESSES.—There is no doubt but that the photo-lithographic process is the most efficient means of obtaining copies for lithography in altered dimensions. There is, however, another process which possesses advantages of its own, and which, unlike photography, can be carried on at any time. It will be easily understood, if a sheet of thin india-rubber be prepared with an elastic transfer composition, and an impression be made upon it in transfer-ink, that by suitable mechanism it may be stretched to a larger size, and while at that size it may be retransferred to stone. In like manner, if the india-rubber be stretched before the impression is taken upon it, it may be allowed to contract to a smaller size before it is retransferred.

Having stated the principle upon which the process depends, we think it unnecessary to describe the various means by which it may be carried out. Those who think of employing this useful method may communicate with either Mr. Joseph Lewis, of Hazlewood House, Ranelagh, Dublin, or Mr. Beattie, of 5, Aston's Quay, Dublin, both of whom furnish effective, though different, apparatus, with complete instructions for use.

24. QUICK-DRYING STOPPING-OUT VARNISH.—Resin dissolved in common benzoline makes a good stopping-out varnish for use in etched-tint making, or for any other purpose where it is necessary to protect the work during etching with strong acid. It dries very quickly—so quickly, indeed, that the stone may be etched a few minutes after it is laid on, and it is easily dissolved by turpentine during the washing-out process.

25. ECONOMY OF RAGS.—Rags are used in washing out the black ink previously to rolling-up the subject in colour, and unless economy be practised, much more will be used than is really necessary. They may be greatly economized by judicious use. Cut them into convenient size pieces. The stone should be sprinkled with a little turpentine and the whole of the ink dissolved before the rag is used to absorb it. The stone is then sprinkled again, and a second rag taken to wipe it with. After the third application, the stone

will probably be clean, and certainly more clean than it would have been if the same amount of rag had been used in one piece.   These dirty rags having been set aside, the second piece may be used for first application on the next occasion ; the third piece for second ; using a clean piece for the third wiping, and so on.   This is a point worth attention.

PART II.

MACHINES AND MACHINE PRINTING.

MACHINE PRINTING.

CHAPTER I.

CONSIDERING the importance of the subject, our task would be incomplete did we not give some practical instructions in the application of the principles laid down in the foregoing pages to printing by means of the many excellent machines now to be had of the various makers. We would especially direct the attention of the young printer to this branch of lithographic printing, because of its daily increasing importance, as machinery is now being generally acknowledged to be equal, under proper management, to the demands of very excellent work either in black or colours. Young men of intelligence whose minds are open to the reception of new ideas should pay great attention to this department of lithography, and should omit no opportunity to qualify themselves for any opening that may occur, because machinery has come so rapidly into use that the number of trained " machine-minders"—as the persons who devote themselves to superintending machines are technically designated—is very far below the actual requirements of the business. Hence, when a machine is newly introduced into an office, it is frequently found necessary to take a printer fresh from the hand-press and place him in the position of manager of a delicate and compli-cated piece of mechanism, with the principles of which he has no acquaintance whatever. To some men who have a mechanical aptitude the change is novel and agreeable, and provided that they have mastered the theory as well as the practice of lithography, they probably soon develop into competent machinists. On the other hand, the newly-appointed machinist may have been chosen merely because he was a good hand-printer, and may have no mechanical proclivities. Such a man will most likely soon feel that he has had a responsibility placed upon him for which he is unsuited, and will wish himself back at his press. To men placed in this position our instructions will, we hope, be of much use; while they may materially help others upon whom the necessity has not actually been imposed of adapting themselves to a novel and unaccustomed calling, yet who are animated by a desire—and a very honourable and worthy one—of understanding every branch, and not merely one department of their business. A great living author and statesman has said that the true secret of "getting on" in the world, is to be ready and qualified for an opportunity of advancement whenever that opportunity presents itself, and an exemplification of the truth of the remark is seen in every large establishment. The man who "gets on" is he who knows *something more* than his actual routine of work demands, and who is conscious that if his employer set him a little higher he would be capable of occupying the place. There are printers at press who think that because they have always made a living hitherto, and most probably will do the same in the future, the acquirement of any further technical knowledge is quite unnecessary and superfluous. There could not be a more decided or a more mischievous mistake. The kind of instruction we are about to give will be found as generally useful as it will most likely some day be absolutely essential, and the intelligent man will avail himself of it beforehand, so as to be ready with it when he is called upon.

2. *The Selection of a Machine.*—It would, of course, be out of our province to recommend the machine of any particular maker. We can say confidently that there is no difficulty in getting a good one. But it is neces-

sary, however, to bear in mind that it will be the truest economy, generally speaking, not to purchase the lowest-priced machine that can be found. When the maker elects to make cheap machines, he is usually compelled to reduce expense of production by the substitution or lightness for massiveness in the framing. It is very essential to a good machine that it should have sufficient weight in this particular. But there are other and worse evils than lightness, in some of the cheap machines that are now being manufactured. These are : heavy and ill-constructed castings in the moving parts; holes cast in the framework instead of being drilled, into which are inserted badly-fitting bolts with nuts of similar character, involving an amount of screwing up nearly sufficient to strip their threads, and ultimately such a degree of instability, that a breakdown is sooner or later the certain consequence. Moreover, the general fitting of such machines is equally bad all through. The *size* of the machine will of course depend upon the work to be performed on it. Where several machines are employed, we recommend that one should be small, say demy folio, *but not driven by a treadle*, for that is unsuitable for litho-printing. A machine of this size will print many little jobs more expeditiously from an original than when two or more are laid down for working at a larger machine, for not only is the time of making up a second stone saved, but the smaller one yields more impressions in the same time with the same speed of table and rolling, on account of the shorter traverse of the table. The demy is a favourite for a moderate-sized machine; but our opinion is that when a printer requires a demy he frequently wants a double-crown or imperial, and he had better order that at once. Upon this size perhaps 90 per cent. of the ordinary machine work in any office can be done.

3. *Second-hand Machines.*—Sometimes a chance presents itself of getting a second-hand machine at a fair price, and to enable the intending purchaser to know what to look for, we give the following hints. It takes a long time to wear out a machine if used properly. We know, for instance, of one of Huguet's first pattern which is still in use, in company with some modern and better machines. It was

never well made, but serves on that account all the better as an instance of what intelligent machine supervision can accomplish, for without this its present state of preservation would not have been possible. In judging of the value of a machine, examine all the wearing parts minutely, and especially note the condition of the bearings; look to the roller spindles and carriages, and note the evidences of wear in the toothed wheels. See if the rollers are *cut*, or whether the seams in them are good. Every machine should have at least *three* inking and two damping rollers, to come in contact with the stone. The framework should be of more massive character than that of the corresponding size of a letterpress machine, as it is subject to immensely greater strains. The ink-table should stand higher than the stone, to enable the rollers to be worked upon it while they are lifted off the latter. There should be adjustable inclines upon the table of the machine to lift the rollers off the stone at the edge; this arrangement saves a lot of trouble in keeping the edges clean. There are many machines in use without this appliance, but we should say there are few to which it could not be applied. A contrivance for raising and lowering the stone should also be looked after, for it is a great convenience, though not essential, as by the help of some half-inch common mahogany boards of equal thickness throughout, supplemented by some thin sheets of zinc, the stone may, effectually, though more slowly, be adjusted to the pressure. See that the gripper answers its purpose of holding the sheet effectually, and that there is a contrivance for instantly throwing the cylinder out of use. If the machine possess these "points," it may be considered one that will prove at least useful, even if not capable of producing the best work.

4. Having made his selection of the machine, the Lithographer requires to know how to make the most of it, or, in other words, *how to keep it in the best working condition.* We would point out, in the first place, that great and unceasing attention must be paid to oiling it and keeping it thoroughly clean. It should be the pride of every machine-minder not only that his machine should *look* clean but that it *be* clean. It is quite possible for it to

look well, and yet be really very dirty in the parts less in sight. For oiling there is perhaps nothing better than Rangoon oil, or lard oil.* These can be had of various qualities, thick and thin, and it will be economical to use both, applying the thick to the parts that are subject to greatest pressure,† and the thin to those of more rapid motion and lighter work. The temperature of the printing-room should also be taken into consideration in the intelligent employment of lubricants. It is not saying too much to assert that a machine will last many years longer when good oil is used than when bad is employed, so that there is no advantage in using the latter because it is low in price.

When a machine is bought new it will not entail much trouble to preserve its good looks. When it is standing still, either from want of work, the setting of the stone, or scraping of the rollers, the boys should be instructed to rub up the bright parts, and wipe away superfluous oil. At least once a week this should be more thoroughly done, giving special attention to the working parts that are out of sight. As often as the work will allow, but at least once in three months, the machine should be well cleaned in every part. Good oil will much facilitate these cleanings, and such attention as we are recommending will cause a machine to work much easier than a badly kept one.

As a rule, too, it may truly be said, that a well-kept machine is *primâ facie* evidence that good work is turned out from it, and that a good man has control of it.

When a machine is newly erected it frequently happens that the vibration in working causes some of the nuts and screws to become loose ; it is very essential, therefore, that

---

* We do not wish to be understood to name these as the only oils fit for machinery, but they are good, moderate in price, and usually kept in stock. Sperm oil is perhaps the best of any, but is very expensive. For very light work, sperm mixed with paraffine or petroleum oil is very good, and will retain its fluidity at very low temperatures when combined in equal parts. Neats-foot oil is also a good lubricant when properly freed from gelatine, which is often only imperfectly removed.

† It is an axiom in mechanics, that, other circumstances being the same, *friction is directly proportionate to pressure.*

the machine-minder should try them occasionally, until he finds from experience that they keep to their work. Should one be found to get easily and frequently loose, it should at once be replaced by a better-fitting one. Attention to these rules would prevent many a break-down. Caution must be observed in the use of the spanner, which must fit the nuts properly, or mischief may be done. We do not however recommend the attendant to loosen or tighten screws and nuts unnecessarily, as that would only tend to bring about the very result we are now cautioning him against.

Having referred to the principal essentials of a good machine, and the general system to be adopted for keeping it in working order, we may proceed to make a few practical remarks on some of the most important parts of the mechanism—viz. the Inking-Rollers, the Damping-Rollers, and the Cylinder and its coverings.

5. *The Inking-Rollers.*—These, when new, require a previous preparation of the same kind as hand-rollers. They may have rubbed into them either tallow, lard, or olive oil, which, after having saturated the skin, is to be well cleaned off by scraping. The rollers are next to be placed in the machine, which must be set running after they have received a supply of medium varnish. After running some hours the varnish must be scraped off, new supplied, and the machine put in motion again. It will be found, upon trying it with the palette-knife, that the new leather has altered the character of the varnish, making it less liable to separate from the rollers. When this effect ceases to be produced the varnish may be thoroughly scraped off, its place supplied with printing-ink, and the rollers tried first upon a heavy job.

6. *The Damping-Rollers.*—If the stocks of these are made of iron, care should be taken to cover them with some waterproof substance, such as red lead paint, indiarubber varnish, oil-cloth, American leather, or any other convenient material. They are then usually supplied with several folds of soft flannel, or some thick soft felt, brought to join neatly without overlapping. The best thing of this class, however, is the fine indiarubber-covered felt known by the name of *spongeo-piline.* The roller must be covered outside

with some cotton or linen fabric. Canvas, a cotton material called swansdown, velveteen, and another named moleskin, are all in use, but we have a decided preference for the latter. It can be bought from the draper or tailor, but must be well washed before use, without soap, to free it from the dressing or sizing which it always contains when new. Unless this is done, much trouble will be experienced in getting the rollers to damp the stone properly. After washing and drying the moleskin, lay it out smoothly on a flat board, and cut one edge straight with a ruler and sharp knife. Having ascertained exactly how much will go round the roller, cut it accurately to that size with the knife and ruler as before. The covering should meet but not overlap, and it will be better to cut it so that a little force is required to bring the edges together, which should be effected by the peculiar stitch known among tailors as "the beggar's ranter," the needle being inserted *under* each edge alternately, and brought out on the top. It is better to have the damping surface of the damping-rollers longer than the inking surface of the inking-rollers.

In regard to the general treatment of damping-rollers, they should be taken out of the machine every evening and set up on end, which will keep them in working condition better than leaving them in the machine. At this time they should be examined to see if they have accumulated any ink upon them, and if they have, it should be at once removed by turpentine or benzoline.

Both when at work and when idle the damping-rollers will accumulate dirt, which should occasionally be removed by washing them with a brush and warm water. They will then be too wet for printing, but if they are scraped with a bone folder or other similar article that will not cut the moleskin, the water will be so much reduced in quantity that they may be at once put into the machine again for use.

7. *The Cylinder and its Covering.*—With an ordinary blanket the cylinder will soon deteriorate, owing to the formation of rust, unless means be used to prevent it, and we recommend the following :—Wash the surface of the iron with turpentine to remove grease, and then intro-

duce some kind of gas arrangement by which the cylinder may be heated. The cylinder having a considerable weight it will take a good while to get the metal warm, and a quantity of moisture will collect inside from the products of combustion, but that will be expelled as the iron gets hot. The surface may now be thinly and evenly painted with a mixture of red lead, drying oil, and brunswick black or copal varnish. This will soon dry hard and prevent the moisture, which penetrates the blanket, attacking the iron.

A fine, but thick, or treble-milled printer's blanket may be used for covering the cylinder. For small machines a finer and thinner blanket may be used, because less variation in the surface of the stone may be expected when it is small. The more true the surface of the cylinder and stone are, the less necessity is there for thick blanket. If they were perfect, all that would be necessary would be something to prevent the stone and cylinder touching in those parts not covered by the paper; but as this perfection cannot be attained in practice, an elastic surface of appreciable thickness is required for the cylinder.

Besides the disadvantages of somewhat rough surface and absorption of moisture, the ordinary blanket, when once it becomes soiled with ink, holds it with such tenacity that it it is only by taking it off and subjecting it to the process of washing that the ink can be effectually removed. When the blanket once catches a little ink from the stone, though the ink may be removed from the latter, the soil on the blanket will become a starting-point for its re-appearance. This may be prevented by attaching to the blanket a sheet of stout smooth paper, somewhat larger than the stone, which can easily be removed when dirty, and upon which anything of the nature of patching may be done, to bring up work in those parts of the stone where corrections have been made.

As a remedy for these inconveniences, some printers use with marked success the indiarubber blanketing, which, though double the price, is found more economical than the woollen one. The advantages of this blanket when used for lithographic printing may be thus summed up as compared with the woollen fabric :—It is more permanently elastic, harder and smoother on the face, quite waterproof, and admits of being cleaned on the cylinders in a few seconds, with a little soft soap and rain water, great care being taken to remove all trace of soap.

CHAPTER II.

Preparation of the Stone—Preparation of the Work—Etching for Machine Printing — Inking — Distribution — Refreshening the Roller's Surface—Quality of Ink—How to reduce the Tenacity of Ink—Setting the Stone in the Machine—Starting the Machine : Inking—Damping.

HAVING selected his machine, and got the rollers and the cylinder into proper order, the printer is ready to begin the actual working of it. The first thing to be attended to is—

8. *The Preparation of the Stone.*— The stone-grinder should remember, when preparing a stone for the machine, that the printer cannot adapt his cylinder to its surface, as is frequently done at hand-press, by means of a scraper. Every care, therefore, must be taken to have the stone true (back as well as front), more especially in the direction of the stone's length, because that is the way in which the cylinder is applied to it. Its two longer edges must also be not only well rounded, but stand fairly the test of the straight-edge along the rounded part. If this be not attended to, the paper will be liable to crease. We know that the paper will sometimes crease from other causes, but this is one that is sometimes overlooked. The stone is easily tested by a straight-edge, which should hold a piece of ordinary post paper when applied at any part between it and the stone. Besides the general evenness of surface, the stone should be well polished, for it then not only receives the drawing or transfer more perfectly, but is less liable in printing to catch the ink in those places which are intended to receive none.

9. *Preparation of the Work.*—Before a drawing or transfer is put upon the stone for machine printing, the size of the

paper on which it is to be printed should be determined.
The width of paper to be held by the gripper should then
be ascertained, and a little more than that width should be
allowed to project over the edge, so that the gripper shall
not come in contact with the stone, which, if allowed to
occur, would roughen it, remove the gum, and cause it at
that part to accumulate ink from the rollers.

10. *Etching for Machine Printing.*—It is usual for machine printers, previously to printing at the machine, to
etch the work into relief, in the following manner :—After
cleaning the work sufficiently, ink it up strongly but clearly,
and dust it with finely-powdered resin or bronze powder,
but preferably with resin ; etch with dilute nitric acid, sufficiently tart to produce a pretty brisk effervescence ; ink
again, and repeat the dusting and etching for a second and
a third time. It must not be understood that we recommend this process to be carried far enough to produce any
considerable amount of relief. As a matter of fact, a
printer used to the work would produce sufficient with one
dusting and etching ; but the beginner is asked to err on
the right side by giving the work plenty of resin. If too
much relief be given, an impression will probably occur
from the sides of the lines as well as from their tops, and
the work will have a thicker appearance than if only etched
in the manner usual for hand-printing. The etching having
been finished, the resin must be removed as follows :—
Wash off all trace of the acid, gum in, and remove the ink
and resin with turpentine, to which some oil, transfer-ink,
or other fatty matter has been added. This is very important, because, as a rule, the work has been newly
transferred or drawn on the stone, and sufficient time
has not been given for the subject to take firm hold of it,
and, under such circumstances, there is great risk in
using turpentine alone.* The stone must now be re-inked,
gummed, and dried, and is then ready for working.

11. *Inking.*—This process naturally divides itself into
three parts—(1) the Distribution ; (2) the Refreshening of

---

* For the same reason it is important that the sponge and cloth used
previously to re-inking should be quite clean and free from any trace of
acid or sour gum.

the surface of the Rollers by means of the "riders"; (3) the quantity and properties of the Ink. We will treat of these *seriatim.*

12. *Distribution.*—By this term is to be understood the spreading of the ink in an even manner over the surface of the ink-table and the rollers. Some patented machines have special contrivances for this purpose, of more or less practical use, but there are tolerably efficient means common to all machines which must be mentioned here. The principal distribution is effected by setting two or more rollers obliquely across the machine, so that when the ink-table passes beneath them they will roll over it in a diagonal direction, and by setting them to run opposite ways, the distribution is doubled. The table then runs under the rollers that ink the work, and they are placed straight across the machine, and thus again change the disposition of the ink upon the table. As a final mode of distribution these rollers have others, usually of smaller diameter, above an 1 in contact with them, which again alter the distribution of the ink. By the combined action of these different rollers the evenness of the impression is maintained, although one part of the stone may take up and transfer to the paper many times the quantity of ink that is sufficient for another.

13. *The Refreshening of the Surface of the Roller* is effected by the riders before mentioned. When the roller passes over the wet stone, it becomes much smoother on its surface, and somewhat damp, which would in a degree render it less effective in leaving its ink upon the drawing in the next revolution, but as soon as it comes in contact with the upper roller, this glazing is destroyed, and a new and more efficient inking power given to it. By the adoption of this simple contrivance, the inking power of the rollers is nearly doubled, and three or four rollers are made to do as much work at one traverse of the table as would be done by a dozen strokes of the hand-roller.

In the arrangement of these riders upon the rollers, a great error is made by some machinists. To effect a more perfect distribution, they set *one* rider on *two* rollers, and, in so doing, they unite all the rollers together as effectually as if they were connected by belts or tooth-wheels, by reason of the adhesive power of the printing ink. Now this system has one very great defect in practice—*one roller cannot move without setting all the rest in motion,*—and the machinist is troubled with the *non-rotation* or *slipping* of the roller that comes first in contact with the stone, ink being taken off instead of being added to it. It is therefore unreasonable to expect the adhesion of *one* greasy roller to a wet stone to set in motion two or three others and their riders. The printer will not be much troubled with rollers slipping if he will set a rider immediately over each roller, so that each pair may work independently, the stone having then to set in motion one pair at a time instead of the whole of them at once.

Machines of recent make are provided with wheels or runners near the ends of the rollers, which run upon guides on the table, about the same height as the stone. In this arrangement, the rollers being constantly in motion, will have less tendency to slip on the stone, because they then run independently of it. Care must, however, be taken that these runners do not become oily, as that has a tendency to make them slip, which, should it begin, will most likely continue and wear flat places upon them. When they once get into that condition, they can no more be depended upon, and must be replaced by new ones.

14. *The Quality of the Ink* to be used for any given job will depend upon various circumstances, which the printer must duly take into account. The chief elements in the calculation are,—quality of paper, speed of machine, quantity of ink requisite for each impression.

As a general rule, *the greater the speed at which the rollers run,* the less tenacious must be the ink.* This may be taken only as a general proposition, because the amount of water used in damping must also be taken into consideration.

---

* The machinist must here be cautioned against confounding this speed of the rollers or table with the number of impressions printed in a given time : it only corresponds in the same or nearly similar-sized machines. If one machine has a traverse of six feet for its table, and another four feet, and both are printing 500 per hour, the rollers of the former will be running at the rate of 100 ft. per minute while the speed of the latter will be only about 66 ft. in the same time.

We may, however, embody this in another proposition : *The more water is used for the purpose of damping the stone, the thinner and more greasy may the ink be.*

How to reduce the tenacity of Ink.—Without specifying in this place the circumstances under which thin ink is to be used, we will give the modes by which the tenacity of ink generally may be reduced.

1st. By thin varnish. We must, however, be cautious not to add too much to the ink, or the impressions will be pale when a proper amount is used on the rollers, while, on the other hand, if sufficient of such thin ink be employed to yield black impressions, they will be so overcharged as to be blurred ; the close parts will run together, and the work will easily set-off when a few sheets are placed upon each other. To combine thinness with depth of colour, we may add—

2ndly. Oil, either raw or boiled. Of course, boiled linseed oil will approach somewhat to thin varnish, but we have a descending scale through raw linseed, olive, and paraffin oils, which may all be used in their place, but it must be remembered that all of them injure the drying quality of the ink, which will therefore require the addition of dryers as a compensation.

3rdly. The addition of certain solid fatty matters will render the ink less tenacious or stringy without increasing its fluidity. The main object is to make the ink part readily from the roller to the stone at an increased speed, and as some solid fatty matters are found to effect this without thinning the ink, they answer some kinds of printing better than the softer and thinner materials. The substance that is found best in practice for this purpose is a little mineral candle, which not only gives a freeness to the ink, but adds to its power of adhering to the greasy drawing on the stone ; but it will be, as a rule, unnecessary to employ such additions to the ink. There are occasions, however, when they may be resorted to with a good result, as, for instance, when using surfaced papers which easily part with their coating. The ordinary ink, when properly used at a fair speed, will behave quite satisfactorily with a person who properly understands his work, and the learner should take this into due consideration and try his best to dispense with the addition of greasy or oily matters.

The less water used in damping the stone, the stronger and stiffer may be the ink. Though this may be remembered as a general rule, yet it ought not to be forgotten that the circumstances of speed, and the nature of the paper and the subject, must also be taken into account.*

15. *Setting the Stone in the Machine.* — When care is exercised in putting the work on the stone, scarcely any alteration is needed in fixing the front stop for different stones, but should any be required, the way to do it will be obvious. For bringing the stone approximately to the proper height, some machines are provided by the makers with a gauge to be set across the table, and to this gauge the stone is raised before being tried by taking an impression. In the absence of such an appliance, a rough estimate of what is wanted may be formed by observing the position of the stone's surface as compared with the teeth of the rack, say to about two-thirds of their height.

Having once got a stone into correct position, an ingenious printer will be able, with such stone as a guide, to contrive a gauge, consisting of a piece of wood about three inches wide and three-quarters of an inch thick, set in a foot at each end, which may rest on the rack or other convenient part of the table.

If the stone is found uneven, packing must be resorted to, as in the hand-press.

All being found correct, the stone is to be held in position by means of the screws, taking care to set the lock-nuts well up, to prevent the screws becoming loose during the working of the machine.

16. *Starting the Machine: Inking.*—When the machine will not permit of the rollers being set so as to run upon the ink-table while they do not touch the stone, the stone should be lowered in its bed, or taken out of the machine while they are being prepared for inking ; or the inking may be seen to before the stone is put in the machine. After the rollers have been scraped, a little ink may be applied to the

---

* For the theory of applying the different kinds of ink, see Part I., par. 116.

wavers or distributors, and the machine set running until it is properly distributed over all the rollers.* This will be facilitated by moving the distributors about and turning them end for end. When it is thought that proper distribution is accomplished, the rollers may be thrown out of use and the attention directed to the

17. *Damping.*—The damping-rollers have already been described in Chap. I., and we have now to speak of the actual wetting of the stone when printing.

Some machines are provided with arrangements for damping, that are intended to be more or less automatic, but, however perfect they may be, they will always require *attention.* The most perfect apparatus can only be expected to work with less frequent attention than is required with the simple arrangement of rollers only, and, if we point out what is necessary for the latter, the knowledge will equally apply to the more complicated methods. We do not wish to be understood as underrating these contrivances, because we know that they are very useful additions when intelligently used.

After the damping-rollers have become dry, care must be taken that the newly-applied water penetrates them thoroughly, before proceeding to print. Having washed the gum from the stone, run it through the machine, without using the inking-rollers, until the stone seems damp enough, but not too wet. Now pass a *dry* sheet round the cylinder to take the water off the stone, and note whether it appears damp enough for printing, after it has returned from a single passage under the rollers; if it is not so, they require another sponging.

The degree of damping will greatly depend on the kind of ink in use. If the ink be strong, very little will do; while the thinner the ink the more water will be required to overcome its tendency to thicken the work. The machine-minder will find it necessary to watch the work sponge in hand, and to apply the water where most wanted,

---

* Though nearly all machines are supplied with an ink duct, the beginner is recommended to apply his ink in this manner until he has mastered the working of the machine in a sufficiently general manner as to be able to turn out a fair quality of work.

which is usually at the edges and sides, and occasionally to sponge the damping slab, or rollers, so as to keep up the supply.

The proper regulation of the water is more difficult than that of the ink, and if too much be applied at a time the succeeding impressions will be paler until the balance between damping and inking be re-established.

* * *

CHAPTER III.

Importance of a proper choice of Paper—Hand-made and Hand-sized Paper very objectionable—Necessity for Absorbency in the Paper —Conditions of Printing on smooth Writing-paper—General Principles involved in Printing dry Paper—Rolled Paper—Registering —Setting a Stone for Register—Colour-Printing—Compo, the "Victory" and glazed Rollers—The Ink-duct—Defects in Ink-ducts.

INTIMATELY connected with the subject of Machine Printing, is that of the proper qualities and descriptions of *paper* to be used, and we may advantageously devote a few paragraphs to it. We may say at the outset, that it is to be regretted that clerks and travellers who take orders for printing do not make themselves better acquainted with the fitness of papers for the various kinds of work. The proper choice of paper in many instances makes all the difference between good and bad printing, and a suggestion from the person who is taking the order would, we think, be generally favourably entertained.

18. Writing, drawing, loan, or other hard-made English-sized papers should never be used for printing upon when beauty of impression is the chief consideration. The use of such papers should be restricted to note, letter, and invoice headings and other similar work, in which the appearance of the printing is secondary to its use for writing upon. Foreign and common English writing-papers are sized less hardly, and take a better impression than the superior makes.

19. To produce the best printing, the paper must be somewhat absorbent, and that is the well-known character

of printing and plate papers, the latter being still less sized than the former. If a good printing paper be well glazed, it will resemble writing-paper sufficiently to be used for circulars and such-like work, and will take a much better impression than can be got upon the harder-sized material; while it will bear writing upon well enough for all ordinary purposes of adding names, prices, &c.

20. Now suppose a smooth, hard-sized writing-paper is. to be printed, let us study the circumstances. 1st. Too much water must not be used, or the surface will be injured. 2nd. The minimum quantity of ink that will produce blackness must only be employed, so as to prevent the setting-off to which such paper is very liable, and to facilitate the drying. Strong and medium varnishes will print cleanly on slightly-damped stones, but would not do for this purpose, because too much ink would be then required for the kind of paper we are supposing is to be used. The ink must therefore be thinned as little as possible with weak varnish, or even oil, with a little dryers, and the machine be run at such a speed as will permit of such ink being used, when, with proper management, good work will be produced.

21. Such being the principles involved in working hard-sized paper, it is not difficult to comprehend what is to be done when the paper is more absorbent, and the following general rule gives the key to the whole. *The more absorbent the paper is, the more water and ink may be used, the thinner the ink may be, and consequently the higher may be the speed of the machine.*

22. We have hitherto spoken of dry papers only, but damp paper is preferable where there is no special objection to its employment. The damping of the paper, by taking away its harshness, enables it to be brought into closer contact with the work, at the same or even a lighter pressure, employed for dry paper; and it is for this reason, rather than for any superior affinity for the ink, that better work is produced upon it.

23. *Registering* at a good machine can be performed with greater facility and exactitude than at hand-press, when once the stone is properly set; but to insure success it must be driven at a moderate and uniform speed, and the stone be so bevelled on the edge that first meets the cylinder, that

it may cause no jolting or other motion tending to move either out of its place.

When the stone is properly adjusted for pressure, the next thing will be to set it for register, and this should be systematized by the machinist so as to perform it in the most ready manner and with the fewest trial-sheets. Machines differ, and what may do for one might be unsuitable for another ; but we should say that a variation of the following might be adapted to any machine.*

24. *Setting a Stone for Register.*—Take a straight, wide, but thin piece of metal long enough to rest on the racks of the table ; through each end and into a tooth of each rack drill a small hole. To each hole of the metal strip fasten a pin to just fit the hole in the tooth of the rack. It should now be easy to set this strip accurately to these holes at any time, and if register-marks be put upon the stone to correspond to the edge of this rule, the stone may be rapidly adjusted in register without taking an impression. In cases where it is desirable to depart from these marks in the first printing, a piece of paper may be cemented to the rule, and marks made upon it corresponding to others upon the stone. This arrangement is then preserved to set the stones by in the subsequent printings.

25. *Colour Printing.*—*Rollers.*—This part of our subject having been fully treated in Chapter XXIII., it only remains to speak of it here in relation to the machine. In colour-printing one of the most essential conditions is clean rollers, and one of the best means of obtaining them is to have two sets (besides the black ones), one set being kept for tints, and another for the stronger and darker colours. When there is much colour-work done, we should even recommend three sets, as it would be very advantageous to keep one for yellow, red, and orange inks, and another for dark blue, green, purple, and the tertiary colours. By this arrangement dark and light, or colours which are complementary to each other, would be used on the same rollers ; the saving of time and turps would pay for them, and the quality of work turned out would be

---

* The observations made upon paper, in relation to register, in par. 154, Part I., apply equally to machine-printing.

far superior to that which has been done from one set of rollers for all colours. We here refer to what are called "nap" rollers, which are suitable for the very highest class of chalk colour-work. For ink-work, the "Victory" rollers mentioned in next paragraph may be highly recommended.

26. *Washable Rollers.*—Attempts have from time to time been made to manufacture rollers for lithographic printing, having the advantages of the composition of glue, treacle, &c., used by letterpress printers, and thus making one set do for all purposes; but on account of the soluble nature of the materials, much difficulty has been experienced in making them work upon the wet stone. We have in our possession, however, a hand-roller covered with a composition possessing almost identical qualities with those used in type-printing, but which is *quite unaffected* by the water used on the stone. It can be perfectly cleaned with turps in a few seconds, but our experience leads us to the conclusion that at present these rollers are not sufficiently durable to be well recommended, because, although they well retain their elasticity, they crack upon the surface. The cracks then absorb the ink and render the rollers difficult to cleanse.

There has lately been introduced to the trade the "Victory" roller, manufactured by Messrs. Blades, East, & Blades, under LANHAM'S patent. These are made with an india-rubber covering, and are entirely free from the objections previously mentioned. They possess all the advantages of the glazed rollers with others peculiarly their own. The cleaning of them is accomplished by washing them in turpentine, which in its turn requires to be removed to prevent it making them too soft and tacky. This can readily be done by sponging them with water, and then wiping them with a dry cloth. The more quickly the turpentine is used and removed from the rollers the better for them; but should they at any time become too dry, their tackiness may be restored by the application of a small quantity of turpentine. The fibre of the finishing cloth sometimes attaches itself too firmly, and causes annoyance, by creating fine white streaks upon the stone, if the work be of a broad character, such as a dark tint. This may be avoided by using a soft woollen cloth for the final wiping;

or making sure that the rollers and with them the fibres are thoroughly inked by the inking slab previous to letting them run over the damp stone. These rollers have such an impervious surface that they may be cleaned up from black to a delicate colour in a very short space of time.

Glazed rollers were spoken of in par. 52, Part I., and instructions given for preparing them. They are much used on machines and may be prepared for such use in a similar manner to hand-rollers. After the drying ink has been well distributed upon them, the riders (if used) are to be taken off them, and the rollers run over a *wet* stone until they become nicely smooth, they are then allowed to dry, after which the operation may be repeated, alternately rolling them up and drying them until they are quite smooth upon the surface.

27. *The Ink-Duct.*—There is great difference of opinion among lithographic machinists as to the value to a machine of the ink-duct. It is no uncommon thing for ink-ducts to remain totally unused, thereby representing so much unremunerative capital. We know good printers who say such things are useless, while other good printers regard them as indispensable, especially in printing heavy masses of colour. We think their non-use may be traced to three causes :—1st, The printer does not like to grind a large quantity of ink, to add dryers which prevent its keeping, and then have to throw the unused portion away ; 2nd, A want of mechanical knowledge of the capabilities of this part of the machine, and a lack of delicacy in regulating the adjusting screws ; 3rd, Faulty construction of the mechanism.

28. *Defects in Ink-Ducts.*— Passing over causes No. 1 and No. 2, we have something to say as to No. 3. The ink-duct may be faulty by reason of the knife not fitting the ink-cylinder, but this may be cured by grinding the knife. The greatest fault, however, is that of the ink-cylinder being kept constantly running, as it is in some machines. In this case, the ink, having dryers in it, and being constantly and freshly exposed to the oxidizing influence of the air, becomes pasty, as well as dirty, and no longer performs properly on the stone. This action goes on upon the ink-slab and rollers, but is there inevitable. The ink can be scraped

off the rollers as often as necessary, but they are usually kept in good order by receiving a new film of ink from the duct, when that is of proper construction. We will now state what we think that should be.

29. The ink-cylinder should be moved intermittently, once for each traverse of the table, and should be capable of being so controlled as to be thrown off instantly, or set to work through a very small space. The feed-roller should be kept in contact with the ink-cylinder while the latter moves, and should always fall upon the ink-table at the proper time. If the machinist has at his command an apparatus of this kind (and it is to be had), we think it only wants a little patience to overcome the difficulties of controlling it; but in first taking to a machine we should recommend him to work without it, so as to reduce as much as possible the number of things to attend to. When he finds he can do good work, he may then profitably turn his attention to this means of ink-supply.

We think we have now given nearly all the information on this subject that can be conveyed by means of writing, and we hope we have not been unsuccessful in our efforts. For the rest, we have to recommend *practice*, *study*, and *perseverance;* and with these may be built up a valuable experience.

THE BIBLIOGRAPHY OF LITHOGRAPHY.

IKE older industrial arts, Lithography possesses a special literature of its own. In the "Biblio-graphy of Printing," now being published in the *Printing Times and Lithographer*, a complete bibliographical account, with critical, technical, and historical annotations, is given of all such books, in alphabetical order. Mean-while, it has been thought that a list of abridged titles of books on the subject of Lithography would be found useful in a practical work like the present. The following com-pilation is, probably, the fullest that has appeared, but it is, no doubt, capable of considerable extension.

ARESTI (Joseph). Lithozographia ; or, Aquatinta stippled gradations produced upon drawings washed or painted on stone. London : 1856. 8vo.

BANKES (H.). Lithography ; or, the art of making drawings on stone for the purpose of being multiplied by printing. London : 1813. 8vo.

—— Lithography ; or, the art of taking impressions from drawings and writing made on stone, with specimens of the art. Second edition. London : 1816. 8vo.

CHEVALLIER (J. B. A.), chemist, and Langlumé (—). Traité complet de la Lithographie, ou Manuel du Lithograph, avec des notes de MM. Mantoux et Joumar. Paris : 1838. 8vo.

DOYEN (Camillo). Trattato di Litografia Storico, Teorico, Pratico ed Economico. Torino : 1877. 4to.

ENGELMANN (Godefroi). Recueil d'Essais Lithographiques. Paris : 1817. 4to.

—— Manuel du Dessinateur Lithographe, ou description des meilleurs moyens à employer pour faire des Dessins sur Pierre dans tous les genres connus. Paris : 1823. 8vo.——Second edition, to which is added "Instruction sur le nouveau procédé du lavis lithographique.   Paris : 1824.   8vo.——Third edition. Paris, &c. : 1830. 8vo.

ENGELMANN (Godefroi).   Handbuch für Steinzeichner und Beschreibung der besten Mittel um in allen bekannten Manieren auf Stein zu zeichnen.   Berlin : 1834.   8vo.

——— Traité théoretique et pratique de Lithographie.   Mulhouse : [1840].   4to. ; and Paris.

——— Das Gesammtgebiet der Lithographie ; oder theoretische und praktische Anleitung zur Ausübung der Lithographie in ihrem ganzen Umfange.   Chemnitz : 1840.   4to.——Second edition. Leipzig : 1843.   4to.   A German translation of the "Traité Théorétique."

EXPOSITION Universelle de 1855 à Paris.   Explication des Ouvrages de Lithographie.   Paris : 1855.   12mo.

EXPOSITION Universelle de 1867 à Paris.   Rapports des Délégations Ouvrières-lithographes.   Paris : 1867.   4to.

FERCHL (Franz Maria).   Uebersicht der einzig bestähenden, vollständigen Incunabel-Sammlung der Lithographie und der übrigen Senefelderschen Erfindungen, als Metallographie, Papyrographie, Papierstereotypen und Oelgemälde (ohne Presse).   Mit einem Vorworte begleitet zur 60jährigen Gedächtnissfeier der Münchner Erfindung der Lithographie vom Sammler und lebenslänglichen Hausfreund des Erfinders.   Munic : 1856.   8vo. pp. 91, and 4 plates.

——— Geschichte der Errichtung der ersten lithographischen Kunstanstalt bei der Feiertags-Schule für Künstler und Techniker in München.   Auf Auftrag des hohen Magistrat von München bei Gelegenheit des 90. Geburtstages des Erfinders der Lithographie Johann Aloys Senefelder verfasst und mit einer kurzen Geschichte dieser ruhmvollen Münchener Erfindung, nebst einer Uebersicht der einzig bestehenden, vollständigen Incunabel-Sammlung der Lithographie begleitet.   Mit Abbildungen der seltensten lithogr. Incunabeln.   Munic : 1862.   8vo. With a portrait of Heinr. Jos. Mitterer.

FOREIGN REVIEW (The).   London [vol. for] 1829.   8vo. A reply to this was published ; see HULLMANDEL.

H[ANHART] (M[ichael]).   Article headed " Chemical Printing " in " A Dictionary of Chemistry and the allied Branches of the Sciences," by Henry Watts, vol. iv., p. 726.   London : 1865.   8vo. A new edition of this Dictionary was commenced in 1872.

HULLMANDEL (Charles).   Manual of Lithography ; or, Memoir on the Lithographic Experiments made in Paris at the Royal School of the Roads and Bridges.   Translated from the French. London : 1820.   8vo. A third edition of this work appeared in 1832, with a slightly varied title.

HULLMANDEL (Charles). The Art of Drawing on Stone ; giving a full explanation of the various styles of the different methods to be employed to ensure success, and of the modes of correcting, as well as causes of failure. London : [1824]. 4to.——Second edition. London : 1833. 8vo.——Third edition. London : 1835.

——— On some further improvements in Lithographic Printing. [London : 1827]. 8vo.

——— [Lithographic Circular, explaining his improvements.] [London: 1829.] s. sh. 4to.

——— Reply to . . . . " The History of Lithography " [in *Foreign Review*]. London : 1829. 8vo.

HUSNIK (J.). Das Gesammtgebiet des Lichtdrucks, nebst einer vollständigen, theoretisch-praktischen Anleitung zur Ausübung der Photolithographie, Emailphotographie, Chemigraphie (Zinkographie). With 4 illustrations. Vienna : 1877. 16mo. pp. iv. 170.

ISERMANN (A.). Anleitung zur Chemitypie. Leipsic : 1869. 32mo. pp. iv., 42.

KRAUSS (F.), and MATTÉ (F.). Handbuch für Lithographen. Stuttgart : 1853. 8vo.

KNECHT (M). Nouveau Manuel complet du Dessinateur et de l'Imprimeur lithographe. Nouvelle édition, entièrement réfondue, mise au courant de l'industrie actuelle, et augmentée de plusieurs procédés nouveaux concernant la Lithographie mécanique, la Chromo-Lithographie, la Litho-Photographie, la Zincographie, et traitant des papiers de sureté. Paris : 1867. 12mo. With atlas. pp. xx. 403. Atlas pp. 7, and six folding plates.

LITHO-OMNICHROME COMPANY. Book of Monograms of Litho-omnichrome Company. London : 1868. 8vo.

MARCUARD (C.). Specimens of Lithography, printed by C. Marcuard. London : 1819. 4to.

MOOCK (L.). Traité pratique complet d'impression photographique aux encres grasses. Paris : 1874. 12mo.

NAGLER (G. K.). Aloys Senefelder. Munchen : 1862. 8vo.

NICHOL (W.). Treatise on Lithographic Printing. Forming part of Treatises on Printing by T. C. Hansard [jun.], reprinted from the seventh edition of the " Encyclopædia Britannica." Edinburgh : 1841.

RAPPORT de la Lithographie, et particulièrement sur un recueil de Dessins lithographies par M. Engelmann. Paris : 1816. 4to.

RAUCOURT (Col.). Manual of Lithography. Translated by Charles Hullmandel. London : 1820. 8vo.

RUSE (G.), and STRAKER (C.). Articles headed " Practical Instructions in lithography, ink, chalk, and chromo, with descriptive illustrations and various receipts in connection therewith " in " Printing and its Accessories." London : [1860]. 8vo.

SCHLOTKE (Ferdinand).   Senefelder-Album.   Hamburg : [1871].
4to.

SENEFELDER (Alois).   Vollständiges Lehrbuch der Steindruckerey,
enthaltend eine richtige und deutliche Anweisung zu den verschie-
denen Manipulations-Arten derselben in allen ihren Zweigen und
Manieren, belegt mit den nöthigen Musterblättern, nebst einer vor-
angehenden ausführlichen Geschichte · dieser Kunst von ihrem
Entstehen bis auf gegenwärtige Zeit.   Verfasst und herausgegeben
von dem Erfinder der Lithographie und chemischen Druckerey
Alois Senefelder.   Mit einer Vorrede des General-Secretärs der
Königl. Akademie der Wiss. zu München, des Directors Friederich
von Schlichtegroll.   München, bey Karl Thienemann.   Wien,
bey Karl Gerold : 1818.   (4to. pp. xvi. and 372 and 19 plates).
The work is dedicated to Maximilian Joseph, King of Bavaria.

—————— L'Art de la Lithographie, ou instruction pratique contenant la
description claire et succincte des différens procédés à suivre pour
dessiner, graver, et imprimer sur pierre.   Précédée d'une histoire de
la lithographie et de ses divers progrès.   Par M. Aloys Senefelder,
inventeur de l'art lithographique.   Paris : 1819.   (4to. pp. iv.
and 226 and 20 plates.

—————— A complete course of Lithography ; containing clear and
explicit instructions in all the different branches and manners of
that art, accompanied by illustrative specimens of drawings.
To which is prefixed a History of Lithography, from its origin to
the present time.   With a preface by F. von Schlichtegroll.
Translated from the original German by A. S.   London : 1819.
4to.

See also articles in " Encyclopædia Metropolitana," " Encyclopædia
Britannica," " English Encyclopædia," Chambers's "Information for
the People," Tomlinson's " Cyclopædia of Useful Arts," Knight's
" Dictionary of Mechanics," " Penny Cyclopædia," &c.

LITHOGRAPHIC PERIODICALS.

AT Hamburg there is published a monthly journal called *La
Lithographia*, exclusively devoted to the art.   Printers acquainted
with the German language will find in it from time to time valuable
practical articles.

In 1870 appeared the first English technical journal of the art.
It was called *The Lithographer*, and was published monthly under that
sole heading up to 1874, when Messrs. Wyman, into whose hands
it had passed, incorporated it with the *Printing Times*.   The two
have since been carried on under the title of *The Printing Times
and Lithographer* (monthly, price 6d.).   A New Series was begun in
1875, and the bound yearly volumes form a complete repertory of
practical information, instruction, news, &c., connected with the art
in its various branches.   It was in this journal that the " Grammar of
Lithography " originally appeared.

INDEX.

THE END.

WYMAN AND SONS, PRINTERS, GREAT QUEEN STREET, LONDON, W.C.

For EU product safety concerns, contact us at Calle de José Abascal, 56–1°,
28003 Madrid, Spain or eugpsr@cambridge.org.

www.ingramcontent.com/pod-product-compliance
Ingram Content Group UK Ltd.
Pitfield, Milton Keynes, MK11 3LW, UK
UKHW010344140625
459647UK00010B/806